Math
ADVANTAGE

Test Copying Masters

- **MULTIPLE-CHOICE (STANDARDIZED) FORMAT TESTS**
- **FREE-RESPONSE FORMAT TESTS**
- **ANSWER KEYS**
- **MANAGEMENT FORMS**

Grade 1

Harcourt Brace & Company

Orlando • Atlanta • Austin • Boston • San Francisco • Chicago • Dallas • New York • Toronto • London

http://www.hbschool.com

Printed in the United States of America

ISBN 0-15-311170-4

6 7 8 9 10 073C 2000

CONTENTS

▶ Formal Assessment

▶ Management Forms

Multiple-Choice Format Tests (Standardized)

The multiple-choice format is provided to assess mastery of the learning goals of the program. These tests assess concepts, skills, and problem solving. The use of these tests helps prepare students for standardized achievement tests.

There is an Inventory Test which tests the learning goals from the previous grade level. This can be used at the beginning of the year or as a placement test when a new student enters your class.

There is a Chapter Test for each chapter and a Multi-Chapter Test to be used as review after several chapters in a content cluster. Also, there are Cumulative Tests at the same point as the Multi-Chapter Tests. The Cumulative Test reviews content from Chapter 1 through the current chapter.

Math Advantage also provides free-response format tests that parallel the multiple-choice tests. You may wish to use one form as a pretest and one form as a posttest.

Name _____

1.

Ⓐ   Ⓑ

2.

Ⓐ   Ⓑ

3.

Ⓐ   Ⓑ

4.

Ⓐ   Ⓑ

5.

Ⓐ
Ⓑ

6.

Ⓐ
Ⓑ

(1, 2) Which shape belongs in the group? (3) Which toy comes next in the pattern? (4) Which puppy is on the left? (5) Which group has fewer? (6) Which group has one more?

Form A • Multiple-Choice   A1   **Go on.**

Name ____

7.

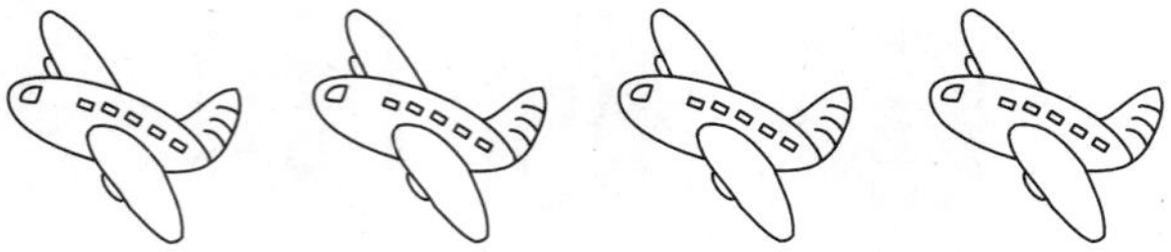

Ⓐ 3 Ⓑ 4

8.

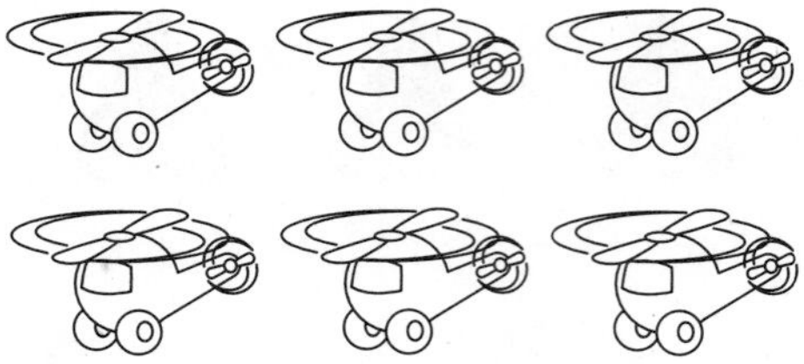

Ⓐ 6 Ⓑ 7

9.

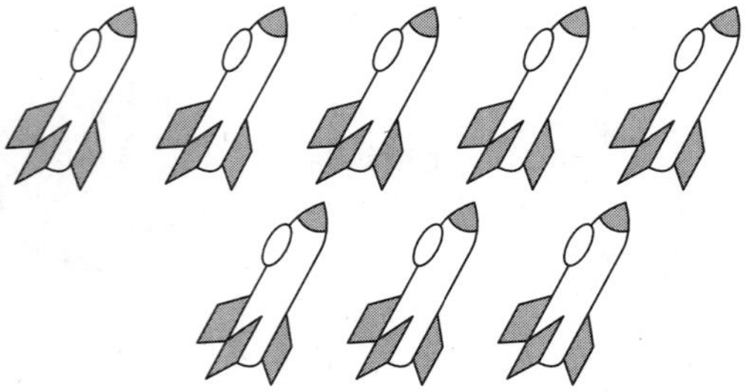

Ⓐ 8 Ⓑ 9

10.

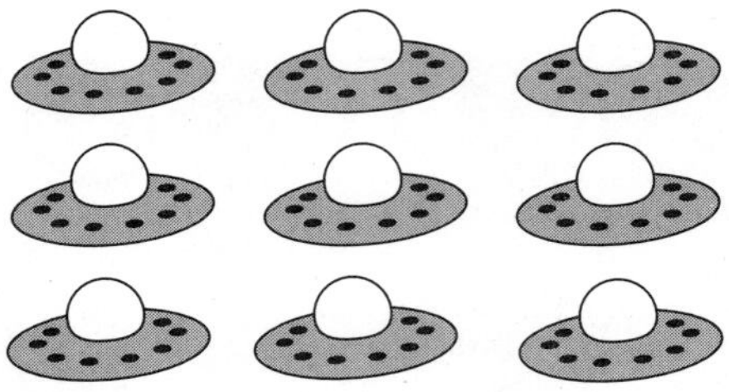

Ⓐ 8 Ⓑ 9

11.

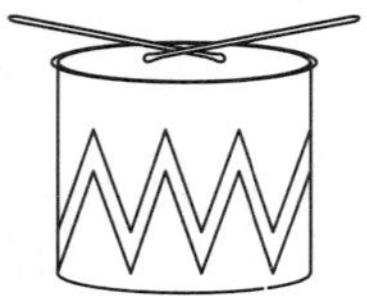

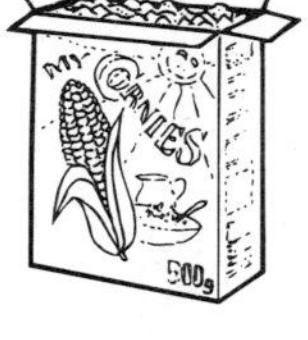

Ⓐ Ⓑ

12.

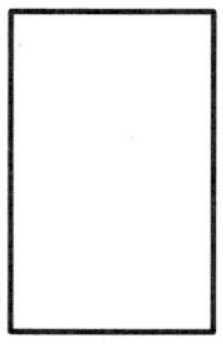

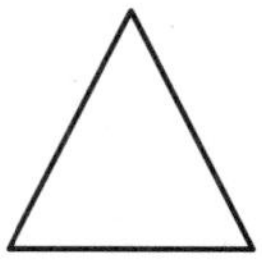

Ⓐ Ⓑ

(7–10) Which number tells how many things are in the group? (11) Which object is shaped like a can? (12) Which shape is a triangle?

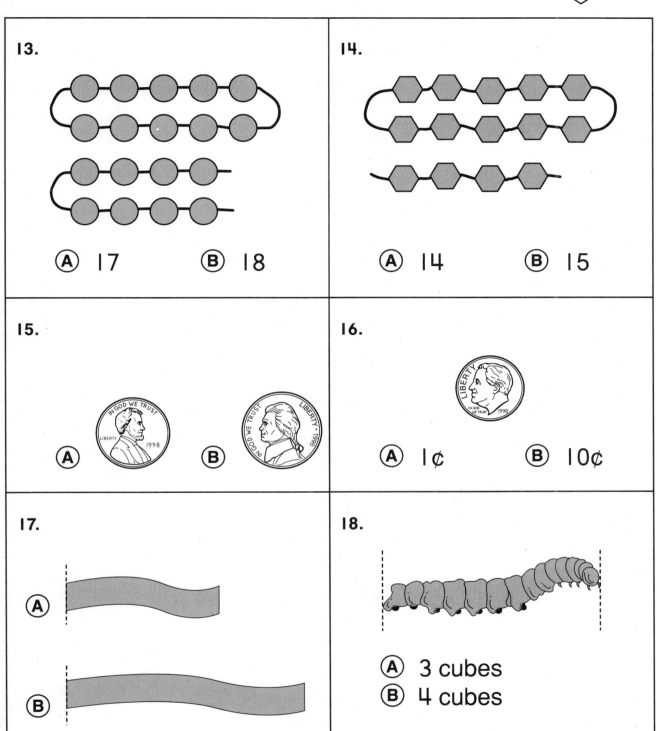

13.

Ⓐ 17   Ⓑ 18

14.

Ⓐ 14   Ⓑ 15

15.

Ⓐ   Ⓑ

16.

Ⓐ 1¢   Ⓑ 10¢

17.

Ⓐ

Ⓑ

18.

Ⓐ 3 cubes
Ⓑ 4 cubes

(13, 14) Which number tells how many beads there are? (15) Which is the penny? (16) How many cents are there? (17) Which ribbon is longer? (18) How many connecting cubes long is the caterpillar?

19.

Ⓐ   Ⓑ

20.

Ⓐ 4 o'clock
Ⓑ 12 o'clock

21.

Ⓐ $2 + 2 = 4$
Ⓑ $2 + 4 = 6$

22.

Ⓐ $5 - 3 = 2$
Ⓑ $3 - 2 = 1$

(19) Which child is second in line? (20) Which time does the clock show?
(21) Which addition sentence tells the story? (22) Which subtraction sentence tells the story?

Name _____

Choose the correct answer.

1.

1 girl jumps.
2 girls run.
How many in all?

(A) 3 girls   (B) 4 girls
(C) 5 girls   (D) 6 girls

2.

3 boys go up.
1 boy goes down.
How many in all?

(A) 2 boys   (B) 3 boys
(C) 4 boys   (D) 6 boys

3.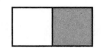

1 + 1 = _____

(A) 1   (B) 2
(C) 3   (D) 4

4.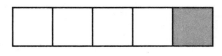

4 + 1 = _____

(A) 3   (B) 4
(C) 5   (D) 6

5.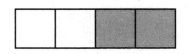

2 + 2 = _____

(A) 3   (B) 4
(C) 5   (D) 6

6.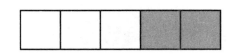

3 + 2 = _____

(A) 2   (B) 3
(C) 4   (D) 5

7.

$4 + 2 =$ _____

Ⓐ 3   Ⓑ 4
Ⓒ 5   Ⓓ 6

8.

$2 + 1 =$ _____

Ⓐ 3   Ⓑ 4
Ⓒ 5   Ⓓ 6

9. Which addition sentence tells how many in all?

Ⓐ $1 + 2 = 3$
Ⓑ $2 + 2 = 4$
Ⓒ $3 + 2 = 5$
Ⓓ $5 + 1 = 6$

10. Which addition sentence tells how many in all?

Ⓐ $2 + 1 = 3$
Ⓑ $2 + 2 = 4$
Ⓒ $2 + 3 = 5$
Ⓓ $3 + 3 = 6$

11. Which addition sentence tells how many in all?

Ⓐ $1 + 3 = 4$
Ⓑ $1 + 4 = 5$
Ⓒ $1 + 5 = 6$
Ⓓ $2 + 4 = 6$

12. Which addition sentence tells how many in all?

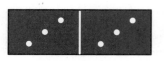

Ⓐ $2 + 2 = 4$
Ⓑ $3 + 2 = 5$
Ⓒ $3 + 3 = 6$
Ⓓ $4 + 2 = 6$

Name _____

Choose the correct answer.

1.

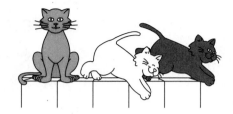

3 cats.
2 go away.
How many are left?

Ⓐ 1 cat   Ⓑ 2 cats
Ⓒ 3 cats   Ⓓ 4 cats

2.

6 frogs.
1 hops away.
How many are left?

Ⓐ 3 frogs   Ⓑ 4 frogs
Ⓒ 5 frogs   Ⓓ 6 frogs

3.

5 − 1 = _____

Ⓐ 3   Ⓑ 4
Ⓒ 5   Ⓓ 6

4.

2 − 1 = _____

Ⓐ 1   Ⓑ 2
Ⓒ 3   Ⓓ 4

5.

6 − 2 = _____

Ⓐ 1   Ⓑ 2
Ⓒ 3   Ⓓ 4

6.

5 − 2 = _____

Ⓐ 2   Ⓑ 3
Ⓒ 4   Ⓓ 5

Form A • Multiple-Choice   A7   **Go on.**

7. Which number sentence tells how many are left?

- Ⓐ 4 – 1 = 3
- Ⓑ 4 – 2 = 2
- Ⓒ 4 – 3 = 1
- Ⓓ 3 – 2 = 1

8. Which number sentence tells how many are left?

- Ⓐ 6 – 5 = 1
- Ⓑ 6 – 4 = 2
- Ⓒ 6 – 3 = 3
- Ⓓ 6 – 2 = 4

9. Which number sentence tells how many are left?

- Ⓐ 5 – 3 = 2
- Ⓑ 5 – 2 = 3
- Ⓒ 5 – 1 = 4
- Ⓓ 6 – 3 = 3

10. Which number sentence tells how many are left?

- Ⓐ 4 – 3 = 1
- Ⓑ 4 – 2 = 2
- Ⓒ 4 – 1 = 3
- Ⓓ 4 – 0 = 4

11. Add or subtract. Use counters.

4 cows walk.

2 more come.

How many in all?

- Ⓐ 2 cows
- Ⓑ 4 cows
- Ⓒ 5 cows
- Ⓓ 6 cows

12. Add or subtract. Use counters.

3 pigs eat corn.

1 goes away.

How many are left?

- Ⓐ 1 pig
- Ⓑ 2 pigs
- Ⓒ 3 pigs
- Ⓓ 4 pigs

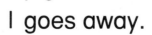

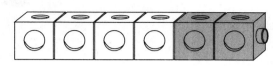

Choose the correct answer.

1.

3 girls play.
1 girl runs.
How many in all?

(A) 3 girls (B) 4 girls
(C) 5 girls (D) 6 girls

2.

4 + 2 = _____

(A) 3 (B) 4
(C) 5 (D) not here

3.

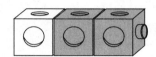

1 + 2 = _____

(A) 3 (B) 4
(C) 5 (D) not here

4.

4 + 1 = _____

(A) 3 (B) 4
(C) 5 (D) not here

5. Which addition sentence
tells how many in all?

(A) 4 + 2 = 6
(B) 3 + 2 = 5
(C) 2 + 2 = 4
(D) 1 + 2 = 3

6. Which addition sentence
tells how many in all?

(A) 2 + 1 = 3
(B) 3 + 1 = 4
(C) 4 + 1 = 5
(D) 5 + 1 = 6

7.

4 pups play.
1 walks away.
How many are left?

Ⓐ 1 pup   Ⓑ 2 pups
Ⓒ 3 pups   Ⓓ 4 pups

8. □ □ □ □ ☒ ☒

6 − 2 = _____

Ⓐ 4   Ⓑ 3
Ⓒ 2   Ⓓ not here

9. Which subtraction sentence shows how many are left?

Ⓐ 6 − 3 = 3
Ⓑ 5 − 2 = 3
Ⓒ 5 − 1 = 4
Ⓓ 4 − 0 = 4

10. Which subtraction sentence shows how many are left?

Ⓐ 6 − 4 = 2
Ⓑ 6 − 3 = 3
Ⓒ 6 − 2 = 4
Ⓓ 6 − 1 = 5

11. Add or subtract. Use counters.

2 fish swim.
2 more come.
How many in all?

Ⓐ 2 fish   Ⓑ 3 fish
Ⓒ 4 fish   Ⓓ 5 fish

12. Add or subtract. Use counters.

3 birds are in a tree.
2 fly away.
How many are left?

Ⓐ 1 bird   Ⓑ 2 birds
Ⓒ 3 birds   Ⓓ 4 birds

Choose the correct answer.

1.

2 cats play.
I cat sleeps.
How many in all?
- (A) 3 cats
- (B) 4 cats
- (C) 5 cats
- (D) 6 cats

2.

2 frogs sit.
2 frogs jump.
How many in all?
- (A) 2 frogs
- (B) 3 frogs
- (C) 4 frogs
- (D) 5 frogs

3.

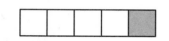

$4 + 1 = $ _____
- (A) 2
- (B) 3
- (C) 4
- (D) 5

4.

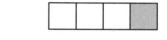

$3 + 1 = $ _____
- (A) 2
- (B) 3
- (C) 4
- (D) 5

5.

$1 + 1 = $ _____
- (A) 2
- (B) 3
- (C) 4
- (D) 5

6.

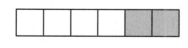

$4 + 2 = $ _____
- (A) 3
- (B) 4
- (C) 5
- (D) 6

Name _____

CUMULATIVE TEST
PAGE 2

7.

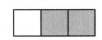

$1 + 2 =$ _____

Ⓐ 3   Ⓑ 4
Ⓒ 5   Ⓓ 6

8.

$3 + 2 =$ _____

Ⓐ 3   Ⓑ 4
Ⓒ 5   Ⓓ 6

9.

$5 + 1 =$ _____

Ⓐ 3   Ⓑ 4
Ⓒ 5   Ⓓ 6

10.

$1 + 3 =$ _____

Ⓐ 3   Ⓑ 4
Ⓒ 5   Ⓓ 6

11. Which addition sentence tells how many in all?

Ⓐ $1 + 2 = 3$
Ⓑ $1 + 3 = 4$
Ⓒ $2 + 3 = 5$
Ⓓ $2 + 4 = 6$

12. Which addition sentence tells how many in all?

Ⓐ $2 + 2 = 4$
Ⓑ $3 + 2 = 5$
Ⓒ $3 + 3 = 6$
Ⓓ $2 + 4 = 6$

13.

3 boys play.
1 goes away.
How many are left?
Ⓐ 1 boy   Ⓑ 2 boys
Ⓒ 3 boys   Ⓓ 4 boys

14.

6 birds sit.
3 fly away.
How many are left?
Ⓐ 3 birds   Ⓑ 4 birds
Ⓒ 5 birds   Ⓓ 6 birds

15.

$6 - 1 = \underline{\hspace{1cm}}$

Ⓐ 3   Ⓑ 4
Ⓒ 5   Ⓓ 6

16.

$4 - 1 = \underline{\hspace{1cm}}$

Ⓐ 2   Ⓑ 3
Ⓒ 4   Ⓓ 5

17.

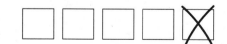

$5 - 1 = \underline{\hspace{1cm}}$

Ⓐ 1   Ⓑ 2
Ⓒ 3   Ⓓ 4

18.

$4 - 2 = \underline{\hspace{1cm}}$

Ⓐ 2   Ⓑ 3
Ⓒ 4   Ⓓ 5

19.

$$5 - 2 = \underline{\quad}$$

(A) 1 (B) 2
(C) 3 (D) 4

20.

$$3 - 2 = \underline{\quad}$$

(A) 1 (B) 2
(C) 3 (D) 4

21. Which subtraction sentence tells how many are left?

(A) $6 - 1 = 5$
(B) $6 - 2 = 4$
(C) $5 - 1 = 4$
(D) $5 - 2 = 3$

22. Which subtraction sentence tells how many are left?

(A) $5 - 2 = 3$
(B) $5 - 3 = 2$
(C) $4 - 2 = 2$
(D) $4 - 3 = 1$

23. Add or subtract. Use counters.

3 ducks are swimming.
3 more come.
How many
in all?

(A) 3 ducks (B) 4 ducks
(C) 5 ducks (D) 6 ducks

24. Add or subtract. Use counters.

6 cats drink milk.
5 go away.
How many
are left?

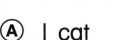

(A) 1 cat (B) 2 cats
(C) 3 cats (D) 4 cats

Name _____

Choose the correct answer.

1.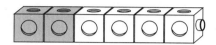

$4 + 2 = 6$

$2 + 4 =$ _____

(A) 2   (B) 6
(C) 7   (D) 8

2.

$3 + 6 = 9$

$6 + 3 =$ _____

(A) 3   (B) 6
(C) 8   (D) 9

3. Use counters.
Which is a way to
make 7?

(A) $5 + 2$ (B) $7 + 1$
(C) $4 + 5$ (D) $2 + 8$

4. Use counters.
Which is a way to
make 8?

(A) $4 + 6$ (B) $5 + 4$
(C) $3 + 5$ (D) $1 + 6$

5. Use counters.
Which is a way to
make 10?

(A) $3 + 4$ (B) $4 + 4$
(C) $6 + 3$ (D) $1 + 9$

6. Use counters.
Which is a way to
make 9?

(A) $8 + 2$ (B) $7 + 2$
(C) $5 + 3$ (D) $4 + 4$

7.

$2 + 6 =$ _____

Ⓐ 7 Ⓑ 8
Ⓒ 9 Ⓓ 10

8.

$5 + 5 =$ _____

Ⓐ 7 Ⓑ 8
Ⓒ 9 Ⓓ 10

9.

$\begin{array}{r} 4 \\ +3 \\ \hline \end{array}$

Ⓐ 7 Ⓑ 8
Ⓒ 9 Ⓓ 10

10.

$\begin{array}{r} 5 \\ +4 \\ \hline \end{array}$

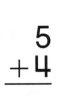

Ⓐ 7 Ⓑ 8
Ⓒ 9 Ⓓ 10

11. Use pennies. Find the total amount.

Ⓐ 3¢ Ⓑ 6¢
Ⓒ 7¢ Ⓓ 8¢

12. Use pennies. Find the total amount.

Ⓐ 3¢ Ⓑ 6¢
Ⓒ 8¢ Ⓓ 9¢

Choose the correct answer.

1.

$$5 + 1 = \underline{\qquad}$$

- Ⓐ 3
- Ⓑ 4
- Ⓒ 6
- Ⓓ 7

2.

$$3 + 2 = \underline{\qquad}$$

- Ⓐ 4
- Ⓑ 5
- Ⓒ 6
- Ⓓ 7

3.

$$4 + 3 = \underline{\qquad}$$

- Ⓐ 7
- Ⓑ 8
- Ⓒ 9
- Ⓓ 10

4.

$$6 + 3 = \underline{\qquad}$$

- Ⓐ 6
- Ⓑ 7
- Ⓒ 8
- Ⓓ 9

5.

$$\begin{array}{r} 7 \\ +2 \\ \hline \end{array}$$

- Ⓐ 7
- Ⓑ 8
- Ⓒ 9
- Ⓓ 10

6.

$$\begin{array}{r} 5 \\ +3 \\ \hline \end{array}$$

- Ⓐ 8
- Ⓑ 7
- Ⓒ 6
- Ⓓ 5

7. Which doubles fact goes with the picture?

Ⓐ 2 + 1 = 3
Ⓑ 3 + 3 = 6
Ⓒ 4 + 4 = 8
Ⓓ 5 + 5 = 10

8. Which doubles fact goes with the picture?

Ⓐ 2 + 2 = 4
Ⓑ 4 + 2 = 6
Ⓒ 3 + 3 = 6
Ⓓ 4 + 4 = 8

9.
$$\begin{array}{r} 2 \\ +6 \\ \hline \end{array}$$

Ⓐ 4   Ⓑ 7
Ⓒ 8   Ⓓ 9

10.
$$\begin{array}{r} 3 \\ +7 \\ \hline \end{array}$$

Ⓐ 10   Ⓑ 9
Ⓒ 8   Ⓓ 4

11. Add or subtract.

I have 6 balloons.

I lose 3.

How many do I have left?

Ⓐ 9   Ⓑ 5
Ⓒ 4   Ⓓ 3

12. Add or subtract.

I have 4 peanuts.

Mom gives me 2 more.

How many do I have in all?

Ⓐ 5   Ⓑ 6
Ⓒ 7   Ⓓ 8

Choose the correct answer.

1.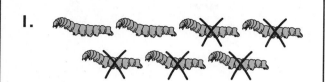

$$7 - 5 = \underline{\hphantom{00}}$$

Ⓐ 2   Ⓑ 3
Ⓒ 5   Ⓓ 7

2.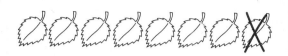

$$8 - 1 = \underline{\hphantom{00}}$$

Ⓐ 5   Ⓑ 6
Ⓒ 7   Ⓓ 9

3.

$$10 - 4 = \underline{\hphantom{00}}$$

Ⓐ 3   Ⓑ 4
Ⓒ 5   Ⓓ 6

4.

$$9 - 5 = \underline{\hphantom{00}}$$

Ⓐ 5   Ⓑ 4
Ⓒ 3   Ⓓ 2

5.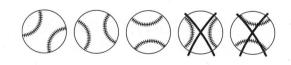

$$\begin{array}{r} 5 \\ -2 \\ \hline \end{array}$$

Ⓐ 1   Ⓑ 2
Ⓒ 3   Ⓓ 4

6.

$$\begin{array}{r} 7 \\ -6 \\ \hline \end{array}$$

Ⓐ 1   Ⓑ 2
Ⓒ 3   Ⓓ 6

7.

$$5 - 4$$

(A) 0   (B) 1
(C) 8   (D) 9

8.

$$10 - 2$$

(A) 2   (B) 6
(C) 7   (D) 8

9. Complete the fact family.

$$2 + 4 = 6$$
$$6 - 4 = 2$$
$$4 + 2 = 6$$
$$6 - 2 = \_\_\_$$

(A) 4   (B) 3
(C) 2   (D) 1

10. Complete the fact family.

$$\begin{array}{r} 5 \\ +3 \\ \hline 8 \end{array} \quad \begin{array}{r} 3 \\ +5 \\ \hline 8 \end{array} \quad \begin{array}{r} 8 \\ -5 \\ \hline 3 \end{array} \quad \begin{array}{r} 8 \\ -3 \\ \hline \end{array}$$

(A) 3   (B) 5
(C) 8   (D) 9

11. How many more ?

$$5 - 3 = \_\_\_$$

(A) 8 more
(B) 5 more
(C) 2 more
(D) 1 more

12. How many more  ?

$$7 - 4 = \_\_\_$$

(A) 9 more
(B) 7 more
(C) 4 more
(D) 3 more

Form A • Multiple-Choice   **A20**   **Stop!**

Choose the correct answer.

1.

$$4 - 2 = \underline{}$$

(A) 6 (B) 3
(C) 2 (D) 1

2.

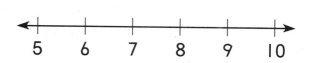

$$8 - 1 = \underline{}$$

(A) 7 (B) 8
(C) 9 (D) 10

3.

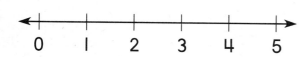

$$5 - 3 = \underline{}$$

(A) 1 (B) 2
(C) 4 (D) 8

4.

$$8 - 3 = \underline{}$$

(A) 10 (B) 9
(C) 6 (D) 5

5.

$$\begin{array}{r} 9 \\ -\,1 \\ \hline \end{array}$$

(A) 10 (B) 9
(C) 8 (D) 7

6.

$$\begin{array}{r} 10 \\ -\,3 \\ \hline \end{array}$$

(A) 7 (B) 8
(C) 9 (D) 10

7.

$$\begin{array}{r} 8 \\ -8 \\ \hline \end{array}$$

Ⓐ 10   Ⓑ 5
Ⓒ 1   Ⓓ 0

8.

$$\begin{array}{r} 4 \\ -0 \\ \hline \end{array}$$

Ⓐ 0   Ⓑ 1
Ⓒ 4   Ⓓ 5

9.

$$\begin{array}{r} 6 \\ +2 \\ \hline \end{array}$$

Ⓐ 4   Ⓑ 8
Ⓒ 9   Ⓓ 10

10.

$$\begin{array}{r} 9 \\ -3 \\ \hline \end{array}$$

Ⓐ 6   Ⓑ 5
Ⓒ 4   Ⓓ 3

11.

6 fish are in a pond.

3 swim away.

How many now?

Ⓐ 2 fish   Ⓑ 3 fish
Ⓒ 8 fish   Ⓓ 9 fish

12.

5 bugs are on a leaf.

2 more come.

How many now?

Ⓐ 3 bugs   Ⓑ 4 bugs
Ⓒ 6 bugs   Ⓓ 7 bugs

Name _____

TEST • CHAPTERS 3–6
PAGE 1

Choose the correct answer.

1. Find the missing sum.

$3 + 2 = 5$

$2 + 3 =$ _____

(A) 5   (B) 6
(C) 7   (D) 8

2. Use counters.

Which is a way to make 7?

(A) $4 + 2$ (B) $5 + 2$
(C) $5 + 3$ (D) $6 + 2$

3.

$4 + 5 =$ _____

(A) 6   (B) 7
(C) 8   (D) 9

4. Count on to add.

$7 + 1 =$ _____

(A) 6   (B) 7
(C) 8   (D) 9

5. Find the doubles fact that goes with the picture.

(A) $2 + 2 = 4$
(B) $3 + 3 = 6$
(C) $4 + 4 = 8$
(D) not here

6.

Sue has 8 dolls.
Mom gives her 2 more.
How many dolls
does Sue have now?

(A) 7   (B) 8
(C) 9   (D) not here

7.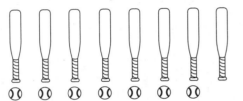

$$\begin{array}{r} 7 \\ -5 \\ \hline \end{array}$$

(A) 0   (B) I
(C) 2   (D) 3

8.
$$6 + 3 = 9$$
$$3 + 6 = 9$$
$$9 - 3 = 6$$
$$9 - 6 = \underline{\hspace{1cm}}$$

(A) 2   (B) 3
(C) 4   (D) 5

9. How many more 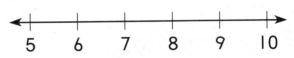 ?

$$8 - 7 = \underline{\hspace{1cm}}$$

(A) I more
(B) 2 more
(C) 3 more
(D) 4 more

10.

(number line showing 5 6 7 8 9 10)

$$9 - 3 = \underline{\hspace{1cm}}$$

(A) 5   (B) 6
(C) 7   (D) 8

11.

$$\begin{array}{r} 3 \\ -3 \\ \hline \end{array}$$

(A) 0   (B) I
(C) 2   (D) 3

12.

6 frogs are on a log.
2 jump off.
How many frogs now?
(A) 2 frogs   (B) 3 frogs
(C) 4 frogs   (D) not here

Choose the correct answer.

1.

4 horses eat.
I horse runs.
How many in all?

Ⓐ 2 horses   Ⓑ 3 horses
Ⓒ 4 horses   Ⓓ 5 horses

2.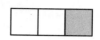

$2 + 1 =$ _____

Ⓐ I   Ⓑ 2
Ⓒ 3   Ⓓ 4

3.

$2 + 2 =$ _____

Ⓐ 4   Ⓑ 5
Ⓒ 6   Ⓓ 7

4.

$3 - 1 =$ _____

Ⓐ I   Ⓑ 2
Ⓒ 3   Ⓓ 4

5.

$5 - 2 =$ _____

Ⓐ 3   Ⓑ 4
Ⓒ 5   Ⓓ 6

6. Add or subtract. Use counters.

6 pigs are in
a pen.
I gets out.
How many are left?

Ⓐ 2 pigs   Ⓑ 3 pigs
Ⓒ 4 pigs   Ⓓ 5 pigs

7.

$$3 + 2 = 5$$

$$2 + 3 = \underline{\hspace{1cm}}$$

Ⓐ 1   Ⓑ 4
Ⓒ 5   Ⓓ 6

8. Use counters. Which is a way to make 7?

Ⓐ 3 + 3   Ⓑ 3 + 4
Ⓒ 4 + 4   Ⓓ 1 + 5

9. Use counters. Which is a way to make 9?

Ⓐ 4 + 5   Ⓑ 4 + 3
Ⓒ 5 + 3   Ⓓ 5 + 5

10.

$$4 + 6 = \underline{\hspace{1cm}}$$

Ⓐ 7   Ⓑ 8
Ⓒ 9   Ⓓ 10

11. Use pennies. Find the total amount.

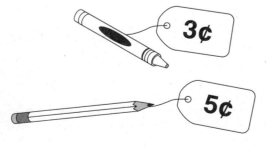

3¢

5¢

Ⓐ 6¢   Ⓑ 7¢
Ⓒ 8¢   Ⓓ 9¢

12.

$$3 + 1 = \underline{\hspace{1cm}}$$

Ⓐ 3   Ⓑ 4
Ⓒ 6   Ⓓ 7

13. Count on to add.

$$6 + 3 = \underline{}$$

Ⓐ 7   Ⓑ 8
Ⓒ 9   Ⓓ 10

14. Which doubles fact goes with the picture?

Ⓐ 4 + 4 = 8
Ⓑ 3 + 3 = 6
Ⓒ 2 + 2 = 4
Ⓓ 1 + 1 = 2

15.

$$\begin{array}{r} 2 \\ + 8 \\ \hline \end{array}$$

Ⓐ 7   Ⓑ 8
Ⓒ 9   Ⓓ 10

16. Add or subtract.

I have 5 blocks.
Dad gives me 2 more.
How many do
I have in all?

Ⓐ 5   Ⓑ 6
Ⓒ 7   Ⓓ 8

17.

$$8 - 5 = \underline{}$$

Ⓐ 2   Ⓑ 3
Ⓒ 5   Ⓓ 7

18.

$$10 - 6 = \underline{}$$

Ⓐ 4   Ⓑ 5
Ⓒ 6   Ⓓ 7

19.

$$-\ \begin{array}{r} 8 \\ 2 \end{array}$$

Ⓐ 3 Ⓑ 4
Ⓒ 5 Ⓓ 6

20. How many more  ?

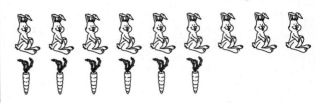

$$9 - 6 = \underline{\qquad}$$

Ⓐ 1 more Ⓑ 2 more
Ⓒ 3 more Ⓓ 4 more

21.

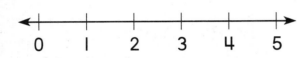

$$5 - 1 = \underline{\qquad}$$

Ⓐ 6 Ⓑ 4
Ⓒ 2 Ⓓ 1

22.

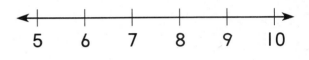

$$10 - 3 = \underline{\qquad}$$

Ⓐ 7 Ⓑ 8
Ⓒ 9 Ⓓ 10

23.

$$+\ \begin{array}{r} 6 \\ 0 \end{array}$$

Ⓐ 0 Ⓑ 1
Ⓒ 6 Ⓓ 10

24.

8 bugs are on a leaf.
4 fly away.
How many now?
Ⓐ 1 bug Ⓑ 2 bugs
Ⓒ 3 bugs Ⓓ 4 bugs

Choose the correct answer.

1. Which object has the same shape?

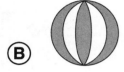

Ⓐ

Ⓑ

Ⓒ

2. Which object has the same shape?

Ⓐ

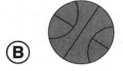

Ⓑ

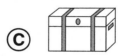

Ⓒ

3. Which object has the same shape?

Ⓐ

Ⓑ

Ⓒ

4. Which object has the same shape?

Ⓐ

Ⓑ

Ⓒ

Form A • Multiple-Choice   **A29**   Go on.

5. Which object has the same shape?

(A) TUNA

(B)

(C)

(D)

6. Which object has the same shape?

(A)

(B)

(C)

(D)

7. Which will roll?

(A)

(B)

(C)

8. Which will stack?

(A)

(B)

(C)

9. Which has all flat faces?

(A)

(B)

(C)

10. How many cubes?

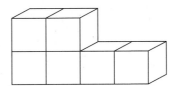

(A) 3 cubes   (B) 4 cubes
(C) 5 cubes   (D) 6 cubes

Name _____

Choose the correct answer.

1. Which plane figure matches the face of the solid figure?

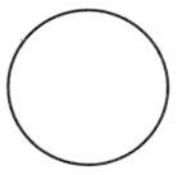

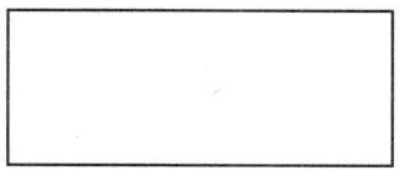

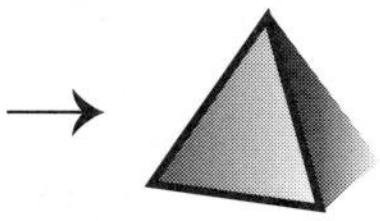

Ⓐ ◯   Ⓑ ▭
Ⓒ ☐   Ⓓ △

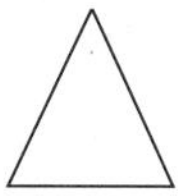

2. Which plane figure matches the face of the solid figure?

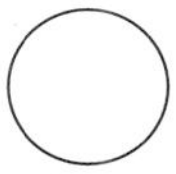

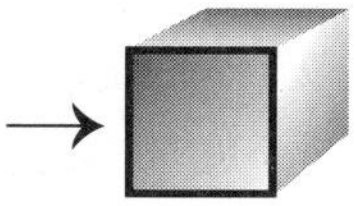

Ⓐ ☐   Ⓑ ◯
Ⓒ △   Ⓓ ▭

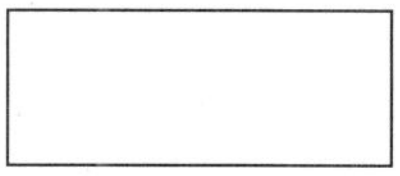

3. Which plane figure matches the face of the solid figure?

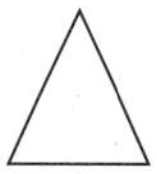

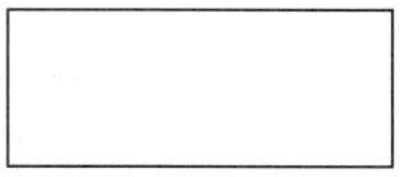

Ⓐ △   Ⓑ ▭
Ⓒ ☐   Ⓓ ◯

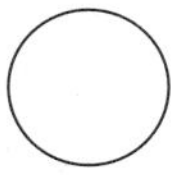

4. Which plane figure matches the face of the solid figure?

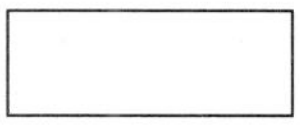

Ⓐ ◯   Ⓑ ▭
Ⓒ △   Ⓓ ☐

5. How many sides does this figure have?

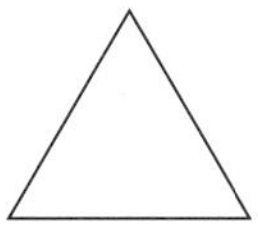

Ⓐ 0 sides   Ⓑ 2 sides
Ⓒ 3 sides   Ⓓ 4 sides

6. How many corners does this figure have?

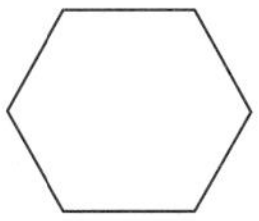

Ⓐ 3 corners
Ⓑ 4 corners
Ⓒ 5 corners
Ⓓ 6 corners

7. Which figure has 5 sides and 5 corners?

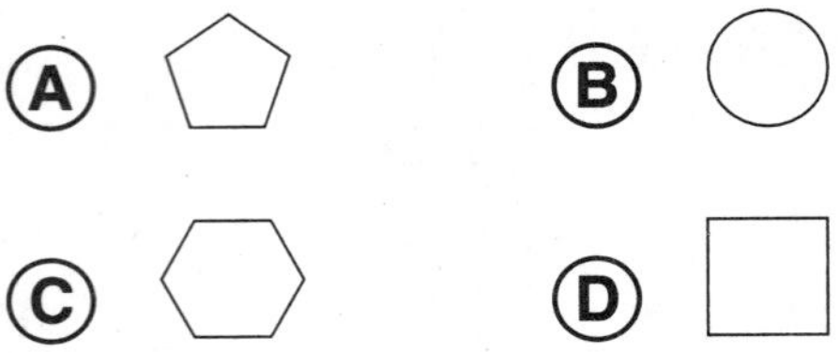

(A)   (B) ◯

(C) ⬡   (D) ▢

8. Which figure has 0 sides and 0 corners?

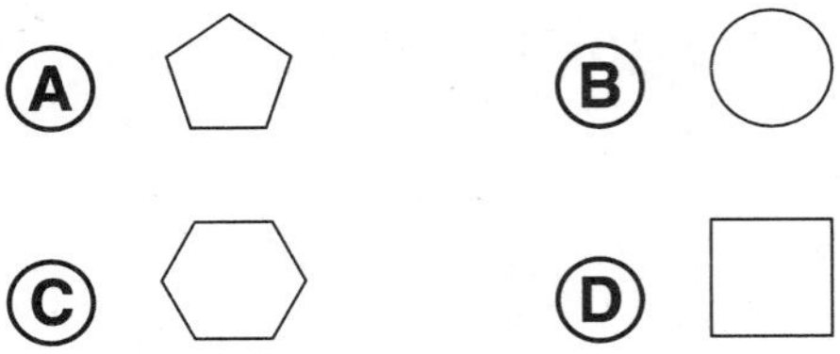

(A) ⬠   (B) ◯

(C) ⬡   (D) ▢

9. Which figure is the same size and shape as this one?

(A) 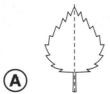   (B)

(C) 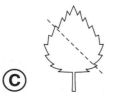   (D)

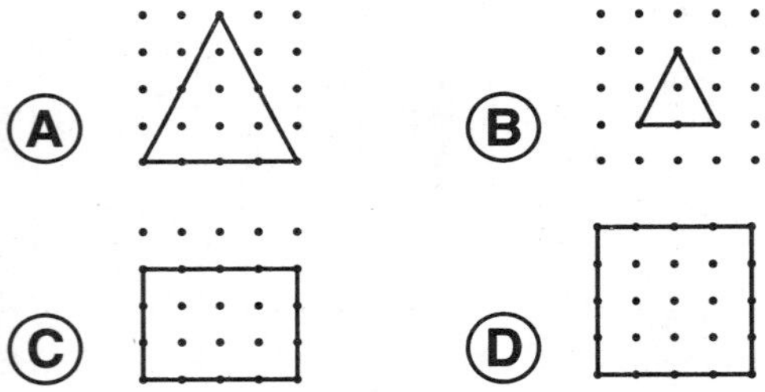

10. Which figure is the same size and shape as this one?

(A)   (B)

(C)   (D)

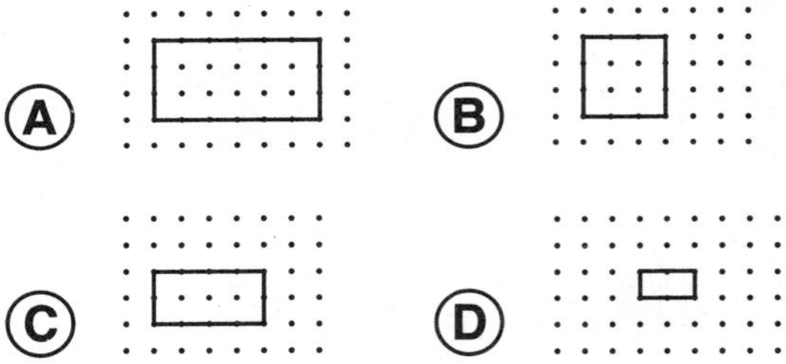

11. Which line makes two sides that match?

(A)   (B)

(C)   (D)

12. Which line makes two sides that match?

(A) 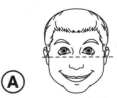   (B)

(C) 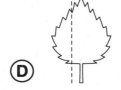   (D)

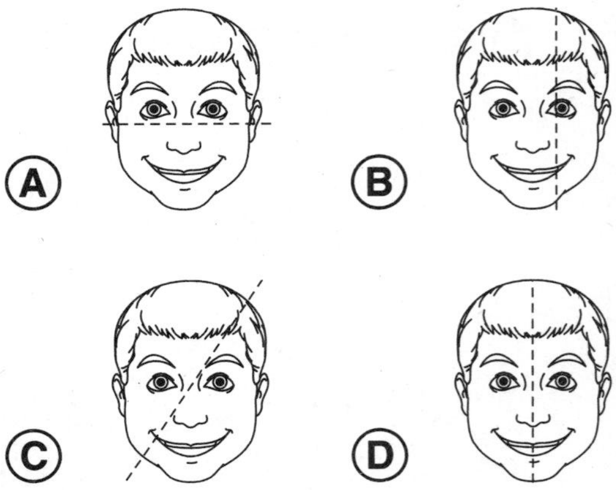

Name _____

Choose the correct answer.

1. Which is a closed figure?

   Ⓐ   Ⓑ

   Ⓒ   Ⓓ

2. Which is an open figure?

   Ⓐ  Ⓑ

   Ⓒ   Ⓓ

3. Which is inside the �"?

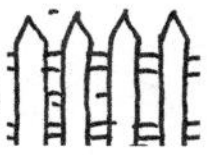

   Ⓐ   Ⓑ

   Ⓒ  Ⓓ

4. Which is outside the ◯?

   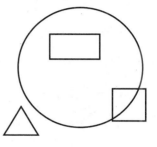

   Ⓐ △ Ⓑ ◯

   Ⓒ ▢ Ⓓ ▭

Use the grid for
questions 5 and 6.

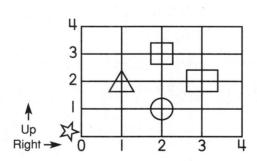

5. Start at ☆. Go right 2.
   Go up 1. Which shape
   is there?

   Ⓐ △ Ⓑ ▢
   Ⓒ ◯ Ⓓ ▭

6. Start at ☆. Go right 3.
   Go up 2. Which shape is
   there?

   Ⓐ △ Ⓑ ▢
   Ⓒ ◯ Ⓓ ▭

Use the picture for questions 7 to 10.

<Left

Right >

---

7. Which is to the **left** of the ?

Ⓐ

Ⓑ

Ⓒ

Ⓓ

---

8. Which is to the **right** of the ?

Ⓐ

Ⓑ

Ⓒ

Ⓓ

---

9. Which is to the **right** of the

the  ?

Ⓐ

Ⓑ

Ⓒ

Ⓓ

---

10. Which is to the **left** of the

the ?

Ⓐ

Ⓑ

Ⓒ

Ⓓ

Form A • Multiple-Choice   A34   **Stop!**

Choose the correct answer.

1. Which is the pattern?

Ⓐ ▦

Ⓑ ▨

Ⓒ ▬

Ⓓ ▤

2. Which is the pattern?

Ⓐ ◇ ◈

Ⓑ ◈ ◈

Ⓒ ◈ ◇

Ⓓ ◇ ◇

3. Which shape comes next in the pattern?

Ⓐ △

Ⓑ ◯

Ⓒ ▭

Ⓓ ☐

4. Which shape comes next in the pattern?

Ⓐ ☐

Ⓑ ■

Ⓒ ▮

Ⓓ ▲

5. Which shapes come next in the pattern?

□ ○ □ ○ □ ○ _?_ _?_

Ⓐ ○ ○   Ⓑ □ □

Ⓒ △ ○   Ⓓ □ ○

6. Which shapes come next in the pattern?

⊘ ⊙ ⊜ ⊘ ⊙ ⊘ ⊙ ⊜ _?_ _?_

Ⓐ ⊙ ⊜   Ⓑ ⊜ ⊙

Ⓒ ⊘ ⊙   Ⓓ ⊜ ⊘

7. Find a different pattern that uses the same shapes as this one.

○ □ △ ○ □ △ ○ □ △

Ⓐ □ ○ □ ○ □ ○

Ⓑ ○ □ □ ○ □ □

Ⓒ □ ○ △ □ ○ △

8. Find a different pattern that uses the same shapes as this one.

△ △ □ △ △ □ △ △ □

Ⓐ △ △ ○ △ △ ○

Ⓑ △ □ △ □ △ □

Ⓒ □ ◇ □ ◇ □ ◇

9. Which shape is a mistake in the pattern?

□ □ □ □ □ ○

Ⓐ □   Ⓑ □

Ⓒ ○   Ⓓ △

10. Which shape fixes the mistake in the pattern?

□ ○ ○ □ ○ ○ ✗ ○ ○

Ⓐ ○   Ⓑ □

Ⓒ △   Ⓓ □

Choose the correct answer.

1. Which object has the same shape?

A
B
C
D

2. Which object has the same shape?

A
B
C
D

3. Which solid figure will stack?

A
B
C
D

4. Which plane figure matches the face of the solid figure?

A
B
C
D

5. Which figure has 4 sides and 4 corners?

A
B
C
D

6. Which line makes two sides that match?

A
B
C
D

Use the grid for questions 7 and 8.

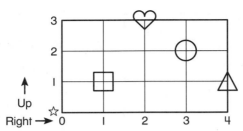

7. Start at ☆. Go right 3. Go up 2. Which shape is there?

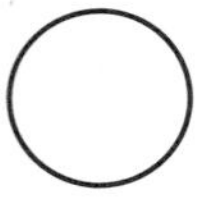

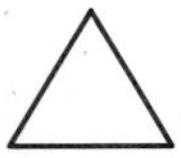

(A) ◯ (B) ♡ (C) △ (D) □

8. Start at ☆. Go right 4. Go up 1. Which shape is there?

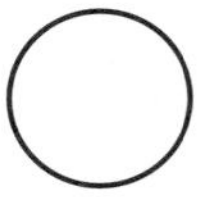

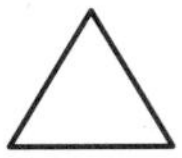

(A) ◯ (B) ♡ (C) △ (D) □

9. Which is an open figure?

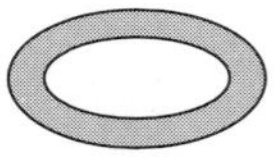

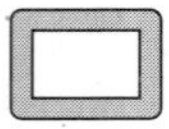

(A) □ (B) ⬭ (C) ⬠ (D) ◯

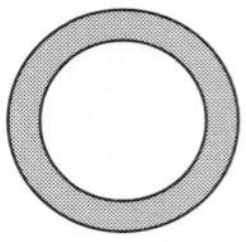

10. Which is next in the pattern?

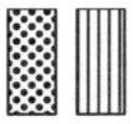

(A)   (B)   (C)   (D)

11. Find a different pattern that uses the same shapes as this one.

△◯□△◯□△◯□

(A) △□□□△□□□

(B) ◯△□◯△□

(C) □◯◇□◯◇

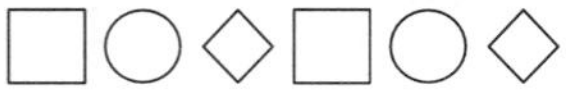

12. Which shape is a mistake in the pattern?

(A) ◇ (B) △ (C) ◯ (D) □

Choose the correct answer.

I.

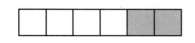

$$4 + 2 = \underline{\qquad}$$

(A) 3 (B) 4
(C) 5 (D) 6

2. Which addition sentence tells how many in all?

(A) $1 + 2 = 3$
(B) $3 + 1 = 4$
(C) $4 + 1 = 5$
(D) $5 + 1 = 6$

3.

5 fish swim in a group.
2 swim away.
How many are left?

(A) 1 fish (B) 2 fish
(C) 3 fish (D) 4 fish

4. Which subtraction sentence tells how many are left?

(A) $6 - 1 = 5$
(B) $6 - 2 = 4$
(C) $6 - 3 = 3$
(D) $6 - 4 = 2$

5.

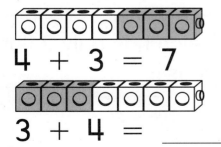

$$4 + 3 = 7$$

$$3 + 4 = \underline{\qquad}$$

(A) 5 (B) 6
(C) 7 (D) 8

6.

$$\begin{array}{r} 9 \\ -\ 5 \\ \hline \end{array}$$

(A) 1 (B) 2
(C) 3 (D) 4

7. Complete the fact family.

6 + 2 = 8   8 − 2 = 6

2 + 6 = 8   8 − 6 = __

Ⓐ 1   Ⓑ 2

Ⓒ 3   Ⓓ 4

8.

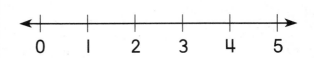

4 − 3 = _____

Ⓐ 1   Ⓑ 2

Ⓒ 3   Ⓓ 4

9. Which object has the same shape?

Ⓐ   Ⓑ

Ⓒ   Ⓓ

10. Which object has the same shape?

Ⓐ   Ⓑ

Ⓒ   Ⓓ

11. Which will roll?

Ⓐ

Ⓑ   Ⓒ

12. Which has only 2 flat faces?

Ⓐ

Ⓑ   Ⓒ

13. Which plane figure matches the face of the solid figure?

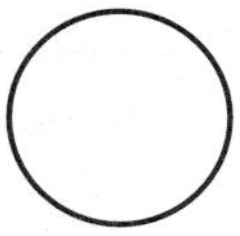

Ⓐ (circle)

Ⓑ (rectangle)

Ⓒ (triangle)

Ⓓ (square)

14. Which figure is the same size and shape as this one?

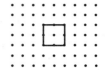

Ⓐ

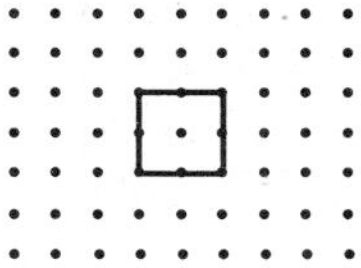

Ⓑ

Ⓒ

Ⓓ

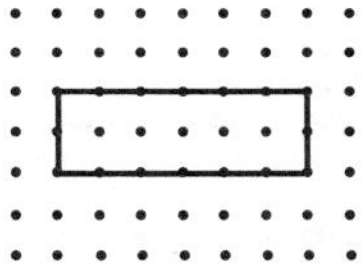

15. Which line makes two sides that match?

 Ⓐ   Ⓑ

 Ⓒ   Ⓓ

16. Which is a closed figure?

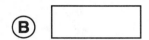 Ⓐ   Ⓑ

 Ⓒ   Ⓓ

17. Which is outside the ?

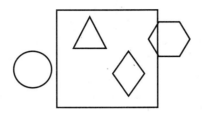

(A) △   (B) ⬡

(C) ◯   (D) ◇

18. Start at ☆. Go right 2. Go up 3. Which shape is there?

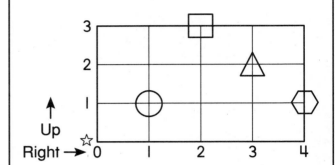

(A) ▢   (B) ⬡

(C) ◯   (D) △

19. Which shape comes next in the pattern?

 ?

(A) ◯

(B) △

(C) ▢

(D) ◇

20. Which shape is a mistake in the pattern?

(A) △

(B) ◯

(C) ⬡

(D) ▢

Choose the correct answer.

1. Count on to add.

$9 + 2 =$ _____

Ⓐ 10   Ⓑ 11
Ⓒ 12   Ⓓ 13

2. Count on to add.

$6 + 1 =$ _____

Ⓐ 5   Ⓑ 6
Ⓒ 7   Ⓓ 8

3. Count on to add.

$7 + 3 =$ _____

Ⓐ 4   Ⓑ 10
Ⓒ 11   Ⓓ 12

4. Count on to add.

$8 + 2 =$ _____

Ⓐ 6   Ⓑ 9
Ⓒ 10   Ⓓ 11

5.

$$\begin{array}{r} 3 \\ +3 \\ \hline \end{array}$$

Ⓐ 5   Ⓑ 6
Ⓒ 7   Ⓓ not here

6.

$$\begin{array}{r} 5 \\ +5 \\ \hline \end{array}$$

Ⓐ 0   Ⓑ 11
Ⓒ 12   Ⓓ not here

7. Ben spent 7¢.

Amy spent 2¢.

How much did they spend in all?

Ⓐ 6¢   Ⓑ 7¢
Ⓒ 8¢   Ⓓ 9¢

8. Sal saved 6¢.

Rosa saved 6¢.

How much did they save in all?

Ⓐ 10¢   Ⓑ 11¢
Ⓒ 12¢   Ⓓ 13¢

9.

$$\begin{array}{r} 4 \\ 3 \\ +2 \\ \hline \end{array}$$

Ⓐ 9   Ⓑ 10
Ⓒ 11   Ⓓ not here

10.

$$\begin{array}{r} 5 \\ 1 \\ +5 \\ \hline \end{array}$$

Ⓐ 10   Ⓑ 11
Ⓒ 12   Ⓓ not here

11.

$$\begin{array}{r} 7 \\ +5 \\ \hline \end{array}$$

Ⓐ 9   Ⓑ 10
Ⓒ 11   Ⓓ not here

12.

$$\begin{array}{r} 6 \\ +2 \\ \hline \end{array}$$

Ⓐ 8   Ⓑ 9
Ⓒ 10   Ⓓ not here

13.

$5 + 1 = \underline{\hspace{1.5cm}}$

Ⓐ 4   Ⓑ 5
Ⓒ 6   Ⓓ not here

14.

$8 + 3 = \underline{\hspace{1.5cm}}$

Ⓐ 5   Ⓑ 11
Ⓒ 12   Ⓓ not here

15. 4 pigs ride in the boat.
3 pigs get in with them.
How many are in the
boat?

Ⓐ 5 pigs   Ⓑ 6 pigs
Ⓒ 7 pigs   Ⓓ 8 pigs

16. 8 dogs are in the yard.
2 more come to play.
How many are in the
yard?

Ⓐ 9 dogs   Ⓑ 10 dogs
Ⓒ 11 dogs   Ⓓ 12 dogs

Name _____

Choose the correct answer.

1.

$7 + 4 = 11$

$11 - 4 = $ _____

Ⓐ 5   Ⓑ 6
Ⓒ 7   Ⓓ 8

2.

$8 + 2 = 10$

$10 - 2 = $ _____

Ⓐ 7   Ⓑ 8
Ⓒ 9   Ⓓ 10

3.

$$\begin{array}{r} 9 \\ +3 \\ \hline 12 \end{array} \qquad \begin{array}{r} 12 \\ -\ 3 \\ \hline \end{array}$$

Ⓐ 9   Ⓑ 10
Ⓒ 11   Ⓓ not here

4.

$$\begin{array}{r} 5 \\ +6 \\ \hline 11 \end{array} \qquad \begin{array}{r} 11 \\ -\ 6 \\ \hline \end{array}$$

Ⓐ 6   Ⓑ 7
Ⓒ 8   Ⓓ not here

5. Count back to subtract.

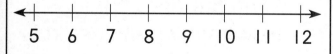

$9 - 3 = $ _____

Ⓐ 4   Ⓑ 5
Ⓒ 6   Ⓓ 7

6. Count back to subtract.

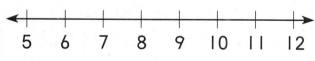

$11 - 2 = $ _____

Ⓐ 10   Ⓑ 9
Ⓒ 8   Ⓓ 2

Form A • Multiple-Choice   **A45**   **Go on.**

7. How many more bananas than pears are there?

$$\begin{array}{r} 8 \\ -4 \\ \hline \end{array}$$

Ⓐ 1 Ⓑ 2
Ⓒ 3 Ⓓ 4

8. How many fewer apples than oranges are there?

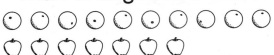

$$\begin{array}{r} 10 \\ -7 \\ \hline \end{array}$$

Ⓐ 2 Ⓑ 3
Ⓒ 4 Ⓓ 5

Which number sentence belongs in the fact family?

9.
8 + 4 = 12
4 + 8 = 12
12 − 4 = 8

Ⓐ 4 + 4 = 8
Ⓑ 8 − 4 = 4
Ⓒ 12 − 6 = 6
Ⓓ 12 − 8 = 4

10.
11 − 2 = 9
11 − 9 = 2
9 + 2 = 11

Ⓐ 2 + 9 = 11
Ⓑ 2 + 7 = 9
Ⓒ 11 − 4 = 7
Ⓓ 9 − 2 = 7

Which number sentence does the story show?

11. Joe had 11 pencils.
He lost 3 of them.
How many pencils does
Joe have left?

Ⓐ 8 + 3 = 11
Ⓑ 11 − 3 = 8
Ⓒ 11 + 3 = 14
Ⓓ not here

12. I have 7 pennies.
I find 5 more pennies.
How many pennies do I
have now?

Ⓐ 7 − 5 = 2
Ⓑ 7 + 2 = 9
Ⓒ 7 + 5 = 12
Ⓓ not here

Choose the correct answer.

1.

$9 + 3 = $ _____

(A) 10   (B) 11
(C) 12   (D) not here

2.

$$\begin{array}{r} 3 \\ +3 \\ \hline \end{array}$$

(A) 0   (B) 6
(C) 7   (D) not here

3.

$$\begin{array}{r} 2 \\ 4 \\ +3 \\ \hline \end{array}$$

(A) 6   (B) 7
(C) 8   (D) not here

4.

$$\begin{array}{r} 9 \\ 2 \\ +1 \\ \hline \end{array}$$

(A) 10   (B) 11
(C) 12   (D) not here

5. Toby spent 4¢.
Ann spent 6¢.
How much did they
spend in all?

(A) 10¢   (B) 11¢
(C) 12¢   (D) 13¢

6. 5 birds are eating.
6 more birds come to eat.
How many birds are
eating?

(A) 11 birds   (B) 12 birds
(C) 13 birds   (D) 14 birds

7.

$$\begin{array}{r} 7 \\ +2 \\ \hline 9 \end{array}$$

$$\begin{array}{r} 9 \\ -2 \\ \hline \end{array}$$

(A) 6   (B) 7

(C) 8   (D) not here

8.

5 6 7 8 9 10 11 12

$$8 - 3 = \_\_\_\_$$

(A) 2   (B) 3

(C) 4   (D) 5

9. How many more oranges than lemons are there?

$$\begin{array}{r} 11 \\ -8 \\ \hline \end{array}$$

(A) 3   (B) 4

(C) 5   (D) 6

10. Which number sentence belongs in this fact family?

$$11 - 4 = 7$$
$$11 - 7 = 4$$
$$7 + 4 = 11$$

(A) $4 + 3 = 7$

(B) $4 + 7 = 11$

(C) $11 - 6 = 5$

(D) $7 - 4 = 3$

11. Which number sentence does the story show?

Max had 12 apples.
He gave away 9.
How many are left?

(A) $6 + 3 = 9$

(B) $12 - 9 = 3$

(C) $9 - 6 = 3$

(D) not here

12. Which number sentence does the story show?

I had 1 penny.
I found 9 more.
How many do I have?

(A) $10 - 9 = 1$

(B) $1 + 8 = 9$

(C) $1 + 9 = 10$

(D) not here

Choose the correct answer.

1.

3 boys draw.
I boy cuts.
How many in all?

Ⓐ 3 boys   Ⓑ 4 boys
Ⓒ 5 boys   Ⓓ 6 boys

2.

5 dogs play.
2 go away.
How many are left?

Ⓐ I dog   Ⓑ 2 dogs
Ⓒ 3 dogs   Ⓓ 4 dogs

3. Use cubes.
Which is a way to
make 8?

Ⓐ 4 + 2   Ⓑ 5 + 1
Ⓒ 6 + 3   Ⓓ 7 + 1

4. Which object has the
same shape?

Ⓐ   Ⓑ

Ⓒ   Ⓓ

5. Which plane figure
matches the face of the
solid figure? →

Ⓐ [rectangle]   Ⓑ [square]

Ⓒ [triangle]   Ⓓ [circle]

6. Which is an open figure?

Ⓐ [square]   Ⓑ [rectangle]

Ⓒ [hexagon]   Ⓓ [open circle / C shape]

7. Which shape comes next in the pattern?

- Ⓐ shape with vertical lines
- Ⓑ ◯
- Ⓒ dotted circle
- Ⓓ ⬤

8. Find a different pattern that uses the same shapes as this one.

- Ⓐ ▢ ⬠ △ ▢ ⬠ △
- Ⓑ ▢ ◯ △ ▢ ◯ △
- Ⓒ ▢ ▭ ◯ ▢ ▭ ◯

9. Count on to add.

$$7 + 3 = \underline{\hspace{1cm}}$$

- Ⓐ 8
- Ⓑ 9
- Ⓒ 10
- Ⓓ 11

10. Count on to add.

$$5 + 2 = \underline{\hspace{1cm}}$$

- Ⓐ 6
- Ⓑ 7
- Ⓒ 8
- Ⓓ 9

11.

$$\begin{array}{r} 6 \\ + 6 \\ \hline \end{array}$$

- Ⓐ 6
- Ⓑ 10
- Ⓒ 11
- Ⓓ not here

12.

$$\begin{array}{r} 9 \\ + 2 \\ \hline \end{array}$$

- Ⓐ 10
- Ⓑ 11
- Ⓒ 12
- Ⓓ not here

13.

$$\begin{array}{r} 3 \\ + 5 \\ \hline \end{array}$$

Ⓐ 8　　　Ⓑ 9
Ⓒ 10　　Ⓓ not here

14.

$$\begin{array}{r} 6 \\ 3 \\ + 1 \\ \hline \end{array}$$

Ⓐ 8　　　Ⓑ 9
Ⓒ 10　　Ⓓ not here

15. 8 pigs are in the pen.
I more pig comes.
How many pigs are
in the pen?

Ⓐ 6 pigs　　Ⓑ 7 pigs
Ⓒ 8 pigs　　Ⓓ 9 pigs

16. 5 bugs sit on a leaf.
2 more bugs come to sit.
How many bugs are
sitting on the leaf?

Ⓐ 6 bugs　　Ⓑ 7 bugs
Ⓒ 8 bugs　　Ⓓ 9 bugs

17.

$$\begin{array}{r} 7 \\ + 4 \\ \hline 11 \end{array} \qquad \begin{array}{r} 11 \\ - 4 \\ \hline \end{array}$$

Ⓐ 10　　　Ⓑ 11
Ⓒ 12　　　Ⓓ not here

18. Count back to subtract.

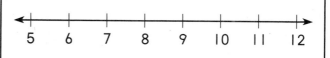

$$8 - 3 = \underline{\qquad}$$

Ⓐ 3　　　Ⓑ 4
Ⓒ 5　　　Ⓓ 6

19. Which number sentence belongs in this fact family?

$$7 + 2 = 9$$
$$2 + 7 = 9$$
$$9 - 2 = 7$$

(A) $9 - 7 = 2$
(B) $11 - 9 = 2$
(C) $9 + 2 = 11$
(D) $2 + 9 = 11$

20. How many fewer oranges than apples are there?

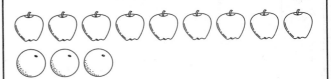

$$\begin{array}{r} 9 \\ -\ 3 \\ \hline \end{array}$$

(A) 6   (B) 7
(C) 8   (D) 9

21. Which number sentence does the story show?

Mary had 10 sheep.

She lost 2 of them.

How many sheep does Mary have left?

(A) $10 + 2 = 12$
(B) $8 + 2 = 10$
(C) $10 - 2 = 8$
(D) not here

22. Which number sentence does the story show?

Tom had 6 shells.

He found 5 more.

How many shells does Tom have now?

(A) $6 - 5 = 1$
(B) $6 + 5 = 11$
(C) $6 + 6 = 12$
(D) not here

Name _____

Choose the correct answer.
How many?

1.

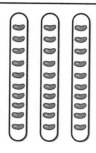

- Ⓐ 3 ones = 3
- Ⓑ 1 ten = 10
- Ⓒ 3 tens = 30
- Ⓓ 4 tens = 40

2.

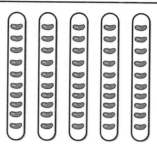

- Ⓐ 5 ones = 5
- Ⓑ 5 tens = 50
- Ⓒ 6 tens = 60
- Ⓓ 7 tens = 70

3.

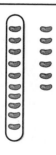

- Ⓐ 1 ten 6 ones = 16
- Ⓑ 1 ten 7 ones = 17
- Ⓒ 6 tens 1 one = 61
- Ⓓ not here

4.

- Ⓐ 1 ten 1 one = 11
- Ⓑ 1 ten 2 ones = 12
- Ⓒ 2 tens 1 one = 21
- Ⓓ not here

5.

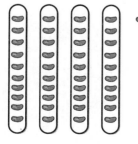

- Ⓐ 14
- Ⓑ 23
- Ⓒ 40
- Ⓓ not here

6.

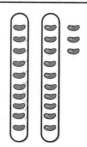

- Ⓐ 23
- Ⓑ 30
- Ⓒ 32
- Ⓓ not here

Form A • Multiple-Choice   A53

7.

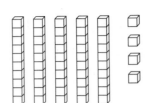

(A) 9   (B) 45
(C) 46   (D) 54

8.

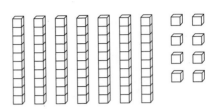

(A) 15   (B) 67
(C) 78   (D) 80

9.

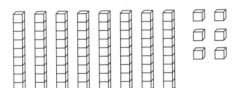

(A) 14   (B) 68
(C) 86   (D) 88

10.

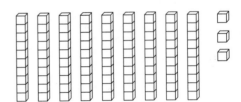

(A) 12   (B) 39
(C) 90   (D) 93

11. Which is the better estimate?

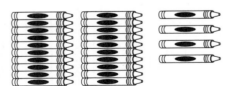

(A) more than ten
(B) fewer than ten

12. Which is the better estimate?

(A) more than ten
(B) fewer than ten

Name _____

Choose the correct answer.
Use this picture for questions 1 and 2.

first

---

1. Which animal is fifth?

 (A)

(B)

(C)

(D)

2. In which place is the

 ?

(A) second
(B) fourth
(C) seventh
(D) eighth

---

3. Which number is **greater**?

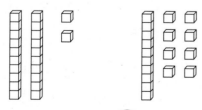

(A) 22   (B) 18

4. Which number is **greater**?

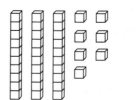 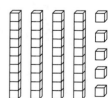

(A) 37   (B) 45

---

5. Which number is **less**?

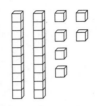

(A) 26   (B) 29

6. Which number is **less**?

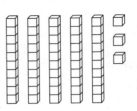 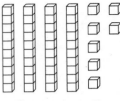

(A) 53   (B) 47

7. Which number comes just **before** 30?

_____, 30

(A) 20   (B) 25
(C) 29   (D) 31

8. Which number comes just **after** 30?

30, _____

(A) 20   (B) 25
(C) 29   (D) 31

9. Which number comes **between** 95 and 97?

95, _____, 97

(A) 94   (B) 96
(C) 98   (D) 99

10. Kurt picked a number **between** 79 and 81. Which number did he pick?

(A) 70   (B) 78
(C) 80   (D) 82

11. Which numbers are in order from **least** to **greatest**?

(A) 42, 46, 48
(B) 42, 48, 46
(C) 48, 46, 42

12. Which numbers are in order from **least** to **greatest**?

(A) 31, 52, 94, 47
(B) 94, 52, 47, 31
(C) 31, 47, 52, 94

Name _____

Choose the correct answer.
Use the chart for questions 1 and 2.

🖐🖐	🖐🖐	🖐🖐	🖐🖐	🖐🖐
10	20	____	40	____

1. Count by tens. Which number comes after 20?

   (A) 21   (B) 25
   (C) 30   (D) not here

2. Count by tens. Which number comes after 40?

   (A) 41   (B) 45
   (C) 51   (D) not here

Use the table for questions 3 and 4.

Sunday	Monday	Tuesday	Wednesday	Thursday	Friday	Saturday
10	20					

Lee saves 10 pennies each day. He starts on Sunday.

3. How many pennies does Lee have on Tuesday?

   (A) 30 pennies
   (B) 40 pennies
   (C) 50 pennies
   (D) 60 pennies

4. How many pennies does Lee have on Friday?

   (A) 50 pennies
   (B) 60 pennies
   (C) 70 pennies
   (D) 80 pennies

Use the chart for questions 5 and 6.

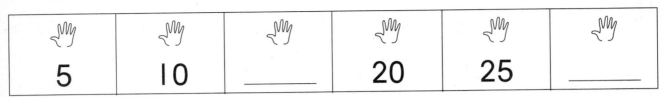

| 5 | 10 | ____ | 20 | 25 | ____ |

5. Count by fives. Which number comes after 10?

   (A) 11   (B) 15
   (C) 20   (D) not here

6. Count by fives. Which number comes after 25?

   (A) 26   (B) 30
   (C) 35   (D) not here

Use the chart for questions 7 and 8.

| 2 | 4 | 6 | ____ | 10 | 12 | ____ |

7. Count by twos. Which number comes after 6?

   (A) 5   (B) 7
   (C) 8   (D) 10

8. Count by twos. Which number comes after 12?

   (A) 11   (B) 14
   (C) 15   (D) 20

9. Even or odd?

   8 �

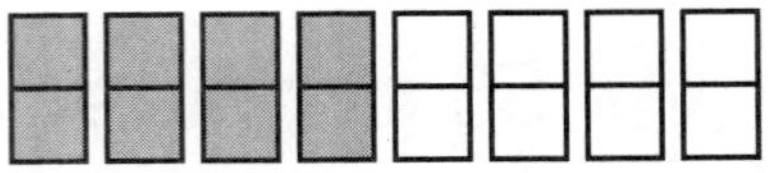

   (A) even   (B) odd

10. Even or odd?

   11

   (A) even   (B) odd

Name _____

Choose the correct answer.

1. How many?

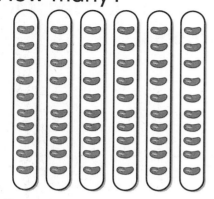

Ⓐ 6 ones = 6
Ⓑ 3 tens = 30
Ⓒ 6 tens = 60
Ⓓ 8 tens = 80

2. How many?

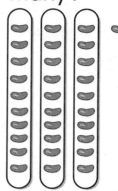

Ⓐ 13   Ⓑ 31
Ⓒ 33   Ⓓ not here

3. How many?

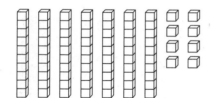

Ⓐ 78   Ⓑ 80
Ⓒ 87   Ⓓ not here

4. Which is the better estimate?

Ⓐ more than ten
Ⓑ fewer than ten

5. Which number is **greater**?

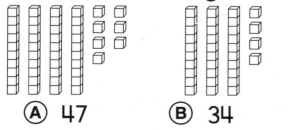

Ⓐ 47   Ⓑ 34

6. Which number comes just **before** 76?

_____, 76

Ⓐ 57   Ⓑ 65
Ⓒ 70   Ⓓ 75

7. Jan picked a number **between** 55 and 57. Which number did she pick?

Ⓐ 54 Ⓑ 56
Ⓒ 58 Ⓓ 60

8. Which numbers are in order from **least** to **greatest**?

Ⓐ 54, 65, 71, 83
Ⓑ 71, 83, 54, 65
Ⓒ 83, 71, 65, 54

9. Count by tens. Which number comes **after** 70?

Ⓐ 60 Ⓑ 71
Ⓒ 90 Ⓓ not here

10. Count by fives. Which number comes **after** 20?

Ⓐ 15 Ⓑ 21
Ⓒ 25 Ⓓ not here

11. Count by twos. Which number comes after 16?

Ⓐ 14 Ⓑ 15
Ⓒ 17 Ⓓ 18

12. Even or odd?

14

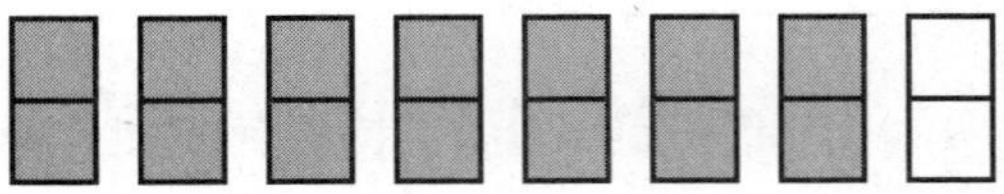

Ⓐ even Ⓑ odd

Name _____

Choose the correct answer.

1.

- (A) 1 + 3 = 4
- (B) 1 + 4 = 5
- (C) 1 + 5 = 6
- (D) 2 + 4 = 6

2. Which figure has 3 sides and 3 corners?

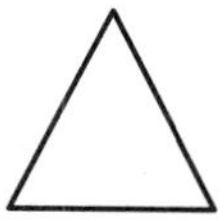

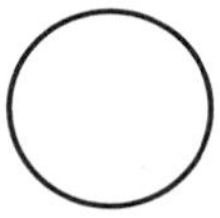

- (A)
- (B)
- (C)
- (D)

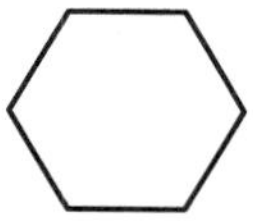

Use the picture for questions 3 and 4.

← Left   Right →

3. Which is to the **left** of the  ?

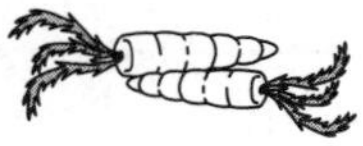

- (A)
- (B)
- (C)
- (D)

4. Which is to the **right** of the ?

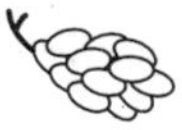

- (A)
- (B)
- (C)
- (D)

5. Count back to subtract.

$$11 - 3 = \underline{\qquad}$$

Ⓐ 4   Ⓑ 6

Ⓒ 8   Ⓓ 9

6. Which number sentence does the story show?
Bess had 9 apples.
She gave away 3.
How many apples does Bess have left?

Ⓐ $6 + 3 = 9$

Ⓑ $9 - 3 = 6$

Ⓒ $9 + 3 = 12$

Ⓓ not here

7. How many?

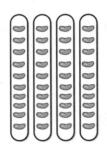

Ⓐ 4 ones = 4

Ⓑ 2 tens = 20

Ⓒ 3 tens = 30

Ⓓ 4 tens = 40

8. How many?

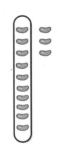

Ⓐ 3 tens 1 one = 31

Ⓑ 1 ten 3 ones = 13

Ⓒ 1 ten 2 ones = 12

Ⓓ not here

9. How many?

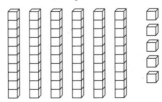

Ⓐ 11   Ⓑ 56

Ⓒ 65   Ⓓ 67

10. Which is the better estimate?

Ⓐ more than ten

Ⓑ fewer than ten

Name _____

Use the picture for questions 11 and 12.

First

---

11. **Which toy is third?**

Ⓐ

Ⓑ

Ⓒ

Ⓓ

12. **In which place is the** **?**

Ⓐ third
Ⓑ fourth
Ⓒ fifth
Ⓓ sixth

---

13. **Which number is greater?**

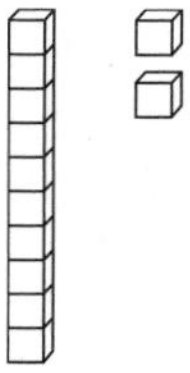

Ⓐ 12   Ⓑ 17

14. **Which number is less?**

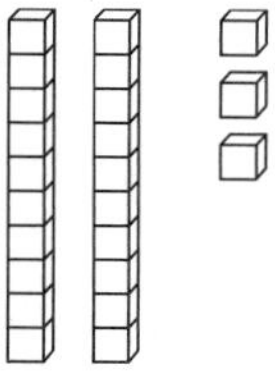

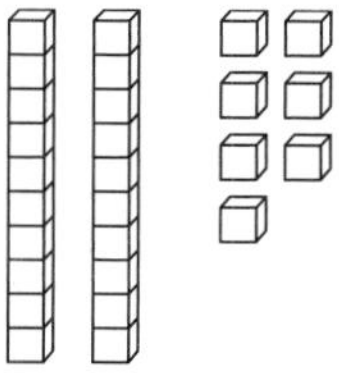

Ⓐ 23   Ⓑ 27

---

15. Kay picked a number **between** 63 and 65. What number did she pick?

Ⓐ 60   Ⓑ 61
Ⓒ 62   Ⓓ 64

16. Which numbers are in order from **least** to **greatest?**

Ⓐ 38, 36, 31
Ⓑ 31, 36, 38
Ⓒ 36, 31, 38

17. Count by tens. Which number comes after 30?

10, 20, 30, _____

Ⓐ 31   Ⓑ 35
Ⓒ 40   Ⓓ not here

18. Count by fives. Which number comes after 15?

5, 10, 15, _____

Ⓐ 16   Ⓑ 21
Ⓒ 30   Ⓓ not here

19. Count by twos. Which number comes after 4?

2, 4, _____, 8

Ⓐ 3   Ⓑ 5
Ⓒ 6   Ⓓ 7

20. Even or odd?

10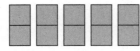

Ⓐ even   Ⓑ odd

Name _____

Choose the correct answer.

1.

Ⓐ 4¢   Ⓑ 20¢
Ⓒ 25¢   Ⓓ 40¢

2.

Ⓐ 2¢   Ⓑ 5¢
Ⓒ 10¢   Ⓓ 20¢

3.

Ⓐ 1¢   Ⓑ 5¢
Ⓒ 10¢   Ⓓ 25¢

4.

Ⓐ 3¢   Ⓑ 15¢
Ⓒ 25¢   Ⓓ 30¢

5. Which shows how to count these coins?

Ⓐ 1¢, 2¢, 3¢
Ⓑ 5¢, 10¢, 11¢
Ⓒ 10¢, 20¢, 25¢
Ⓓ not here

6. Which shows how to count these coins?

Ⓐ 1¢, 2¢, 3¢, 4¢
Ⓑ 5¢, 10¢, 11¢, 12¢
Ⓒ 10¢, 20¢, 21¢, 22¢
Ⓓ not here

7. Which amount do these coins add up to?

Ⓐ 8¢   Ⓑ 13¢
Ⓒ 18¢   Ⓓ not here

8. Which amount do these coins add up to?

Ⓐ 16¢   Ⓑ 21¢
Ⓒ 30¢   Ⓓ not here

9. Which coins add up to the amount on the tag?

 **20¢**

Ⓐ

Ⓑ

Ⓒ

Ⓓ

10. Which coins add up to the amount on the tag?

16¢

Ⓐ

Ⓑ

Ⓒ

Ⓓ

Form A • Multiple-Choice   A66   **Stop!**

Choose the correct answer.

1. Which coins can you trade these pennies for?

(A)

(B)

(C)

(D)

2. Which coins can you trade these pennies for?

(A)

(B)

(C)

(D)

3. Which answer shows the amount using the fewest coins?

20¢

(A)

(B)

(C)

(D)

4. Which answer shows the amount using the fewest coins?

25¢

(A)

(B)

(C)

(D)

5. Which coins do you need?

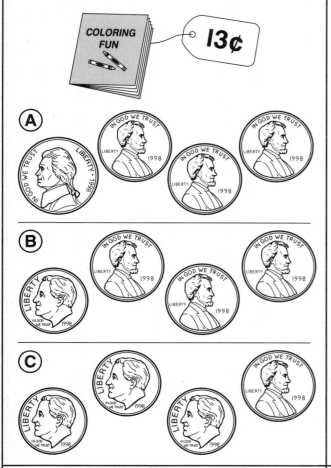

COLORING FUN

13¢

Ⓐ

Ⓑ

Ⓒ

6. Which coins do you need?

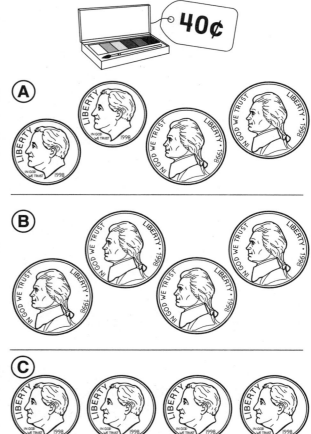

40¢

Ⓐ

Ⓑ

Ⓒ

7. Which coins have the same value as

 ?

Ⓐ 5 pennies
Ⓑ 10 pennies
Ⓒ 20 pennies
Ⓓ 25 pennies

8. Which coins have the same value as

 ?

Ⓐ five nickels
Ⓑ five dimes
Ⓒ 2 nickels and 1 dime
Ⓓ 3 dimes and 1 nickel

9. Which toy can you buy with  ?

Ⓐ 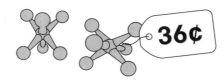 36¢

Ⓑ 29¢

Ⓒ 26¢

Ⓓ 30¢

10. Which toy can you buy with   ?

Ⓐ  40¢

Ⓑ  30¢

Ⓒ 25¢

Ⓓ  20¢

Use the calendar to answer questions 1 to 6.

July

Sunday	Monday	Tuesday	Wednesday	Thursday	Friday	Saturday
		1	2	3	4	5
6	7	8	9	10	11	12
13	14	15	16	17	18	19
20	21	22	23	24	25	26
27	28	29	30	31		

1. How many days are in one week?

   Ⓐ 5 days
   Ⓑ 7 days
   Ⓒ 31 days
   Ⓓ not here

2. Which day comes just before Saturday?

   Ⓐ Friday
   Ⓑ Sunday
   Ⓒ Tuesday
   Ⓓ not here

3. On which day does the month begin?

   Ⓐ Sunday   Ⓑ Monday
   Ⓒ Tuesday Ⓓ Friday

4. On which day is July 19?

   Ⓐ Sunday   Ⓑ Tuesday
   Ⓒ Friday   Ⓓ Saturday

5. What is the date of the first Monday?

   Ⓐ July 1   Ⓑ July 6
   Ⓒ July 7   Ⓓ not here

6. How many days are there in July?

   Ⓐ 7 days   Ⓑ 28 days
   Ⓒ 30 days Ⓓ not here

Choose the correct answer.

7. When does this happen?

Ⓐ In the morning
Ⓑ In the afternoon
Ⓒ In the evening

8. When does this happen?

Ⓐ In the morning
Ⓑ In the afternoon
Ⓒ In the evening

9. Which takes longer?

Ⓐ

Ⓑ

10. Which takes longer?

Ⓐ

Ⓑ

Choose the correct answer.

1. **What time is it?**

Ⓐ 3 o'clock
Ⓑ 4 o'clock
Ⓒ 5 o'clock
Ⓓ not here

2. **What time is it?**

Ⓐ 8 o'clock
Ⓑ 9 o'clock
Ⓒ 12 o'clock
Ⓓ not here

3. **Which clock shows the same time?**

Ⓐ `1:00`

Ⓑ `7:00`

Ⓒ `11:00`

Ⓓ not here

4. **Which clock shows the same time?**

Ⓐ `12:00`

Ⓑ `2:00`

Ⓒ `6:00`

Ⓓ not here

5. Which clock shows the same time?

A   **B**

C   **D**

6. Which clock shows the same time?

A   **B**

C   **D**

7. What time is it?

A 2:00   **B** 2:30
C 3:00   **D** not here

8. What time is it?

A 6:30   **B** 7:00
C 7:30   **D** not here

9. Which takes more than a minute to do?

A   **B**   **C**
patting   waving   reading
a dog   good-bye   a book

10. Which takes less than a minute to do?

A   **B**   **C**
putting   walking   going
on shoes   a dog   to school

Choose the correct answer.

1. Which amount do these coins add up to?

Ⓐ 3¢ Ⓑ 10¢
Ⓒ 15¢ Ⓓ 30¢

2. Which amount do these coins add up to?

Ⓐ 8¢ Ⓑ 10¢
Ⓒ 14¢ Ⓓ not here

3. Which coins add up to the amount on the tag?

16¢

Ⓐ

Ⓑ

4. Which answer shows the amount using the fewest coins?

30¢

Ⓐ

Ⓑ

5. Which coins have the same value as   ?

Ⓐ 1 dime, 1 nickel
Ⓑ 2 dimes, 1 nickel
Ⓒ 2 dimes, 2 pennies
Ⓓ 3 dimes, 5 pennies

6. Which toy can you buy with

 ?

Ⓐ 28¢ Ⓑ  32¢

Ⓒ 37¢ Ⓓ  40¢

Use the calendar to answer questions 7 and 8.

May

S	M	T	W	T	F	S
				1	2	3
4	5	6	7	8	9	10
11	12	13	14	15	16	17
18	19	20	21	22	23	24
25	26	27	28	29	30	31

7. On which day is May 17?

Ⓐ Friday   Ⓑ Saturday
Ⓒ Sunday   Ⓓ Monday

8. What is the date of the last Tuesday?

Ⓐ May 12   Ⓑ May 23
Ⓒ May 27   Ⓓ May 30

9. Which takes longer?

Ⓐ   Ⓑ

10. Which clock shows the same time?

Ⓐ  1:00   Ⓑ 2:00

Ⓒ 3:00   Ⓓ not here

11. What time is it?

Ⓐ 9:30   Ⓑ 10:00
Ⓒ 10:30   Ⓓ not here

12. Which takes more than a minute to do?

Ⓐ   Ⓑ   Ⓒ

winking   buying   opening
an eye   shoes   a door

Choose the correct answer.

1.

$$\begin{array}{r} 3 \\ + \ 5 \\ \hline \end{array}$$

(A) 7   (B) 8
(C) 9   (D) 10

2. Which figure is the same size and shape as this one?

(A)   (B)

(C)   (D)

3. Which shapes come next in the pattern?

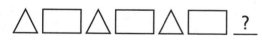 ?

(A) △▭   (B) ○△

(C) ▭○   (D) △△

4.

$$\begin{array}{r} 3 \\ 5 \\ + \ 4 \\ \hline \end{array}$$

(A) 10   (B) 11
(C) 12   (D) not here

5. Which number sentence belongs in this fact family?

$9 - 7 = 2$
$9 - 2 = 7$
$7 + 2 = 9$

(A) $9 + 2 = 11$
(B) $11 - 2 = 9$
(C) $11 - 7 = 4$
(D) $2 + 7 = 9$

6. How many?

(A) 2 ones = 2
(B) 2 tens = 20
(C) 3 tens = 30
(D) 4 tens = 40

7. Jean picked a number **between** 56 and 58. Which number did she pick?

Ⓐ 50　　Ⓑ 55
Ⓒ 57　　Ⓓ 60

8. Which number comes just **after** 29?

29, _____

Ⓐ 30　　Ⓑ 34
Ⓒ 35　　Ⓓ 38

9. Which amount do these coins add up to?

Ⓐ 2¢　　Ⓑ 20¢
Ⓒ 25¢　　Ⓓ 30¢

10. Which shows how to count these coins?

Ⓐ 1¢, 6¢, 7¢
Ⓑ 1¢, 10¢, 11¢
Ⓒ 5¢, 12¢, 13¢
Ⓓ 5¢, 10¢, 15¢

11. Which amount do these coins add up to?

Ⓐ 5¢　　Ⓑ 13¢
Ⓒ 22¢　　Ⓓ not here

12. Which amount do these coins add up to?

Ⓐ 11¢　　Ⓑ 16¢
Ⓒ 20¢　　Ⓓ not here

13. Which toy can you buy
with    ?

Ⓐ   25¢

Ⓑ  35¢

Ⓒ  36¢

Ⓓ  46¢

14. Which coins have
the same value as
 ?

Ⓐ 3 dimes
Ⓑ 2 dimes, 2 nickels
Ⓒ 2 dimes, 5 pennies
Ⓓ 3 nickels

Use the calendar for questions 15 and 16.

October

Sunday	Monday	Tuesday	Wednesday	Thursday	Friday	Saturday
			1	2	3	4
5	6	7	8	9	10	11
12	13	14	15	16	17	18
19	20	21	22	23	24	25
26	27	28	29	30	31	

15. On which day does the
month begin?
Ⓐ Wednesday
Ⓑ Thursday
Ⓒ Friday
Ⓓ Saturday

16. Which is the date of the
second Tuesday?
Ⓐ October 7
Ⓑ October 12
Ⓒ October 14
Ⓓ not here

17. When does this happen?

(A) In the morning
(B) In the afternoon
(C) In the evening

18. Which clock shows the same time?

(A)    (B)

(C)    (D)

19. What time is it?

(A) 6:00   (B) 6:30
(C) 12:00   (D) not here

20. Which takes more than a minute to do?

(A)   (B)
making   eating
a cake   a cookie

(C)
tying a shoe

Name _____

Choose the correct answer.

1. About how many  long?

  Ⓐ about 1 ⬭
  Ⓑ about 2 ⬭
  Ⓒ about 3 ⬭
  Ⓓ about 4 ⬭

2. About how many ⬭ long?

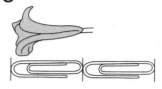

  Ⓐ about 1 ⬭
  Ⓑ about 2 ⬭
  Ⓒ about 3 ⬭
  Ⓓ about 4 ⬭

3. How many inches long?

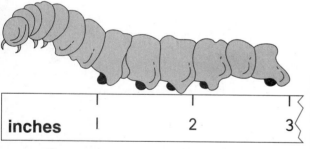

  Ⓐ 1 inch   Ⓑ 2 inches
  Ⓒ 3 inches   Ⓓ 4 inches

4. How many inches long?

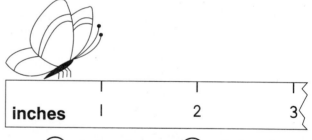

  Ⓐ 1 inch   Ⓑ 2 inches
  Ⓒ 3 inches   Ⓓ 4 inches

5. How many inches long?

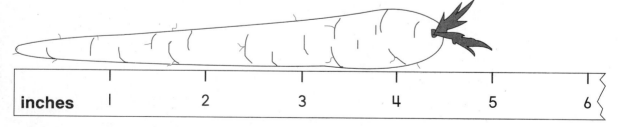

  Ⓐ 3 inches   Ⓑ 4 inches
  Ⓒ 5 inches   Ⓓ 6 inches

6. How many inches long?

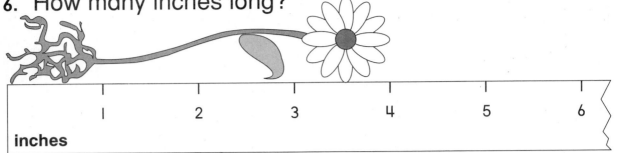

inches

Ⓐ 3 inches   Ⓑ 4 inches
Ⓒ 5 inches   Ⓓ 6 inches

7. How many centimeters long?

Ⓐ I centimeter
Ⓑ 2 centimeters
Ⓒ 3 centimeters
Ⓓ 4 centimeters

8. How many centimeters long?

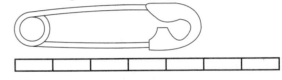

Ⓐ 4 centimeters
Ⓑ 5 centimeters
Ⓒ 6 centimeters
Ⓓ 7 centimeters

9. How many centimeters long?

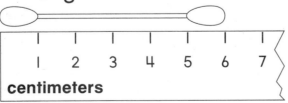

centimeters

Ⓐ 3 centimeters
Ⓑ 4 centimeters
Ⓒ 5 centimeters
Ⓓ 6 centimeters

10. How many centimeters long?

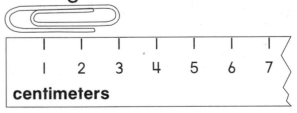

centimeters

Ⓐ I centimeter
Ⓑ 2 centimeters
Ⓒ 3 centimeters
Ⓓ 4 centimeters

Name _____

Choose the correct answer.

1. How will the balance look when the cup and the spoon are on it?

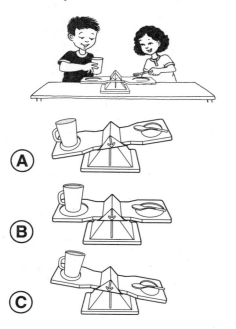

Ⓐ

Ⓑ

Ⓒ

2. How will the balance look when the milk and the straw are on it?

Ⓐ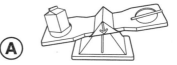

Ⓑ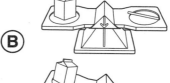

Ⓒ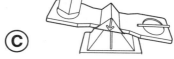

Use the pictures to answer questions 3 and 4.

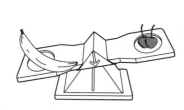  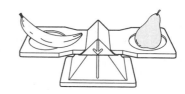

3. Which is heavier than the  ?

Ⓐ   Ⓑ

Ⓒ   Ⓓ not here

4. Which is lighter than the  ?

Ⓐ   Ⓑ

Ⓒ   Ⓓ not here

Use the pictures to answer questions 5 and 6.

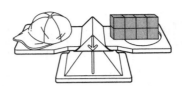 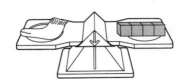 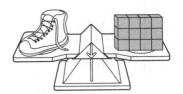

5. Which is the heaviest?

(A)

(B)

(C)

6. Which is the lightest?

(A)

(B)

(C)

7. About how many does the hold?

(A) 1   (B) 4

(C) 6   (D) 8

8. About how many  does the hold?

(A) 1   (B) 2

(C) 8   (D) 10

9. Which picture shows something hot?

(A)   (B)

(C)   (D)

10. Which picture shows something cold?

(A)

(B)

(C)

Choose the correct answer.

1. Which figure shows equal parts?

 Ⓐ   Ⓑ

Ⓒ   Ⓓ

2. Which figure shows equal parts?

Ⓐ 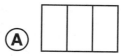   Ⓑ

Ⓒ 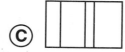   Ⓓ

3. Which picture shows halves?

Ⓐ   Ⓑ

Ⓒ   Ⓓ

4. Which figure shows halves?

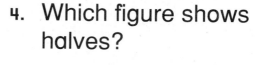

Ⓐ   Ⓑ

Ⓒ   Ⓓ

5. Which figure shows fourths?

 Ⓐ

Ⓑ

Ⓒ

6. Which figure has $\frac{1}{4}$ colored black?

Ⓐ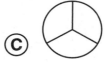

Ⓑ

Ⓒ

7. Which figure shows thirds?

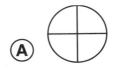 (A)   (B)

 (C)   (D)

8. Which figure has $\frac{1}{3}$ colored black?

 (A)   (B)

 (C)   (D)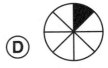

9. There are 4 children. Each gets an equal share. How would you cut the pizza?

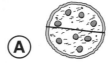 (A)   (B)

 (C)   (D)

10. There are 3 children. Each gets an equal share. How much is 1 equal share?

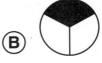 (A)   (B)

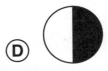 (C)   (D)

11. Which picture shows $\frac{1}{4}$ of the pears colored?

(A)

(B)

(C)

12. Which picture shows $\frac{2}{3}$ of the apples colored?

(A)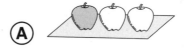

(B)

(C)

Name _____

Choose the correct answer.

1. About how many  long?

(A) about 1   (B) about 2

(C) about 3   (D) about 4

2. How many inches long?

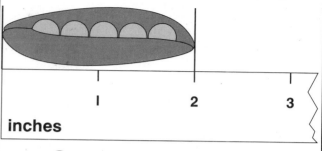

(A) 1 inch   (B) 2 inches
(C) 3 inches   (D) 4 inches

3. How many centimeters long?

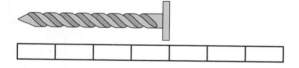

(A) 1 centimeter
(B) 2 centimeters
(C) 3 centimeters
(D) 4 centimeters

4. How many centimeters long?

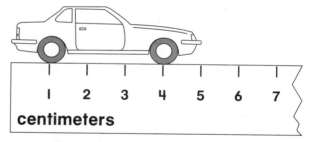

(A) 3 centimeters
(B) 4 centimeters
(C) 5 centimeters
(D) 6 centimeters

Use the pictures to answer questions 5 and 6.

5. Which is the lightest?

(A)   (B)   (C)

6. Which is the heaviest?

(A)   (B)   (C)

7. Which picture shows something hot?

Ⓐ    Ⓑ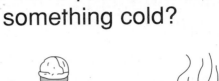

Ⓒ   Ⓓ

8. Which picture shows something cold?

Ⓐ   Ⓑ

Ⓒ   Ⓓ

9. Which figure shows equal parts?

Ⓐ   Ⓑ

Ⓒ   Ⓓ

10. Which figure shows thirds?

Ⓐ   Ⓑ

Ⓒ   Ⓓ

11. There are 2 children. Each gets an equal share.
How would you cut the sandwich?

Ⓐ   Ⓑ

Ⓒ   Ⓓ

12. Which picture shows $\frac{1}{4}$ of the strawberries colored?

Ⓐ

Ⓑ

Ⓒ

Ⓓ

Name _____

Choose the correct answer.

1. Use pennies. Find the total amount.

Ⓐ 5¢   Ⓑ 6¢
Ⓒ 7¢   Ⓓ 8¢

2. Which line makes two sides that match?

Ⓐ   Ⓑ

Ⓒ   Ⓓ

3. 6 girls come to Cam's party. 6 boys come, too. How many children come to Cam's party?

Ⓐ 3 children
Ⓑ 6 children
Ⓒ 10 children
Ⓓ 12 children

4. How many?

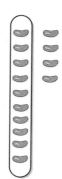

Ⓐ 1 ten 4 ones = 14
Ⓑ 1 ten 5 ones = 15
Ⓒ 4 tens 1 one = 41
Ⓓ not here

5. Which numbers are in order from **least** to **greatest**?

Ⓐ 93, 98, 96
Ⓑ 93, 96, 98
Ⓒ 98, 96, 93

6. Which amount do these coins add up to?

Ⓐ 12¢   Ⓑ 20¢
Ⓒ 22¢   Ⓓ 25¢

7. Which takes more than a minute to do?

Ⓐ
writing
your name

Ⓑ
cleaning
your room

8. About how many  long?

Ⓐ about 1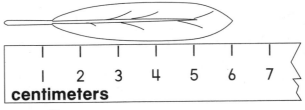
Ⓑ about 2
Ⓒ about 3

9. How many inches long?

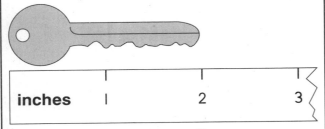

inches   1   2   3

Ⓐ 1 inch   Ⓑ 2 inches
Ⓒ 3 inches   Ⓓ 4 inches

10. How many inches long?

inches   1   2   3

Ⓐ 1 inch   Ⓑ 2 inches
Ⓒ 3 inches   Ⓓ 4 inches

11. How many centimeters long?

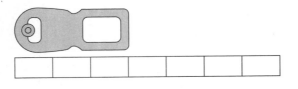

Ⓐ 1 centimeter
Ⓑ 2 centimeters
Ⓒ 3 centimeters

12. How many centimeters long?

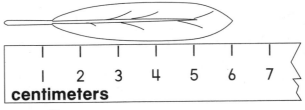

1   2   3   4   5   6   7
centimeters

Ⓐ 4 centimeters
Ⓑ 5 centimeters
Ⓒ 6 centimeters

Use the pictures for questions 13 and 14.

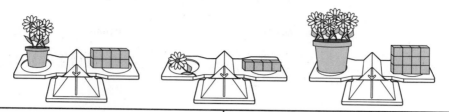

13. Which is the lightest?

Ⓐ   Ⓑ   Ⓒ

14. Which is the heaviest?

Ⓐ   Ⓑ   Ⓒ

15. How will the balance look when the book and the crayon are on it?

Ⓐ

Ⓑ

Ⓒ

16. About how many 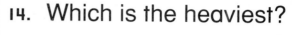 does the  hold?

Ⓐ I

Ⓑ 4

Ⓒ 8

17. Which picture shows something hot?

Ⓐ    Ⓑ

Ⓒ   Ⓓ

18. Which figure shows equal parts?

Ⓐ    Ⓑ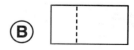

Ⓒ    Ⓓ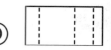

19. Which figure shows halves?

 Ⓐ  Ⓑ

 Ⓒ  Ⓓ

20. Which figure has $\frac{1}{4}$ colored black?

Ⓐ  Ⓑ

Ⓒ Ⓓ

21. Which figure has $\frac{1}{3}$ colored black?

Ⓐ  Ⓑ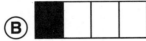

Ⓒ  Ⓓ

22. There are 4 children. Each gets an equal share. How would you cut the pizza?

Ⓐ  Ⓑ

Ⓒ 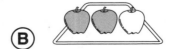 Ⓓ

23. Which picture shows $\frac{1}{3}$ of the apples colored?

Ⓐ

Ⓑ

Ⓒ

24. Which picture shows $\frac{1}{2}$ of the bananas colored?

Ⓐ

Ⓑ

Ⓒ

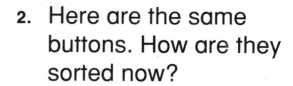

Choose the correct answer.

1. How are the buttons sorted?

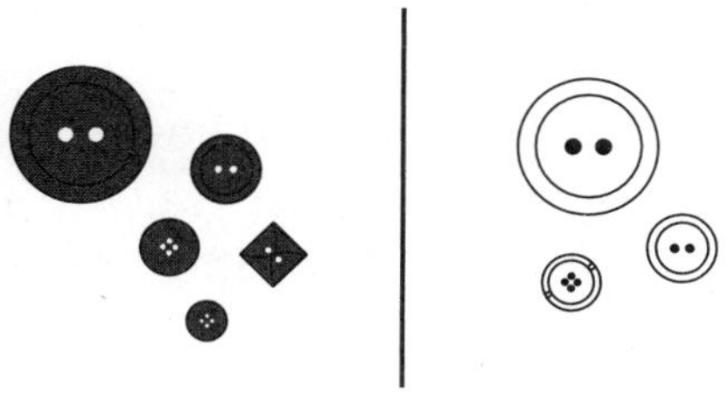

Ⓐ big–little
Ⓑ circle–square
Ⓒ black–white
Ⓓ not here

2. Here are the same buttons. How are they sorted now?

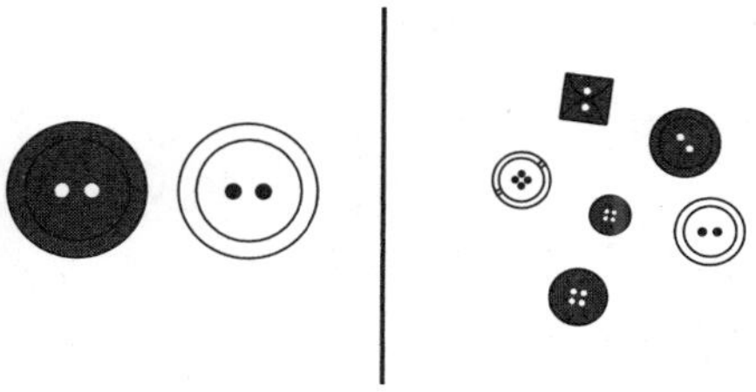

Ⓐ big–little
Ⓑ circle–square
Ⓒ black–white
Ⓓ not here

3. How many buttons are big?

Buttons

big	II
little	卌 I

Ⓐ 2   Ⓑ 6
Ⓒ I I   Ⓓ not here

4. How many buttons are black?

Buttons

black	卌
white	III

Ⓐ 2   Ⓑ 3
Ⓒ 4   Ⓓ not here

5. Which can you choose?

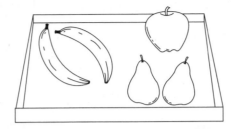

Ⓐ 🍇

Ⓑ 🍒

Ⓒ 🍊

Ⓓ 🍌

6. Which can you choose?

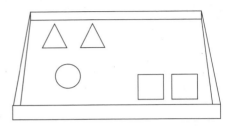

Ⓐ ◯ ◯

Ⓑ ☐ ☐ ☐

Ⓒ ◯ ☐

Ⓓ △ △ △

7. Which one will you pull out most often?

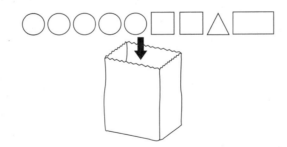

Ⓐ △

Ⓑ ◯

Ⓒ ☐

Ⓓ ▭

8. Which one will you pull out most often?

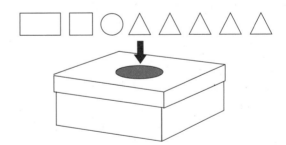

Ⓐ △

Ⓑ ◯

Ⓒ ☐

Ⓓ ▭

9. Which color will the spinner stop on most often?

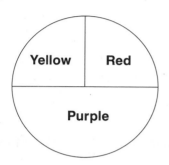

(A) Yellow

(B) Red

(C) Purple

10. Which color will the spinner stop on most often?

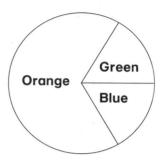

(A) Orange

(B) Green

(C) Blue

11. Which number tells how many △ ?

	Tally Marks	Total
○	|||	3
□	⊞	5
△	⊞ |||	

(A) 7
(B) 8
(C) 9

12. Which number tells how many 🚚 ?

	Tally Marks	Total
🚌	⊞ ||	7
✈	⊞	5
🚚	⊞ ||||	

(A) 7
(B) 8
(C) 9

Choose the correct answer.
Use the graph for questions 1 and 2.

Pets				Total
bird	🐦			1
fish	🐟	🐟	🐟	3
cat	🐱	🐱		2

1. How many cats are there?

Ⓐ 1 cat   Ⓑ 2 cats
Ⓒ 3 cats   Ⓓ 4 cats

2. How many pets in all?

Ⓐ 4 pets   Ⓑ 5 pets
Ⓒ 6 pets   Ⓓ 7 pets

Use the tally table for questions 3 and 4.

	Favorite Fruits		Total
🍌	bananas	IIII	4
🍐	pears	II	2
🍎	apples	ЖIII	5

3. How many children liked pears the best?
Ⓐ 2 children
Ⓑ 3 children
Ⓒ 4 children
Ⓓ 5 children

4. Which tally marks show how many chose apples?
Ⓐ II
Ⓑ III
Ⓒ IIII
Ⓓ ЖII

Name _____

Use the graph for questions 5 and 6.

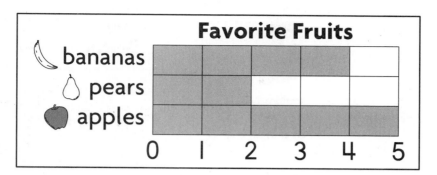

Favorite Fruits

bananas
pears
apples

0 1 2 3 4 5

5. How many children liked bananas the best?
   Ⓐ 2 children
   Ⓑ 4 children
   Ⓒ 5 children
   Ⓓ 6 children

6. Which fruit did the most children choose?
   Ⓐ bananas
   Ⓑ pears
   Ⓒ oranges
   Ⓓ apples

Use the graph for questions 7 and 8.

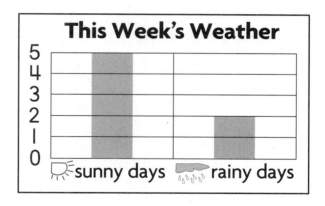

This Week's Weather

5
4
3
2
1
0

sunny days   rainy days

7. How many rainy days were there this week?

   Ⓐ 5 rainy days
   Ⓑ 4 rainy days
   Ⓒ 3 rainy days
   Ⓓ 2 rainy days

8. How many more sunny days than rainy days were there?
   Ⓐ 1 more sunny day
   Ⓑ 2 more sunny days
   Ⓒ 3 more sunny days
   Ⓓ 4 more sunny days

Use the tally table and the graph to answer
questions 9 to 12.

	Books Read	Total
Diane	III	3
Carl	II	2
Bob	IIII	4
Amy	III	

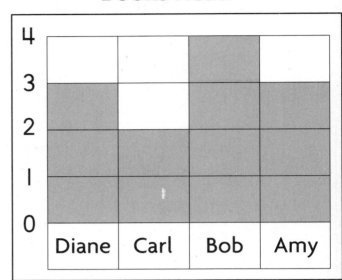

Books Read

9. What number is missing from the tally table?

    (A) 1   (B) 2
    (C) 3   (D) not here

10. How many books did Carl read?

    (A) 1 book   (B) 2 books
    (C) 3 books   (D) not here

11. Who read the fewest books?

    (A) Amy   (B) Bob
    (C) Diane   (D) not here

12. How many more books did Bob read than Amy?

    (A) 1 more   (B) 2 more
    (C) 3 more   (D) not here

Choose the correct answer.

1. How are the bugs sorted?

Ⓐ big–little
Ⓑ circle–square
Ⓒ black–white
Ⓓ not here

2. How many bugs are white?

	Tally Marks	Total
black	II	2
white	IIII	4

Ⓐ I   Ⓑ 2
Ⓒ 3   Ⓓ not here

3. Which can you choose?

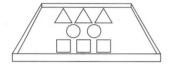

Ⓐ ☐☐☐☐   Ⓑ ○○

Ⓒ △△△△   Ⓓ ○○○△

4. Which will you pull out most often?

Ⓐ △   Ⓑ ⬡

Ⓒ ○   Ⓓ ▭

5. Which color will the spinner stop on most often?

Ⓐ Blue   Ⓑ Red   Ⓒ Green

6. Which number tells how many ?

	Tally Marks	Total
crayon	IIII III	8
pencil	III	3
ruler (inches)	IIII II	

Ⓐ 3   Ⓑ 7   Ⓒ 8

Use the graph for questions 7 and 8.

Balls					Total
baseball	⚾	⚾	⚾		3
football	🏈				1
soccer ball	⚽	⚽	⚽	⚽	4

7. How many footballs are there?
   Ⓐ 1 football
   Ⓑ 2 footballs
   Ⓒ 3 footballs
   Ⓓ 4 footballs

8. How many balls in all?
   Ⓐ 5 balls
   Ⓑ 6 balls
   Ⓒ 7 balls
   Ⓓ 8 balls

Use the tally table and the graph to answer questions 9 to 12.

Favorite Toys		Total
truck	III	3
doll	I	1
drum	IIII	
ball	II	2

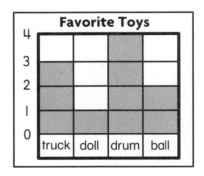

9. Which number is missing from the tally table?
   Ⓐ 2   Ⓑ 3
   Ⓒ 4   Ⓓ not here

10. How many children like dolls the best?
    Ⓐ 1 child   Ⓑ 4 children
    Ⓒ 6 children   Ⓓ not here

11. Which toy do children like the best?
    Ⓐ truck   Ⓑ doll
    Ⓒ drum   Ⓓ ball

12. How many more children like drums than dolls?
    Ⓐ 1 child   Ⓑ 2 children
    Ⓒ 3 children   Ⓓ not here

Stop!

Name _____

Choose the correct answer.

1. Which is outside the ?

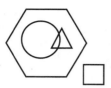

(A) ◯   (B) ☐

(C) △   (D) ⬡

2.

$$\begin{array}{r} 7 \\ + 5 \\ \hline 12 \end{array} \qquad \begin{array}{r} 12 \\ - 5 \\ \hline \end{array}$$

(A) 5   (B) 6

(C) 7   (D) not here

---

3. How many?

(A) 17   (B) 30

(C) 73   (D) not here

---

4. Count by tens. Which number comes after 50?

(A) 60   (B) 61

(C) 70   (D) not here

---

5. Which group shows the amount using the fewest coins?

 11¢

(A)

(B)

(C)

---

6. Which coins have the same value as ?

(A) five dimes

(B) 3 dimes and 1 nickel

(C) five nickels

(D) 2 nickels and 1 dime

---

7. What time is it?

Ⓐ 4:30   Ⓑ 5:00
Ⓒ 5:30   Ⓓ not here

8. How many inches long?

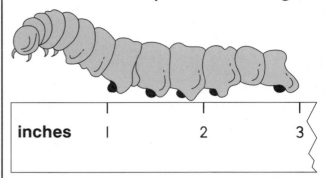

Ⓐ 1 inch   Ⓑ 2 inches
Ⓒ 3 inches   Ⓓ 4 inches

9. About how many does the hold?

Ⓐ 1    Ⓑ 2
Ⓒ 6    Ⓓ 8

10. There are 2 children. Each gets an equal share. How would you cut the sandwich?

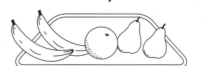

Ⓐ   Ⓑ

Ⓒ   Ⓓ

11. How many cars are red?

CARS	
red	III
white	ℍ I

Ⓐ 2   Ⓑ 3
Ⓒ 4   Ⓓ not here

12. Which can you choose?

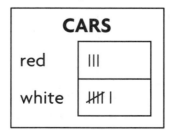

Ⓐ   Ⓑ

Ⓒ   Ⓓ

13. Which one will you pull out most often?

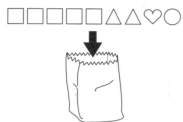

(A) △ (B) ♡
(C) ○ (D) □

14. Which number tells how many ⬠ ?

	Tally Marks	Total
□	卌	5
⬠	||||	
○	卌 |	6

(A) 3 (B) 4
(C) 5 (D) 6

Use the graph for questions 15 and 16.

	Tools			Total
hammer	hammer	hammer	hammer	3
screwdriver	screwdriver	screwdriver		2
pliers	pliers			1

15. How many hammers are there?

(A) 1 hammer
(B) 2 hammers
(C) 3 hammers
(D) 4 hammers

16. How many tools in all?

(A) 3 tools
(B) 4 tools
(C) 5 tools
(D) 6 tools

Use the graph for questions 17 and 18.

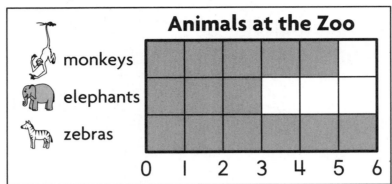

Animals at the Zoo

monkeys
elephants
zebras

0 1 2 3 4 5 6

---

17. How many monkeys were at the zoo?

Ⓐ 4 monkeys
Ⓑ 5 monkeys
Ⓒ 6 monkeys
Ⓓ 7 monkeys

18. Which animal did the zoo have the most of?

Ⓐ monkeys
Ⓑ elephants
Ⓒ lions
Ⓓ zebras

Use the tally table and the graph for questions 19 and 20.

Number of Races Won

	Number of Races Won	Total
Ben	II	2
Lisa	IIII	4
Jeb	III	3
Anna	I	1

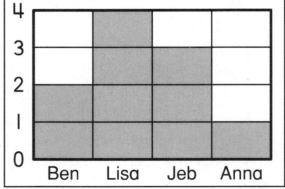

4
3
2
1
0
Ben   Lisa   Jeb   Anna

---

19. How many races did Lisa win?

Ⓐ 1 race   Ⓑ 2 races
Ⓒ 3 races   Ⓓ not here

20. How many more races did Jeb win than Anna?

Ⓐ 1 more   Ⓑ 2 more
Ⓒ 3 more   Ⓓ not here

Name _____

Choose the correct answer.

1.

$$7 \quad \quad 7$$
$$+7 \quad +8$$
$$\overline{14}$$

Ⓐ 15   Ⓑ 16
Ⓒ 17   Ⓓ 18

2.

$$5 + 5 = 10$$
$$5 + 6 = \underline{\quad\quad}$$

Ⓐ 9   Ⓑ 10
Ⓒ 11   Ⓓ 12

3.

$$3 + 3 = 6$$
$$3 + 2 = \underline{\quad\quad}$$

Ⓐ 4   Ⓑ 5
Ⓒ 6   Ⓓ 7

4.

$$9 \quad \quad 9$$
$$+9 \quad +8$$
$$\overline{18}$$

Ⓐ 15   Ⓑ 16
Ⓒ 17   Ⓓ 18

5.

$$7 + 6 = \underline{\quad\quad}$$

Ⓐ 13   Ⓑ 14
Ⓒ 15   Ⓓ not here

6.

$$6 + 5 = \underline{\quad\quad}$$

Ⓐ 9   Ⓑ 10
Ⓒ 11   Ⓓ not here

7.

$$4 + 5 = \underline{\quad\quad}$$

Ⓐ 8   Ⓑ 9
Ⓒ 10   Ⓓ not here

8.

$$8 + 7 = \underline{\quad\quad}$$

Ⓐ 16   Ⓑ 17
Ⓒ 18   Ⓓ not here

9.

$6 + 6 = 12$

$12 - 6 =$ _____

Ⓐ 4   Ⓑ 5
Ⓒ 6   Ⓓ 7

10.

$8 - 4 = 4$

$4 + 4 =$ _____

Ⓐ 7   Ⓑ 8
Ⓒ 9   Ⓓ 10

11.

$9 + 9 = 18$

$18 - 9 =$ _____

Ⓐ 8   Ⓑ 9
Ⓒ 10   Ⓓ not here

12.

$8 + 8 = 16$

$16 - 8 =$ _____

Ⓐ 5   Ⓑ 6
Ⓒ 7   Ⓓ not here

13. Jan has 7 dolls.
Sue has 2 more than Jan.

How many dolls do they have in all?

Ⓐ 13 dolls Ⓑ 14 dolls
Ⓒ 15 dolls Ⓓ 16 dolls

14. Tina had some cars.
Luis gave her 7 more.
Now she has 14.

How many cars did she have to start?

Ⓐ 6 cars   Ⓑ 7 cars
Ⓒ 8 cars   Ⓓ 9 cars

Name ______________________________

Choose the correct answer.

1. Make a 10. Then add.

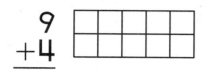

$$\begin{array}{r} 9 \\ +4 \\ \hline \end{array}$$

Ⓐ 12 Ⓑ 13
Ⓒ 14 Ⓓ 15

2. Make a 10. Then add.

$$\begin{array}{r} 8 \\ +7 \\ \hline \end{array}$$

Ⓐ 13 Ⓑ 14
Ⓒ 15 Ⓓ 16

3.

$$\begin{array}{r} 7 \\ +4 \\ \hline \end{array}$$

Ⓐ 11 Ⓑ 12
Ⓒ 13 Ⓓ not here

4.

$$\begin{array}{r} 9 \\ +7 \\ \hline \end{array}$$

Ⓐ 13 Ⓑ 14
Ⓒ 15 Ⓓ not here

5.

$$\begin{array}{r} 8 \\ 2 \\ +4 \\ \hline \end{array}$$

Ⓐ 14 Ⓑ 15
Ⓒ 16 Ⓓ 17

6.

$$\begin{array}{r} 3 \\ 4 \\ +3 \\ \hline \end{array}$$

Ⓐ 8 Ⓑ 9
Ⓒ 10 Ⓓ 11

7.

$$\begin{array}{r} 9 \\ 1 \\ +2 \\ \hline \end{array}$$

Ⓐ 9 Ⓑ 10
Ⓒ 11 Ⓓ 12

8.

$$\begin{array}{r} 5 \\ 5 \\ +3 \\ \hline \end{array}$$

Ⓐ 12 Ⓑ 13
Ⓒ 14 Ⓓ 15

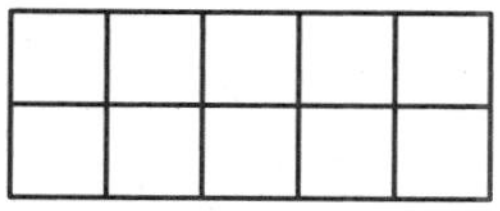

9.
$$\begin{array}{r} 9 \\ +2 \\ \hline 11 \end{array}$$

$$\begin{array}{r} 11 \\ -2 \\ \hline \end{array}$$

(A) 6   (B) 7
(C) 8   (D) 9

10.
$$\begin{array}{r} 6 \\ +7 \\ \hline 13 \end{array}$$

$$\begin{array}{r} 13 \\ -7 \\ \hline \end{array}$$

(A) 4   (B) 5
(C) 6   (D) 7

11.
$$\begin{array}{r} 8 \\ +8 \\ \hline 16 \end{array}$$

$$\begin{array}{r} 16 \\ -8 \\ \hline \end{array}$$

(A) 8   (B) 9
(C) 10   (D) 11

12.
$$\begin{array}{r} 9 \\ +8 \\ \hline 17 \end{array}$$

$$\begin{array}{r} 17 \\ -8 \\ \hline \end{array}$$

(A) 6   (B) 7
(C) 8   (D) 9

13.
$$\begin{array}{r} 5 \\ +9 \\ \hline 14 \end{array}$$

$$\begin{array}{r} 14 \\ -9 \\ \hline \end{array}$$

(A) 4   (B) 5
(C) 6   (D) not here

14.
$$\begin{array}{r} 9 \\ +9 \\ \hline 18 \end{array}$$

$$\begin{array}{r} 18 \\ -9 \\ \hline \end{array}$$

(A) 6   (B) 7
(C) 8   (D) not here

15.
$$\begin{array}{r} 9 \\ +3 \\ \hline 12 \end{array}$$

$$\begin{array}{r} 12 \\ -3 \\ \hline \end{array}$$

(A) 3   (B) 6
(C) 9   (D) not here

16.
$$\begin{array}{r} 6 \\ +9 \\ \hline 15 \end{array}$$

$$\begin{array}{r} 15 \\ -9 \\ \hline \end{array}$$

(A) 5   (B) 6
(C) 7   (D) not here

Name _____

Choose the correct answer.

1.

$$9 + 9 = \overline{18} \qquad 9 + 8$$

Ⓐ 16   Ⓑ 17
Ⓒ 18   Ⓓ 19

2.

$$4 + 4 = 8$$
$$4 + 3 = \underline{\qquad}$$

Ⓐ 5   Ⓑ 6
Ⓒ 7   Ⓓ 8

3.

$$7 + 8 = \underline{\qquad}$$

Ⓐ 12   Ⓑ 13
Ⓒ 14   Ⓓ not here

4.

$$8 + 9 = \underline{\qquad}$$

Ⓐ 17   Ⓑ 18
Ⓒ 19   Ⓓ not here

5.

$$6 + 6 = \underline{\qquad}$$

$$12 - 6 = 6$$

Ⓐ 10   Ⓑ 11
Ⓒ 12   Ⓓ 14

6. Joel had some hats.
Bess gave him 3 more.
Now he has 6.
How many hats did he
have to start?

Ⓐ 2 hats   Ⓑ 3 hats
Ⓒ 4 hats   Ⓓ 5 hats

7. Make a 10. Then add.

$$\begin{array}{r} 8 \\ + 6 \\ \hline \end{array}$$

(A) 11   (B) 12
(C) 13   (D) 14

8.

$$\begin{array}{r} 9 \\ + 2 \\ \hline \end{array}$$

(A) 10   (B) 11
(C) 12   (D) not here

9.

$$\begin{array}{r} 7 \\ 3 \\ + 2 \\ \hline \end{array}$$

(A) 12   (B) 13
(C) 14   (D) 15

10.

$$\begin{array}{r} 4 \\ 4 \\ + 7 \\ \hline \end{array}$$

(A) 13   (B) 14
(C) 15   (D) 16

11.

$$\begin{array}{r} 9 \\ + 4 \\ \hline 13 \end{array} \qquad \begin{array}{r} 13 \\ - 4 \\ \hline \end{array}$$

(A) 6   (B) 7
(C) 8   (D) 9

12.

$$\begin{array}{r} 9 \\ + 9 \\ \hline 18 \end{array} \qquad \begin{array}{r} 18 \\ - 9 \\ \hline \end{array}$$

(A) 8   (B) 9
(C) 10   (D) 11

Name _____

Choose the correct answer.
Use the picture for questions 1 and 2.

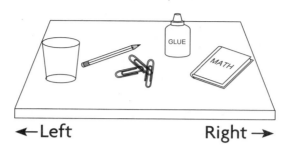

←Left   Right→

---

1. Which is to the **left** of the ?

(A)    (B)

(C)   (D) GLUE

---

2. Which is to the **right** of the GLUE ?

(A)    (B)

(C) MATH   (D)

---

3. How many more birds than nests are there?

$$10 - 5$$

(A) 5   (B) 6
(C) 7   (D) 8

---

4. Which is the better estimate?

(A) more than ten
(B) fewer than ten

---

5. Count by twos. Which number comes after 28?

24, 26, 28, _____

Ⓐ 25   Ⓑ 27

Ⓒ 30   Ⓓ 32

6. Which coins do you need?

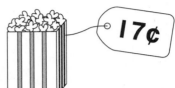

Ⓐ

Ⓑ

Ⓒ

Ⓓ not here

7. Which takes longer?

Ⓐ

Ⓑ

8. How many centimeters long?

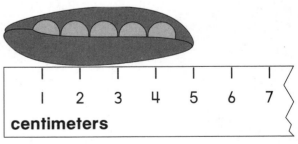

centimeters

Ⓐ 2 centimeters
Ⓑ 3 centimeters
Ⓒ 4 centimeters
Ⓓ 5 centimeters

9. Which figure shows fourths?

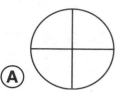

Ⓐ

Ⓑ

Ⓒ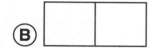

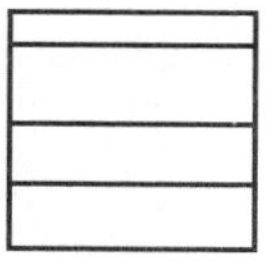

Ⓓ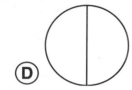

10. Which one will you pull out most often?

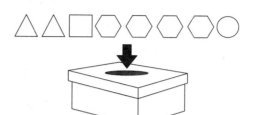

Ⓐ ☐

Ⓑ △

Ⓒ ⬡

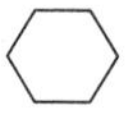

Ⓓ ◯

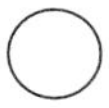

Use the graph for questions 11 and 12.

Farm Animals				Total
cow	 🐄	 🐄		2
chicken	 🐓			1
pig	 🐖	 🐖	 🐖	3

11. How many cows are there?

Ⓐ 2 cows
Ⓑ 3 cows
Ⓒ 4 cows
Ⓓ 5 cows

12. How many animals are there in all?

Ⓐ 5 animals
Ⓑ 6 animals
Ⓒ 7 animals
Ⓓ 8 animals

13.

$$\begin{array}{r} 8 \\ + 8 \\ \hline 16 \end{array} \qquad \begin{array}{r} 9 \\ + 8 \\ \hline \end{array}$$

(A) 14   (B) 15
(C) 16   (D) 17

14. Ken had some books. Jim gave him 8 more. Now he has 16. How many books did Ken have to start?

(A) 7 books   (B) 8 books
(C) 9 books   (D) 10 books

15.

$$\begin{array}{r} 7 \\ + 5 \\ \hline \end{array}$$

(A) 9   (B) 10
(C) 11   (D) not here

16.

$$\begin{array}{r} 9 \\ + 2 \\ \hline \end{array}$$

(A) 9   (B) 10
(C) 11   (D) not here

17.

$$\begin{array}{r} 6 \\ 4 \\ + 2 \\ \hline \end{array}$$

(A) 12   (B) 13
(C) 14   (D) 15

18.

$$\begin{array}{r} 9 \\ + 5 \\ \hline 14 \end{array} \qquad \begin{array}{r} 14 \\ - 5 \\ \hline \end{array}$$

(A) 8   (B) 9
(C) 10   (D) 11

Name _____

Choose the correct answer.

1. How many counters?

  Ⓐ 3 counters
  Ⓑ 7 counters
  Ⓒ 10 counters
  Ⓓ 12 counters

2. How many counters?

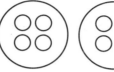

  Ⓐ 1 counter
  Ⓑ 4 counters
  Ⓒ 8 counters
  Ⓓ 12 counters

3. How many in each group?

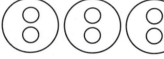

  Ⓐ 2 counters
  Ⓑ 4 counters
  Ⓒ 6 counters
  Ⓓ 8 counters

4. How many in each group?

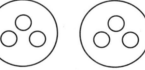

  Ⓐ 2 counters
  Ⓑ 3 counters
  Ⓒ 4 counters
  Ⓓ 6 counters

5. How many in each group?

  Ⓐ 2 counters
  Ⓑ 3 counters
  Ⓒ 4 counters
  Ⓓ 6 counters

6. How many in each group?

  Ⓐ 2 counters
  Ⓑ 3 counters
  Ⓒ 4 counters
  Ⓓ 9 counters

7. How many groups?

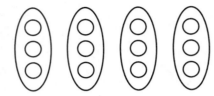

Ⓐ 3 groups
Ⓑ 4 groups
Ⓒ 6 groups
Ⓓ 9 groups

8. How many groups?

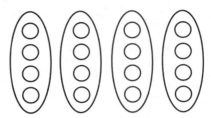

Ⓐ 4 groups
Ⓑ 6 groups
Ⓒ 8 groups
Ⓓ 12 groups

9. How many groups?

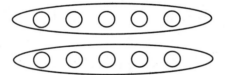

Ⓐ 2 groups
Ⓑ 3 groups
Ⓒ 4 groups
Ⓓ 5 groups

10. How many groups?

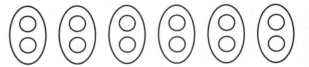

Ⓐ 3 groups
Ⓑ 4 groups
Ⓒ 5 groups
Ⓓ 6 groups

11. There are 3 bird nests.
Each nest has 2 eggs.
How many eggs in all?
Ⓐ 1 egg
Ⓑ 5 eggs
Ⓒ 6 eggs
Ⓓ 9 eggs

12. There are 8 apples.
We eat 4.
How many are left?
Ⓐ 2 apples
Ⓑ 4 apples
Ⓒ 6 apples
Ⓓ 12 apples

Name _____

Choose the correct answer.

1. Add.

$$\begin{array}{r} 30 \\ +20 \\ \hline \end{array}$$

tens	ones

Ⓐ 5 Ⓑ 10
Ⓒ 32 Ⓓ 50

2. Subtract.

$$\begin{array}{r} 70 \\ -60 \\ \hline \end{array}$$

tens	ones

Ⓐ 10 Ⓑ 13
Ⓒ 30 Ⓓ 130

3. Add.

tens	ones
3	2
+1	2

tens	ones

Ⓐ 8 Ⓑ 20
Ⓒ 24 Ⓓ 44

4. Add.

tens	ones
4	7
+2	2

tens	ones

Ⓐ 25 Ⓑ 49
Ⓒ 69 Ⓓ 96

5. Add.

tens	ones
5	1
+1	3

Ⓐ 42 Ⓑ 54
Ⓒ 64 Ⓓ 73

6. Add.

tens	ones
5	6
+3	3

Ⓐ 86 Ⓑ 89
Ⓒ 96 Ⓓ 98

7. Subtract.

tens	ones
6	7
−1	1

tens	ones

Ⓐ 56   Ⓑ 58
Ⓒ 66   Ⓓ 78

8. Subtract.

tens	ones
7	4
−2	3

tens	ones

Ⓐ 15   Ⓑ 51
Ⓒ 57   Ⓓ 97

9. Subtract.

tens	ones
3	5
−1	0

Ⓐ 10   Ⓑ 15
Ⓒ 20   Ⓓ 25

10. Subtract.

tens	ones
9	7
−8	4

Ⓐ 13   Ⓑ 23
Ⓒ 31   Ⓓ 32

Choose the answer that makes sense.

11. Joe had 35 pennies.
He spent 14 pennies.
How many does he have left?

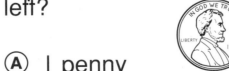

Ⓐ 1 penny
Ⓑ 21 pennies
Ⓒ 49 pennies
Ⓓ 210 pennies

12. Lisa read 16 pages.
Then she read 10 more.
How many pages did she read in all?

Ⓐ 6 pages
Ⓑ 10 pages
Ⓒ 26 pages
Ⓓ 160 pages

Choose the correct answer.

1. How many counters?

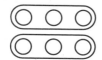

- Ⓐ 3 counters
- Ⓑ 5 counters
- Ⓒ 6 counters
- Ⓓ 8 counters

2. How many in each group?

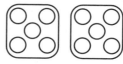

- Ⓐ 4 counters
- Ⓑ 5 counters
- Ⓒ 6 counters
- Ⓓ 7 counters

3. How many in each group?

- Ⓐ 2 counters
- Ⓑ 4 counters
- Ⓒ 6 counters
- Ⓓ 8 counters

4. How many groups?

- Ⓐ 2 groups
- Ⓑ 3 groups
- Ⓒ 4 groups
- Ⓓ 6 groups

5. How many groups?

- Ⓐ 2 groups
- Ⓑ 3 groups
- Ⓒ 4 groups
- Ⓓ 5 groups

6. There are 2 cars. Each has 4 people in it. How many people are there in all?

- Ⓐ 2 people
- Ⓑ 4 people
- Ⓒ 6 people
- Ⓓ 8 people

7. Add.

tens	ones

$$\begin{array}{r} 20 \\ + 10 \\ \hline \end{array}$$

Ⓐ 3   Ⓑ 20
Ⓒ 30   Ⓓ 31

8. Add.

tens	ones
4	1

$$\begin{array}{r} 4\ \ 1 \\ +\ 1\ \ 6 \\ \hline \end{array}$$

tens	ones

Ⓐ 11   Ⓑ 57
Ⓒ 58   Ⓓ 67

9. Add.

tens	ones
3	3

$$\begin{array}{r} 3\ \ 3 \\ +\ 3\ \ 5 \\ \hline \end{array}$$

Ⓐ 14   Ⓑ 67
Ⓒ 68   Ⓓ 86

10. Subtract.

tens	ones
5	8

$$\begin{array}{r} 5\ \ 8 \\ -\ 4\ \ 2 \\ \hline \end{array}$$

tens	ones

Ⓐ 16   Ⓑ 19
Ⓒ 61   Ⓓ 96

11. Subtract.

tens	ones
6	4

$$\begin{array}{r} 6\ \ 4 \\ -\ 2\ \ 1 \\ \hline \end{array}$$

Ⓐ 3   Ⓑ 33
Ⓒ 35   Ⓓ 43

12. Choose the answer that makes sense.

Tim saw 25 birds.
Then 11 birds flew away.
How many birds are left?

Ⓐ 1 bird   Ⓑ 14 birds
Ⓒ 36 birds   Ⓓ 140 birds

Choose the correct answer.

1. Which number sentence belongs in this fact family?

$$9 + 3 = 12$$
$$3 + 9 = 12$$
$$12 - 9 = 3$$

(A) $3 + 3 = 6$
(B) $12 - 4 = 8$
(C) $6 + 3 = 9$
(D) $12 - 3 = 9$

2. How many?

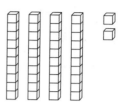

(A) 24　　(B) 42
(C) 43　　(D) 44

3. Count by fives. Which number comes after 30?

20, 25, 30, _____

(A) 40　　(B) 35
(C) 31　　(D) not here

4. Which amount do these coins add up to?

(A) 11¢　　(B) 13¢
(C) 31¢　　(D) 25¢

Name _____

Use the calendar for questions 5 and 6.

April

Sunday	Monday	Tuesday	Wednesday	Thursday	Friday	Saturday
		1	2	3	4	5
6	7	8	9	10	11	12
13	14	15	16	17	18	19
20	21	22	23	24	25	26
27	28	29	30			

5. On which day does the month end?

Ⓐ Wednesday
Ⓑ Thursday
Ⓒ Friday
Ⓓ Saturday

6. Which is the date of the first Thursday in this month?

Ⓐ April 1
Ⓑ April 3
Ⓒ April 17
Ⓓ not here

7. Which clock shows the same time?

Ⓐ 12:00   Ⓑ 1:00

Ⓒ 3:00   Ⓓ not here

8. Which figure shows halves?

Ⓐ   Ⓑ

Ⓒ 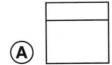   Ⓓ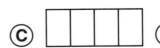

Name _____

9.

$$\begin{array}{r} 5 \\ +5 \\ \hline 10 \end{array} \qquad \begin{array}{r} 5 \\ +4 \\ \hline \end{array}$$

(A) 6   (B) 7
(C) 8   (D) 9

10.

$$\begin{array}{r} 7 \\ 3 \\ +2 \\ \hline \end{array}$$

(A) 10   (B) 11
(C) 12   (D) 13

11. How many?

(A) 2 counters
(B) 4 counters
(C) 8 counters
(D) 10 counters

12. How many in each group?

(A) 2 counters
(B) 3 counters
(C) 4 counters
(D) 5 counters

13. How many groups?

(A) 2 groups
(B) 3 groups
(C) 4 groups
(D) 6 groups

14. There are 2 baskets. Each basket has 5 cupcakes. How many cupcakes in all?

(A) 10 cupcakes
(B) 11 cupcakes
(C) 12 cupcakes
(D) 13 cupcakes

15. There are 11 balloons.
3 pop!
How many are left?

(A) 7 balloons
(B) 8 balloons
(C) 9 balloons
(D) 10 balloons

16. Subtract.

tens	ones
⦀⦀⦀⦀⦀	

$$60$$
$$- 40$$

(A) 12   (B) 20
(C) 22   (D) 120

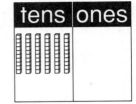

17. Add.

tens	ones
4	7
+ 1	2

(A) 35   (B) 59
(C) 60   (D) 69

18. Subtract.

tens	ones
8	6
− 2	5

(A) 51   (B) 52
(C) 60   (D) 61

19. Van had 73 pennies.
He spent 41 pennies.
How many does he
have left?

(A) 2 pennies
(B) 32 pennies
(C) 70 pennies
(D) 150 pennies

20. Rosa saw 12 birds.
Then she saw 11 more.
How many birds did she
see in all?

(A) 3 birds
(B) 10 birds
(C) 23 birds
(D) 121 birds

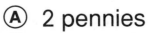

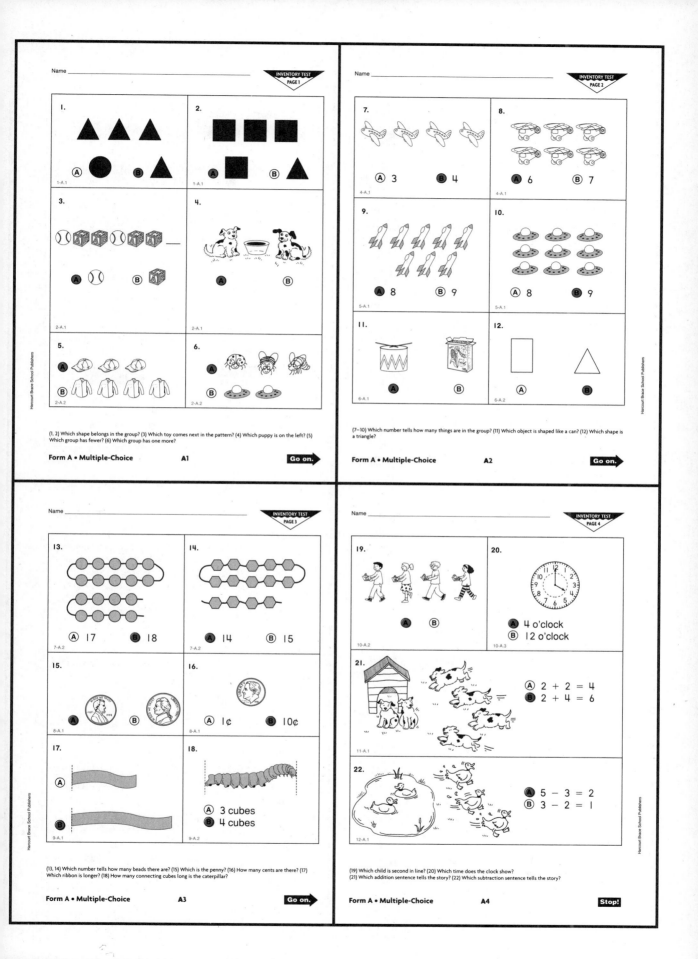

Multiple-Choice Format • Test Answers

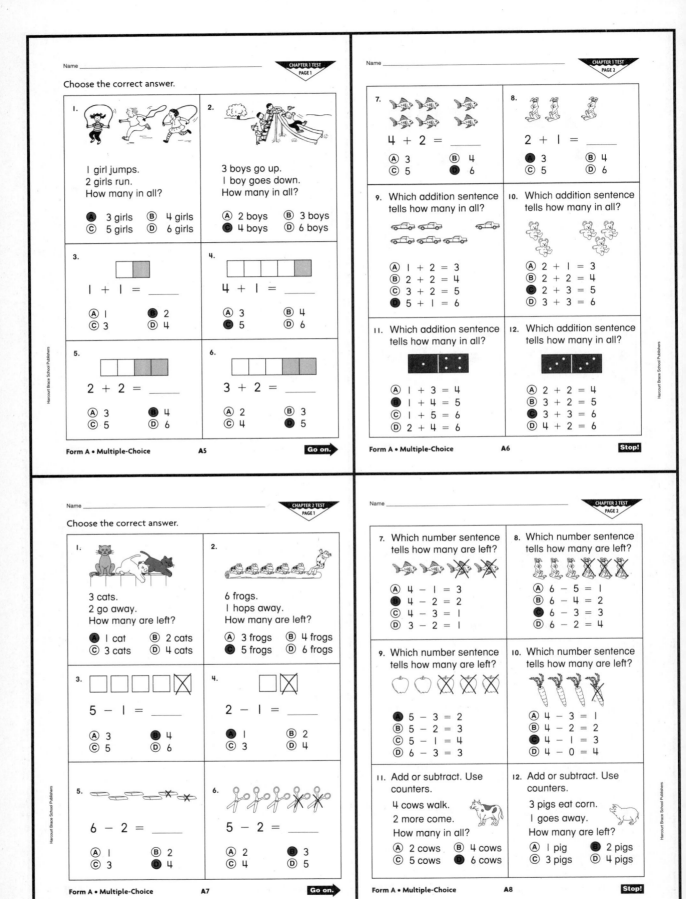

Multiple-Choice Format • Test Answers

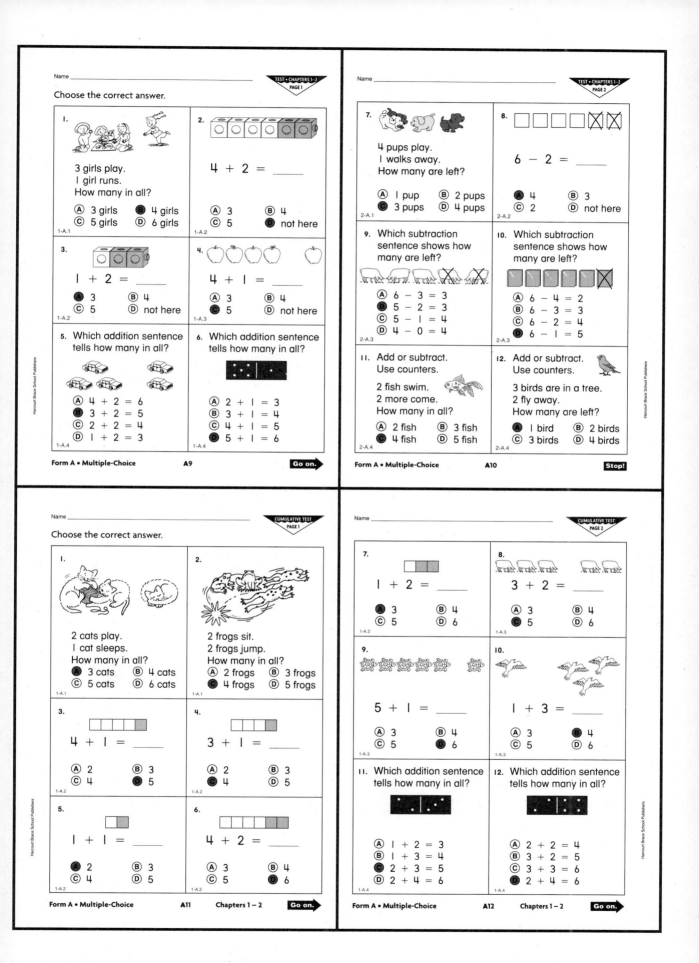

Name _____

Choose the correct answer.

1.
3 girls play.
1 girl runs.
How many in all?
- Ⓐ 3 girls
- ● 4 girls
- Ⓒ 5 girls
- Ⓓ 6 girls

1-A.1

2.
4 + 2 = _____
- Ⓐ 3
- Ⓑ 4
- Ⓒ 5
- ● not here

1-A.2

3.
1 + 2 = _____
- ● 3
- Ⓑ 4
- Ⓒ 5
- Ⓓ not here

1-A.2

4.
4 + 1 = _____
- Ⓐ 3
- Ⓑ 4
- ● 5
- Ⓓ not here

1-A.3

5. Which addition sentence tells how many in all?
- Ⓐ 4 + 2 = 6
- ● 3 + 2 = 5
- Ⓒ 2 + 2 = 4
- Ⓓ 1 + 2 = 3

1-A.4

6. Which addition sentence tells how many in all?
- Ⓐ 2 + 1 = 3
- Ⓑ 3 + 1 = 4
- Ⓒ 4 + 1 = 5
- ● 5 + 1 = 6

1-A.4

Form A • Multiple-Choice   A9   **Go on.**

Name _____

7.
4 pups play.
1 walks away.
How many are left?
- Ⓐ 1 pup
- Ⓑ 2 pups
- ● 3 pups
- Ⓓ 4 pups

2-A.1

8.
6 − 2 = _____
- ● 4
- Ⓑ 3
- Ⓒ 2
- Ⓓ not here

2-A.2

9. Which subtraction sentence shows how many are left?
- Ⓐ 6 − 3 = 3
- ● 5 − 2 = 3
- Ⓒ 5 − 1 = 4
- Ⓓ 4 − 0 = 4

2-A.3

10. Which subtraction sentence shows how many are left?
- Ⓐ 6 − 4 = 2
- Ⓑ 6 − 3 = 3
- Ⓒ 6 − 2 = 4
- ● 6 − 1 = 5

2-A.3

11. Add or subtract. Use counters.
2 fish swim.
2 more come.
How many in all?
- Ⓐ 2 fish
- Ⓑ 3 fish
- ● 4 fish
- Ⓓ 5 fish

2-A.4

12. Add or subtract. Use counters.
3 birds are in a tree.
2 fly away.
How many are left?
- ● 1 bird
- Ⓑ 2 birds
- Ⓒ 3 birds
- Ⓓ 4 birds

2-A.4

Form A • Multiple-Choice   A10   **Stop!**

Name _____

Choose the correct answer.

1.
2 cats play.
1 cat sleeps.
How many in all?
- ● 3 cats
- Ⓑ 4 cats
- Ⓒ 5 cats
- Ⓓ 6 cats

1-A.1

2.
2 frogs sit.
2 frogs jump.
How many in all?
- Ⓐ 2 frogs
- Ⓑ 3 frogs
- ● 4 frogs
- Ⓓ 5 frogs

1-A.1

3.
4 + 1 = _____
- Ⓐ 2
- Ⓑ 3
- Ⓒ 4
- ● 5

1-A.2

4.
3 + 1 = _____
- Ⓐ 2
- Ⓑ 3
- ● 4
- Ⓓ 5

1-A.2

5.
1 + 1 = _____
- ● 2
- Ⓑ 3
- Ⓒ 4
- Ⓓ 5

1-A.2

6.
4 + 2 = _____
- Ⓐ 3
- Ⓑ 4
- Ⓒ 5
- ● 6

1-A.2

Form A • Multiple-Choice   A11   Chapters 1 – 2   **Go on.**

Name _____

7.
1 + 2 = _____
- ● 3
- Ⓑ 4
- Ⓒ 5
- Ⓓ 6

1-A.2

8.
3 + 2 = _____
- Ⓐ 3
- Ⓑ 4
- ● 5
- Ⓓ 6

1-A.3

9.
5 + 1 = _____
- Ⓐ 3
- Ⓑ 4
- Ⓒ 5
- ● 6

1-A.3

10.
1 + 3 = _____
- Ⓐ 3
- ● 4
- Ⓒ 5
- Ⓓ 6

1-A.3

11. Which addition sentence tells how many in all?
- Ⓐ 1 + 2 = 3
- Ⓑ 1 + 3 = 4
- ● 2 + 3 = 5
- Ⓓ 2 + 4 = 6

1-A.4

12. Which addition sentence tells how many in all?
- Ⓐ 2 + 2 = 4
- Ⓑ 3 + 2 = 5
- ● 3 + 3 = 6
- Ⓓ 2 + 4 = 6

1-A.4

Form A • Multiple-Choice   A12   Chapters 1 – 2   **Go on.**

Multiple-Choice Format • Test Answers   127

13.

3 boys play.
I goes away.
How many are left?
Ⓐ I boy 🅑 2 boys
Ⓒ 3 boys Ⓓ 4 boys
2-A.1

14.

6 birds sit.
3 fly away.
How many are left?
🅐 3 birds Ⓑ 4 birds
Ⓒ 5 birds Ⓓ 6 birds
2-A.1

15.

6 − 1 = _____
Ⓐ 3 Ⓑ 4
🅒 5 Ⓓ 6
2-A.2

16.

4 − 1 = _____
Ⓐ 2 🅑 3
Ⓒ 4 Ⓓ 5
2-A.2

17.

5 − 1 = _____
Ⓐ I Ⓑ 2
Ⓒ 3 🅓 4
2-A.2

18.

4 − 2 = _____
🅐 2 Ⓑ 3
Ⓒ 4 Ⓓ 5
2-A.2

Form A • Multiple-Choice   A13   Chapters 1 – 2   **Go on.**

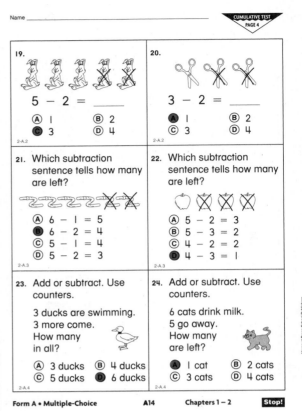

19.

5 − 2 = _____
🅐 I Ⓑ 2
Ⓒ 3 Ⓓ 4
2-A.2

20.

3 − 2 = _____
🅐 I Ⓑ 2
Ⓒ 3 Ⓓ 4
2-A.2

21. Which subtraction
sentence tells how many
are left?

Ⓐ 6 − 1 = 5
🅑 6 − 2 = 4
Ⓒ 5 − 1 = 4
Ⓓ 5 − 2 = 3
2-A.3

22. Which subtraction
sentence tells how many
are left?

Ⓐ 5 − 2 = 3
Ⓑ 5 − 3 = 2
Ⓒ 4 − 2 = 2
🅓 4 − 3 = I
2-A.3

23. Add or subtract. Use
counters.

3 ducks are swimming.
3 more come.
How many
in all?
Ⓐ 3 ducks Ⓑ 4 ducks
Ⓒ 5 ducks 🅓 6 ducks
2-A.4

24. Add or subtract. Use
counters.

6 cats drink milk.
5 go away.
How many
are left?
🅐 I cat Ⓑ 2 cats
Ⓒ 3 cats Ⓓ 4 cats
2-A.4

Form A • Multiple-Choice   A14   Chapters 1 – 2   **Stop!**

Choose the correct answer.

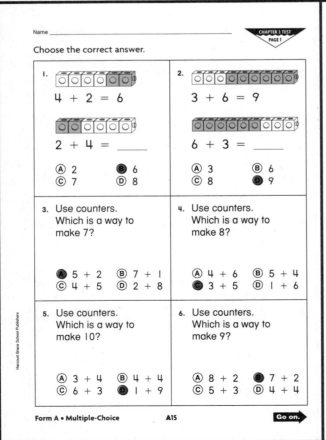

1.

4 + 2 = 6

2 + 4 = _____
Ⓐ 2 🅑 6
Ⓒ 7 Ⓓ 8

2.

3 + 6 = 9

6 + 3 = _____
Ⓐ 3 Ⓑ 6
Ⓒ 8 🅓 9

3. Use counters.
Which is a way to
make 7?

🅐 5 + 2 Ⓑ 7 + 1
Ⓒ 4 + 5 Ⓓ 2 + 8

4. Use counters.
Which is a way to
make 8?

Ⓐ 4 + 6 Ⓑ 5 + 4
🅒 3 + 5 Ⓓ I + 6

5. Use counters.
Which is a way to
make 10?

Ⓐ 3 + 4 Ⓑ 4 + 4
Ⓒ 6 + 3 🅓 I + 9

6. Use counters.
Which is a way to
make 9?

Ⓐ 8 + 2 🅑 7 + 2
Ⓒ 5 + 3 Ⓓ 4 + 4

Form A • Multiple-Choice   A15   **Go on.**

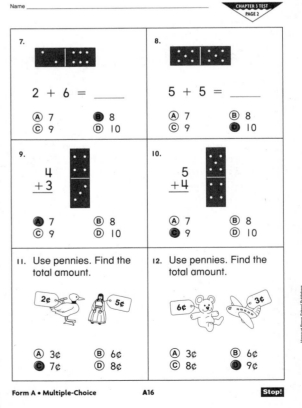

7.

2 + 6 = _____
Ⓐ 7 🅑 8
Ⓒ 9 Ⓓ 10

8.

5 + 5 = _____
Ⓐ 7 Ⓑ 8
Ⓒ 9 🅓 10

9.

4
+3
_____
🅐 7 Ⓑ 8
Ⓒ 9 Ⓓ 10

10.

5
+4
_____
Ⓐ 7 Ⓑ 8
🅒 9 Ⓓ 10

11. Use pennies. Find the
total amount.

2¢   5¢
Ⓐ 3¢ Ⓑ 6¢
🅒 7¢ Ⓓ 8¢

12. Use pennies. Find the
total amount.

6¢   3¢
Ⓐ 3¢ Ⓑ 6¢
Ⓒ 8¢ 🅓 9¢

Form A • Multiple-Choice   A16   **Stop!**

Choose the correct answer.

1.

5 + 1 = _____

Ⓐ 3   Ⓑ 4
● C 6   Ⓓ 7

2.

3 + 2 = _____

Ⓐ 4   ● B 5
Ⓒ 6   Ⓓ 7

3.

④

4 + 3 = _____

● A 7   Ⓑ 8
Ⓒ 9   Ⓓ 10

4.

⑥

6 + 3 = _____

Ⓐ 6   Ⓑ 7
Ⓒ 8   ● D 9

5.

$$\begin{array}{r} 7 \\ +2 \\ \hline \end{array}$$

Ⓐ 7   Ⓑ 8
● C 9   Ⓓ 10

6.

$$\begin{array}{r} 5 \\ +3 \\ \hline \end{array}$$

● A 8   Ⓑ 7
Ⓒ 6   Ⓓ 5

Form A • Multiple-Choice   A17   **Go on.**

---

7. Which doubles fact goes with the picture?

△△△ △△△

Ⓐ 2 + 1 = 3
● B 3 + 3 = 6
Ⓒ 4 + 4 = 8
Ⓓ 5 + 5 = 10

8. Which doubles fact goes with the picture?

◯◯◯◯ ◯◯◯◯

Ⓐ 2 + 2 = 4
Ⓑ 4 + 2 = 6
Ⓒ 3 + 3 = 6
● D 4 + 4 = 8

9.

$$\begin{array}{r} 2 \\ +6 \\ \hline \end{array}$$

Ⓐ 4   Ⓑ 7
● C 8   Ⓓ 9

10.

$$\begin{array}{r} 3 \\ +7 \\ \hline \end{array}$$

● A 10   Ⓑ 9
Ⓒ 8   Ⓓ 4

11. Add or subtract.

I have 6 balloons.
I lose 3.
How many do I have left?

Ⓐ 9   Ⓑ 5
Ⓒ 4   ● D 3

12. Add or subtract.

I have 4 peanuts.
Mom gives me 2 more.
How many do I have in all?

Ⓐ 5   ● B 6
Ⓒ 7   Ⓓ 8

Form A • Multiple-Choice   A18   **Stop!**

Choose the correct answer.

1.

7 – 5 = _____

● A 2   Ⓑ 3
Ⓒ 5   Ⓓ 7

2.

8 – 1 = _____

Ⓐ 5   Ⓑ 6
● C 7   Ⓓ 9

3.

10 – 4 = _____

Ⓐ 3   Ⓑ 4
Ⓒ 5   ● D 6

4.

9 – 5 = _____

Ⓐ 5   ● B 4
Ⓒ 3   Ⓓ 2

5.

$$\begin{array}{r} 5 \\ -2 \\ \hline \end{array}$$

Ⓐ 1   Ⓑ 2
● C 3   Ⓓ 4

6.

$$\begin{array}{r} 7 \\ -6 \\ \hline \end{array}$$

● A 1   Ⓑ 2
Ⓒ 3   Ⓓ 6

Form A • Multiple-Choice   A19   **Go on.**

7.

$$\begin{array}{r} 5 \\ -4 \\ \hline \end{array}$$

Ⓐ 0   ● B 1
Ⓒ 8   Ⓓ 9

8.

$$\begin{array}{r} 10 \\ -2 \\ \hline \end{array}$$

Ⓐ 2   Ⓑ 6
Ⓒ 7   ● D 8

9. Complete the fact family.

2 + 4 = 6
6 – 4 = 2
4 + 2 = 6
6 – 2 = _____

● A 4   Ⓑ 3
Ⓒ 2   Ⓓ 1

10. Complete the fact family.

$$\begin{array}{r} 5 \\ +3 \\ \hline 8 \end{array} \quad \begin{array}{r} 3 \\ +5 \\ \hline 8 \end{array} \quad \begin{array}{r} 8 \\ -5 \\ \hline 3 \end{array} \quad \begin{array}{r} 8 \\ -3 \\ \hline \end{array}$$

Ⓐ 3   ● B 5
Ⓒ 8   Ⓓ 9

11. How many more ?

5 – 3 = _____

Ⓐ 8 more
Ⓑ 5 more
● C 2 more
Ⓓ 1 more

12. How many more 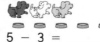 ?

7 – 4 = _____

Ⓐ 9 more
Ⓑ 7 more
Ⓒ 4 more
● D 3 more

Form A • Multiple-Choice   A20   **Stop!**

Multiple-Choice Format • Test Answers

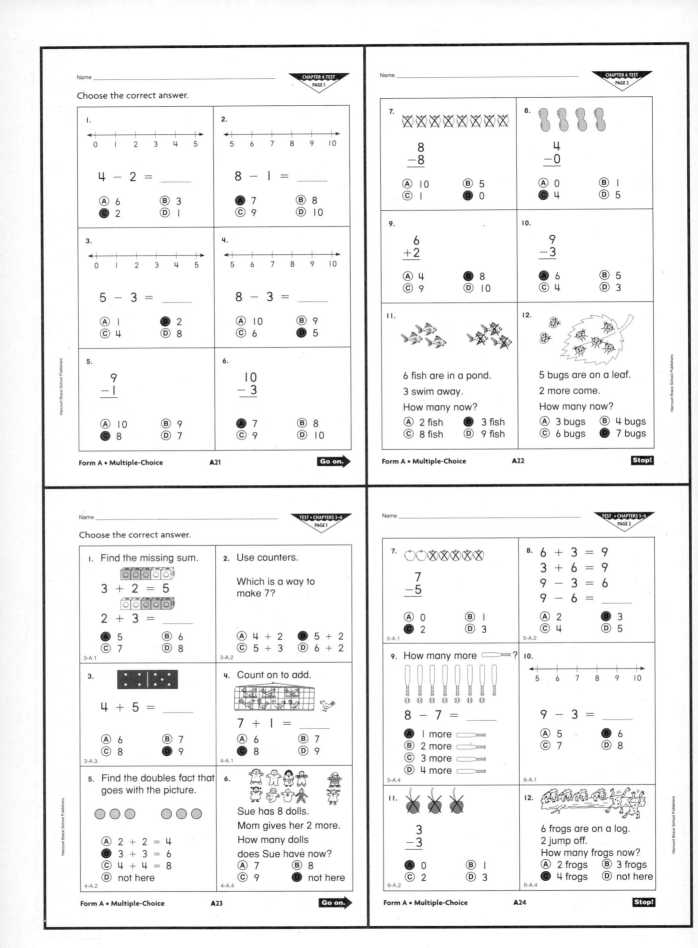

Multiple-Choice Format • Test Answers

Choose the correct answer.

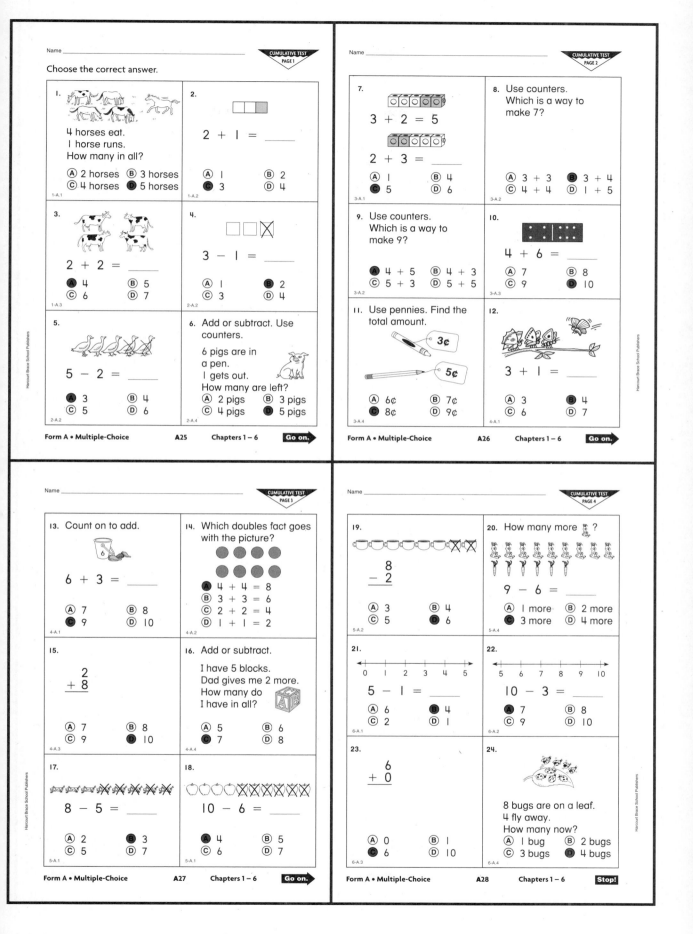

1.

4 horses eat.
1 horse runs.
How many in all?

- (A) 2 horses
- (B) 3 horses
- (C) 4 horses
- (D) 5 horses

1-A.1

2.

$2 + 1 =$ _____

- (A) 1
- (B) 2
- (C) 3
- (D) 4

1-A.2

3.

$2 + 2 =$ _____

- (A) 4
- (B) 5
- (C) 6
- (D) 7

1-A.3

4.

$3 - 1 =$ _____

- (A) 1
- (B) 2
- (C) 3
- (D) 4

2-A.2

5.

$5 - 2 =$ _____

- (A) 3
- (B) 4
- (C) 5
- (D) 6

2-A.2

6. Add or subtract. Use counters.

6 pigs are in a pen.
1 gets out.
How many are left?

- (A) 2 pigs
- (B) 3 pigs
- (C) 4 pigs
- (D) 5 pigs

2-A.4

Form A • Multiple-Choice A25 Chapters 1 – 6 **Go on.**

7.

$3 + 2 = 5$

$2 + 3 =$ _____

- (A) 1
- (B) 4
- (C) 5
- (D) 6

3-A.1

8. Use counters.
Which is a way to make 7?

- (A) 3 + 3
- (B) 3 + 4
- (C) 4 + 4
- (D) 1 + 5

3-A.2

9. Use counters.
Which is a way to make 9?

- (A) 4 + 5
- (B) 4 + 3
- (C) 5 + 3
- (D) 5 + 5

3-A.2

10.

$4 + 6 =$ _____

- (A) 7
- (B) 8
- (C) 9
- (D) 10

3-A.3

11. Use pennies. Find the total amount.

3¢
5¢

- (A) 6¢
- (B) 7¢
- (C) 8¢
- (D) 9¢

3-A.4

12.

$3 + 1 =$ _____

- (A) 3
- (B) 4
- (C) 6
- (D) 7

4-A.1

Form A • Multiple-Choice A26 Chapters 1 – 6 **Go on.**

13. Count on to add.

6

$6 + 3 =$ _____

- (A) 7
- (B) 8
- (C) 9
- (D) 10

4-A.1

14. Which doubles fact goes with the picture?

- (A) 4 + 4 = 8
- (B) 3 + 3 = 6
- (C) 2 + 2 = 4
- (D) 1 + 1 = 2

4-A.2

15.

$\begin{array}{r} 2 \\ + 8 \\ \hline \end{array}$

- (A) 7
- (B) 8
- (C) 9
- (D) 10

4-A.3

16. Add or subtract.

I have 5 blocks.
Dad gives me 2 more.
How many do
I have in all?

- (A) 5
- (B) 6
- (C) 7
- (D) 8

4-A.4

17.

$8 - 5 =$ _____

- (A) 2
- (B) 3
- (C) 5
- (D) 7

5-A.1

18.

$10 - 6 =$ _____

- (A) 4
- (B) 5
- (C) 6
- (D) 7

5-A.1

Form A • Multiple-Choice A27 Chapters 1 – 6 **Go on.**

19.

$\begin{array}{r} 8 \\ - 2 \\ \hline \end{array}$

- (A) 3
- (B) 4
- (C) 5
- (D) 6

5-A.2

20. How many more ?

$9 - 6 =$ _____

- (A) 1 more
- (B) 2 more
- (C) 3 more
- (D) 4 more

5-A.4

21.

0 1 2 3 4 5

$5 - 1 =$ _____

- (A) 6
- (B) 4
- (C) 2
- (D) 1

6-A.1

22.

5 6 7 8 9 10

$10 - 3 =$ _____

- (A) 7
- (B) 8
- (C) 9
- (D) 10

6-A.2

23.

$\begin{array}{r} 6 \\ + 0 \\ \hline \end{array}$

- (A) 0
- (B) 1
- (C) 6
- (D) 10

6-A.3

24.

8 bugs are on a leaf.
4 fly away.
How many now?

- (A) 1 bug
- (B) 2 bugs
- (C) 3 bugs
- (D) 4 bugs

6-A.4

Form A • Multiple-Choice A28 Chapters 1 – 6 **Stop!**

Multiple-Choice Format • Test Answers

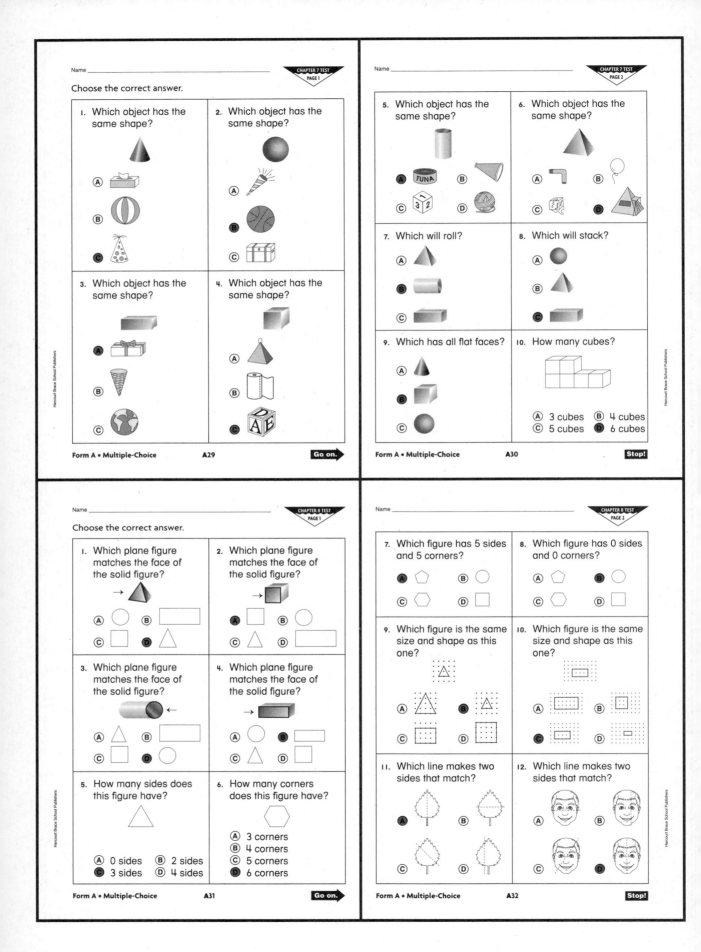

CHAPTER 7 TEST
PAGE 1

Choose the correct answer.

1. Which object has the same shape?

Ⓐ
Ⓑ
Ⓒ

2. Which object has the same shape?

Ⓐ
Ⓑ
Ⓒ

3. Which object has the same shape?

Ⓐ
Ⓑ
Ⓒ

4. Which object has the same shape?

Ⓐ
Ⓑ
Ⓒ

Form A • Multiple-Choice   A29   Go on.

CHAPTER 7 TEST
PAGE 2

5. Which object has the same shape?

Ⓐ TUNA   Ⓑ
Ⓒ 3 2   Ⓓ

6. Which object has the same shape?

Ⓐ   Ⓑ
Ⓒ   Ⓓ

7. Which will roll?

Ⓐ
Ⓑ
Ⓒ

8. Which will stack?

Ⓐ
Ⓑ
Ⓒ

9. Which has all flat faces?

Ⓐ
Ⓑ
Ⓒ

10. How many cubes?

Ⓐ 3 cubes   Ⓑ 4 cubes
Ⓒ 5 cubes   Ⓓ 6 cubes

Form A • Multiple-Choice   A30   Stop!

CHAPTER 8 TEST
PAGE 1

Choose the correct answer.

1. Which plane figure matches the face of the solid figure?

Ⓐ   Ⓑ
Ⓒ   Ⓓ

2. Which plane figure matches the face of the solid figure?

Ⓐ   Ⓑ
Ⓒ   Ⓓ

3. Which plane figure matches the face of the solid figure?

Ⓐ   Ⓑ
Ⓒ   Ⓓ

4. Which plane figure matches the face of the solid figure?

Ⓐ   Ⓑ
Ⓒ   Ⓓ

5. How many sides does this figure have?

Ⓐ 0 sides   Ⓑ 2 sides
Ⓒ 3 sides   Ⓓ 4 sides

6. How many corners does this figure have?

Ⓐ 3 corners
Ⓑ 4 corners
Ⓒ 5 corners
Ⓓ 6 corners

Form A • Multiple-Choice   A31   Go on.

CHAPTER 8 TEST
PAGE 2

7. Which figure has 5 sides and 5 corners?

Ⓐ   Ⓑ
Ⓒ   Ⓓ

8. Which figure has 0 sides and 0 corners?

Ⓐ   Ⓑ
Ⓒ   Ⓓ

9. Which figure is the same size and shape as this one?

Ⓐ   Ⓑ
Ⓒ   Ⓓ

10. Which figure is the same size and shape as this one?

Ⓐ   Ⓑ
Ⓒ   Ⓓ

11. Which line makes two sides that match?

Ⓐ   Ⓑ
Ⓒ   Ⓓ

12. Which line makes two sides that match?

Ⓐ   Ⓑ
Ⓒ   Ⓓ

Form A • Multiple-Choice   A32   Stop!

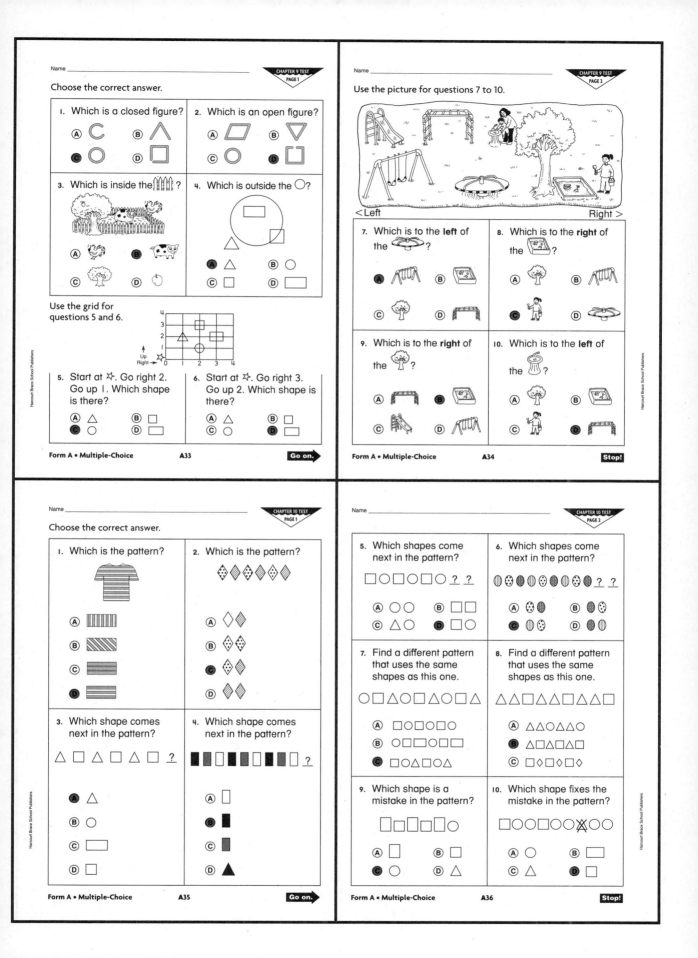

Name _____

Choose the correct answer.

1. Which is a closed figure?
- Ⓐ C
- Ⓑ △
- Ⓒ ○
- Ⓓ □

2. Which is an open figure?
- Ⓐ ▱
- Ⓑ ▽
- Ⓒ ○
- Ⓓ ⊓

3. Which is inside the 🗍 ?
- Ⓐ 🐓
- Ⓑ 🐄
- Ⓒ 🌳
- Ⓓ 🍎

4. Which is outside the ○?
- Ⓐ △
- Ⓑ ○
- Ⓒ □
- Ⓓ ▭

Use the grid for questions 5 and 6.

5. Start at ✩. Go right 2. Go up 1. Which shape is there?
- Ⓐ △
- Ⓑ □
- Ⓒ ○
- Ⓓ ▭

6. Start at ✩. Go right 3. Go up 2. Which shape is there?
- Ⓐ △
- Ⓑ □
- Ⓒ ○
- Ⓓ ▭

Form A • Multiple-Choice   A33   **Go on.**

Name _____

Use the picture for questions 7 to 10.

< Left   Right >

7. Which is to the **left** of the 🎠 ?
- Ⓐ swings
- Ⓑ sandbox
- Ⓒ tree
- Ⓓ bars

8. Which is to the **right** of the 🧰 ?
- Ⓐ tree
- Ⓑ swings
- Ⓒ girl
- Ⓓ merry-go-round

9. Which is to the **right** of the 🌳 ?
- Ⓐ bars
- Ⓑ sandbox
- Ⓒ slide
- Ⓓ swings

10. Which is to the **left** of the 🎠 ?
- Ⓐ tree
- Ⓑ sandbox
- Ⓒ girl
- Ⓓ bars

Form A • Multiple-Choice   A34   **Stop!**

Name _____

Choose the correct answer.

1. Which is the pattern?
- Ⓐ
- Ⓑ
- Ⓒ
- Ⓓ

2. Which is the pattern?
- Ⓐ ◇ ◇
- Ⓑ ◈ ◆
- Ⓒ ◈ ◆
- Ⓓ ◈ ◈

3. Which shape comes next in the pattern?
△ □ △ □ △ □ ?
- Ⓐ △
- Ⓑ ○
- Ⓒ ▭
- Ⓓ □

4. Which shape comes next in the pattern?
- Ⓐ □
- Ⓑ ■
- Ⓒ ▪
- Ⓓ ▲

Form A • Multiple-Choice   A35   **Go on.**

Name _____

5. Which shapes come next in the pattern?
□ ○ □ ○ □ ○ ? ?
- Ⓐ ○ ○
- Ⓑ □ □
- Ⓒ △ ○
- Ⓓ □ ○

6. Which shapes come next in the pattern?
- Ⓐ
- Ⓑ
- Ⓒ
- Ⓓ

7. Find a different pattern that uses the same shapes as this one.
○ □ △ ○ □ △ ○ □ △
- Ⓐ □ ○ □ ○ □ ○
- Ⓑ ○ □ ○ □ ○ □
- Ⓒ □ ○ △ □ ○ △

8. Find a different pattern that uses the same shapes as this one.
△ △ □ △ △ □ △ △ □
- Ⓐ △ △ ○ △ △ ○
- Ⓑ △ □ △ □ △ □
- Ⓒ □ ◇ □ ◇ □ ◇

9. Which shape is a mistake in the pattern?
□ □ □ □ □ ○
- Ⓐ □
- Ⓑ □
- Ⓒ ○
- Ⓓ △

10. Which shape fixes the mistake in the pattern?
□ ○ ○ □ ○ ○ ✖ ○ ○
- Ⓐ ○
- Ⓑ ▭
- Ⓒ △
- Ⓓ □

Form A • Multiple-Choice   A36   **Stop!**

Multiple-Choice Format • Test Answers   **133**

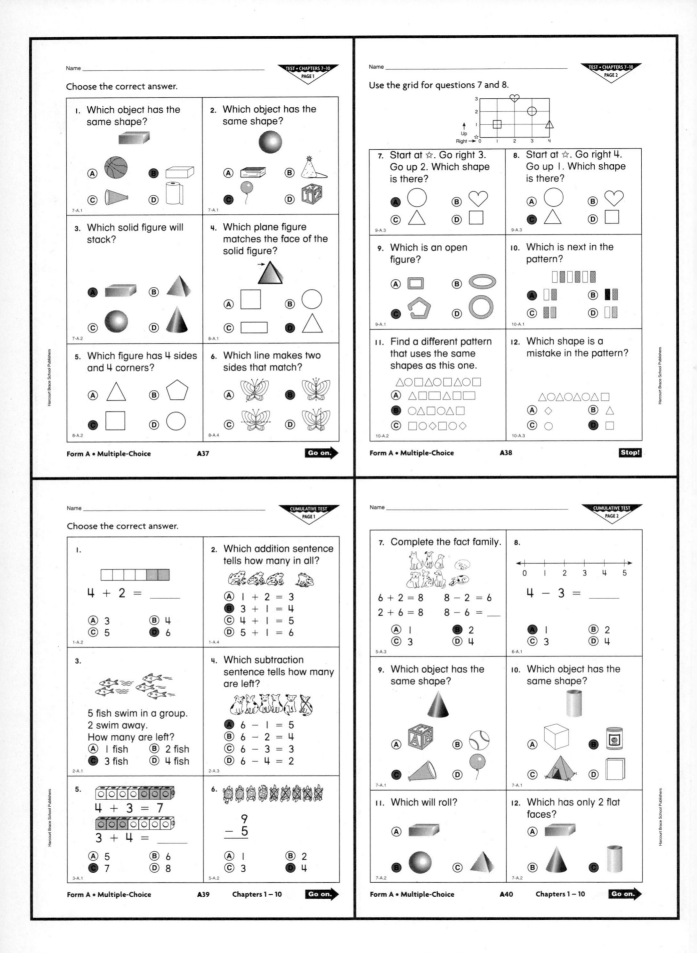

Multiple-Choice Format • Test Answers

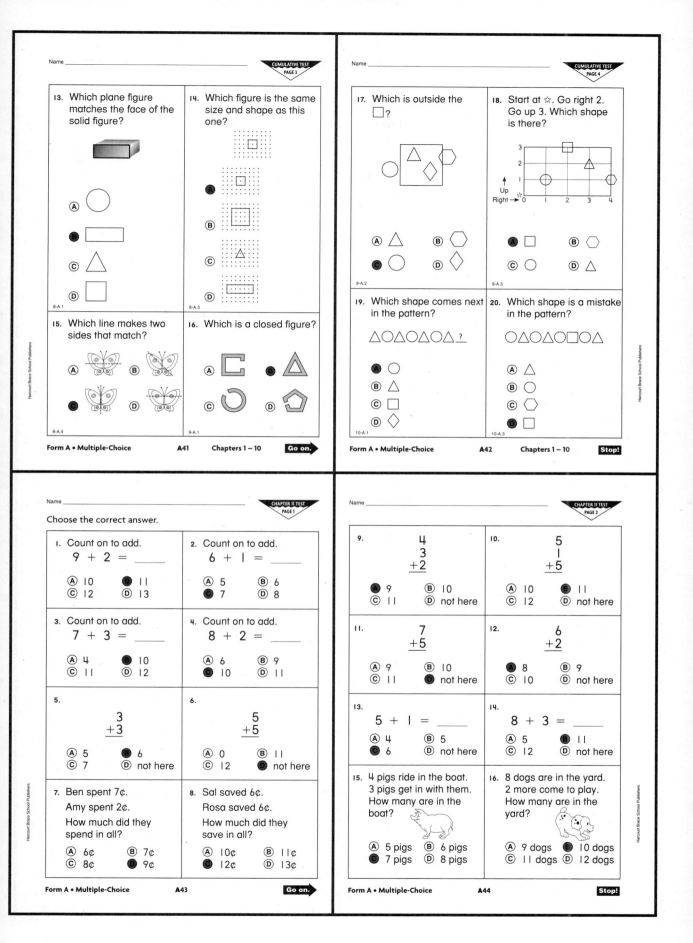

Choose the correct answer.

1.
○○○○○○○
○·○○○

$7 + 4 = 11$
$11 - 4 = $ ____

Ⓐ 5   Ⓑ 6
Ⓒ 7   Ⓓ 8

2.
○○○○○○○○
○○

$8 + 2 = 10$
$10 - 2 = $ ____

Ⓐ 7   Ⓑ 8
Ⓒ 9   Ⓓ 10

3.
$\begin{array}{r} 9 \\ +3 \\ \hline 12 \end{array}$ $\begin{array}{r} 12 \\ - 3 \\ \hline \end{array}$

Ⓐ 9   Ⓑ 10
Ⓒ 11   Ⓓ not here

4.
$\begin{array}{r} 5 \\ +6 \\ \hline 11 \end{array}$ $\begin{array}{r} 11 \\ - 6 \\ \hline \end{array}$

Ⓐ 6   Ⓑ 7
Ⓒ 8   Ⓓ not here

5. Count back to subtract.
5 6 7 8 9 10 11 12

$9 - 3 = $ ____

Ⓐ 4   Ⓑ 5
Ⓒ 6   Ⓓ 7

6. Count back to subtract.
5 6 7 8 9 10 11 12

$11 - 2 = $ ____

Ⓐ 10   Ⓑ 9
Ⓒ 8   Ⓓ 2

Form A • Multiple-Choice   A45   Go on.

7. How many more bananas than pears are there?

$\begin{array}{r} 8 \\ -4 \\ \hline \end{array}$
Ⓐ 1   Ⓑ 2
Ⓒ 3   Ⓓ 4

8. How many fewer apples than oranges are there?
○○○○○○○○○○
○○○

$\begin{array}{r} 10 \\ - 7 \\ \hline \end{array}$
Ⓐ 2   Ⓑ 3
Ⓒ 4   Ⓓ 5

Which number sentence belongs in the fact family?

9.
$8 + 4 = 12$
$4 + 8 = 12$
$12 - 4 = 8$

Ⓐ $4 + 4 = 8$
Ⓑ $8 - 4 = 4$
Ⓒ $12 - 6 = 6$
Ⓓ $12 - 8 = 4$

10.
$11 - 2 = 9$
$11 - 9 = 2$
$9 + 2 = 11$

Ⓐ $2 + 9 = 11$
Ⓑ $2 + 7 = 9$
Ⓒ $11 - 4 = 7$
Ⓓ $9 - 2 = 7$

Which number sentence does the story show?

11. Joe had 11 pencils. He lost 3 of them. How many pencils does Joe have left?

Ⓐ $8 + 3 = 11$
Ⓑ $11 - 3 = 8$
Ⓒ $11 + 3 = 14$
Ⓓ not here

12. I have 7 pennies. I find 5 more pennies. How many pennies do I have now?

Ⓐ $7 - 5 = 2$
Ⓑ $7 + 2 = 9$
Ⓒ $7 + 5 = 12$
Ⓓ not here

Form A • Multiple-Choice   A46   Stop!

Choose the correct answer.

1.
$9 + 3 = $ ____

Ⓐ 10   Ⓑ 11
Ⓒ 12   Ⓓ not here
11-A.1

2.
$\begin{array}{r} 3 \\ +3 \\ \hline \end{array}$

Ⓐ 0   Ⓑ 6
Ⓒ 7   Ⓓ not here
11-A.1

3.
$\begin{array}{r} 2 \\ 4 \\ +3 \\ \hline \end{array}$

Ⓐ 6   Ⓑ 7
Ⓒ 8   Ⓓ not here
11-A.2

4.
$\begin{array}{r} 9 \\ 2 \\ +1 \\ \hline \end{array}$

Ⓐ 10   Ⓑ 11
Ⓒ 12   Ⓓ not here
11-A.2

5. Toby spent 4¢. Ann spent 6¢. How much did they spend in all?

Ⓐ 10¢   Ⓑ 11¢
Ⓒ 12¢   Ⓓ 13¢
11-A.3

6. 5 birds are eating. 6 more birds come to eat. How many birds are eating?

Ⓐ 11 birds   Ⓑ 12 birds
Ⓒ 13 birds   Ⓓ 14 birds
11-A.3

Form A • Multiple-Choice   A47   Go on.

7.
$\begin{array}{r} 7 \\ +2 \\ \hline 9 \end{array}$ $\begin{array}{r} 9 \\ -2 \\ \hline \end{array}$

Ⓐ 6   Ⓑ 7
Ⓒ 8   Ⓓ not here
12-A.1

8.
5 6 7 8 9 10 11 12

$8 - 3 = $ ____

Ⓐ 2   Ⓑ 3
Ⓒ 4   Ⓓ 5
12-A.1

9. How many more oranges than lemons are there?

$\begin{array}{r} 11 \\ - 8 \\ \hline \end{array}$

Ⓐ 3   Ⓑ 4
Ⓒ 5   Ⓓ 6
12-A.2

10. Which number sentence belongs in this fact family?
$11 - 4 = 7$
$11 - 7 = 4$
$7 + 4 = 11$

Ⓐ $4 + 3 = 7$
Ⓑ $4 + 7 = 11$
Ⓒ $11 - 6 = 5$
Ⓓ $7 - 4 = 3$
12-A.1

11. Which number sentence does the story show?

Max had 12 apples. He gave away 9. How many are left?

Ⓐ $6 + 3 = 9$
Ⓑ $12 - 9 = 3$
Ⓒ $9 - 6 = 3$
Ⓓ not here
12-A.3

12. Which number sentence does the story show?

I had 1 penny. I found 9 more. How many do I have?

Ⓐ $10 - 9 = 1$
Ⓑ $1 + 8 = 9$
Ⓒ $1 + 9 = 10$
Ⓓ not here
12-A.3

Form A • Multiple-Choice   A48   Stop!

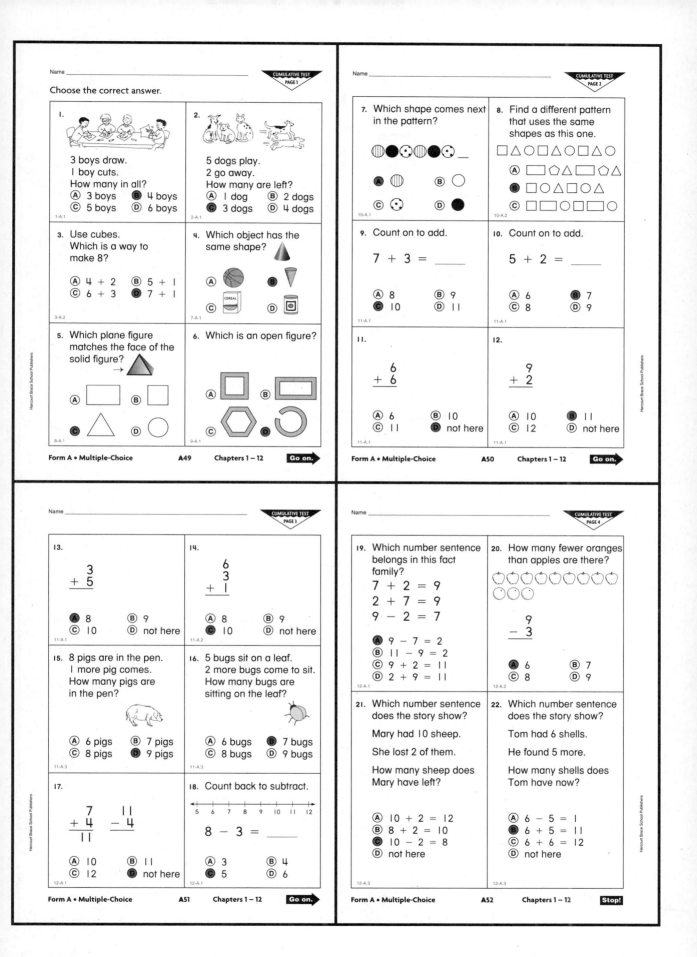

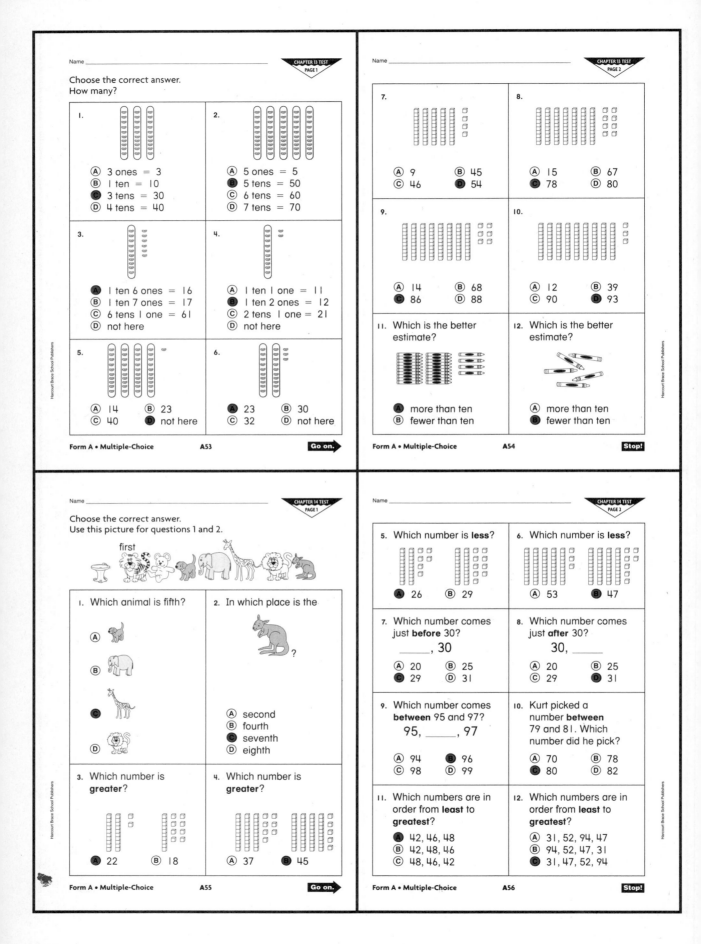

Multiple-Choice Format • Test Answers

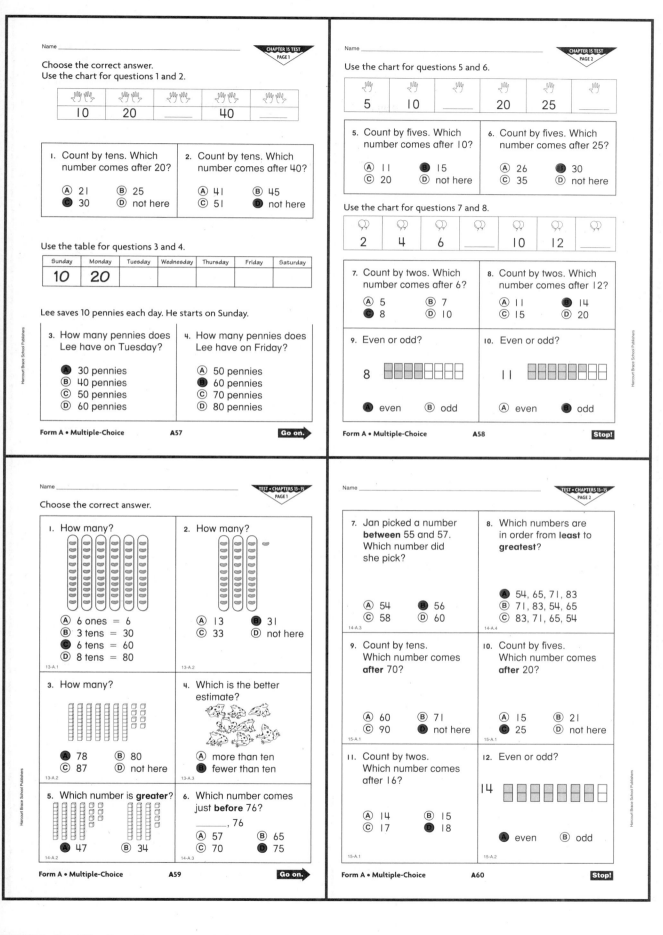

Page 1 — Chapter 15 Test (A57)

Name _____

Choose the correct answer.
Use the chart for questions 1 and 2.

🖐🖐	🖐🖐	🖐🖐	🖐🖐	🖐🖐
10	20	___	40	___

1. Count by tens. Which number comes after 20?
- Ⓐ 21
- Ⓑ 25
- ● 30
- Ⓓ not here

2. Count by tens. Which number comes after 40?
- Ⓐ 41
- Ⓑ 45
- Ⓒ 51
- ● not here

Use the table for questions 3 and 4.

Sunday	Monday	Tuesday	Wednesday	Thursday	Friday	Saturday
10	20					

Lee saves 10 pennies each day. He starts on Sunday.

3. How many pennies does Lee have on Tuesday?
- Ⓐ 30 pennies
- Ⓑ 40 pennies
- Ⓒ 50 pennies
- Ⓓ 60 pennies

4. How many pennies does Lee have on Friday?
- Ⓐ 50 pennies
- Ⓑ 60 pennies
- Ⓒ 70 pennies
- Ⓓ 80 pennies

Form A • Multiple-Choice   A57   **Go on.**

Page 2 — Chapter 15 Test (A58)

Name _____

Use the chart for questions 5 and 6.

🖐	🖐	🖐	🖐	🖐	🖐
5	10	___	20	25	___

5. Count by fives. Which number comes after 10?
- Ⓐ 11
- Ⓑ 15
- Ⓒ 20
- Ⓓ not here

6. Count by fives. Which number comes after 25?
- Ⓐ 26
- ● 30
- Ⓒ 35
- Ⓓ not here

Use the chart for questions 7 and 8.

🍷	🍷	🍷	🍷	🍷	🍷
2	4	6	___	10	12

7. Count by twos. Which number comes after 6?
- Ⓐ 5
- Ⓑ 7
- ● 8
- Ⓓ 10

8. Count by twos. Which number comes after 12?
- Ⓐ 11
- ● 14
- Ⓒ 15
- Ⓓ 20

9. Even or odd?

8
- ● even
- Ⓑ odd

10. Even or odd?

11
- Ⓐ even
- ● odd

Form A • Multiple-Choice   A58   **Stop!**

Page 1 — Test Chapters 13–15 (A59)

Name _____

Choose the correct answer.

1. How many?
- Ⓐ 6 ones = 6
- Ⓑ 3 tens = 30
- ● 6 tens = 60
- Ⓓ 8 tens = 80

13-A.1

2. How many?
- Ⓐ 13
- ● 31
- Ⓒ 33
- Ⓓ not here

13-A.2

3. How many?
- ● 78
- Ⓑ 80
- Ⓒ 87
- Ⓓ not here

13-A.2

4. Which is the better estimate?
- Ⓐ more than ten
- ● fewer than ten

13-A.3

5. Which number is **greater**?
- ● 47
- Ⓑ 34

14-A.2

6. Which number comes just **before** 76?
___, 76
- Ⓐ 57
- Ⓑ 65
- Ⓒ 70
- ● 75

14-A.3

Form A • Multiple-Choice   A59   **Go on.**

Page 2 — Test Chapters 13–15 (A60)

Name _____

7. Jan picked a number **between** 55 and 57. Which number did she pick?
- Ⓐ 54
- ● 56
- Ⓒ 58
- Ⓓ 60

14-A.3

8. Which numbers are in order from **least** to **greatest**?
- ● 54, 65, 71, 83
- Ⓑ 71, 83, 54, 65
- Ⓒ 83, 71, 65, 54

14-A.4

9. Count by tens. Which number comes **after** 70?
- Ⓐ 60
- Ⓑ 71
- Ⓒ 90
- ● not here

15-A.1

10. Count by fives. Which number comes **after** 20?
- Ⓐ 15
- Ⓑ 21
- ● 25
- Ⓓ not here

15-A.1

11. Count by twos. Which number comes after 16?
- Ⓐ 14
- Ⓑ 15
- Ⓒ 17
- ● 18

15-A.1

12. Even or odd?

14
- ● even
- Ⓑ odd

15-A.2

Form A • Multiple-Choice   A60   **Stop!**

Multiple-Choice Format • Test Answers

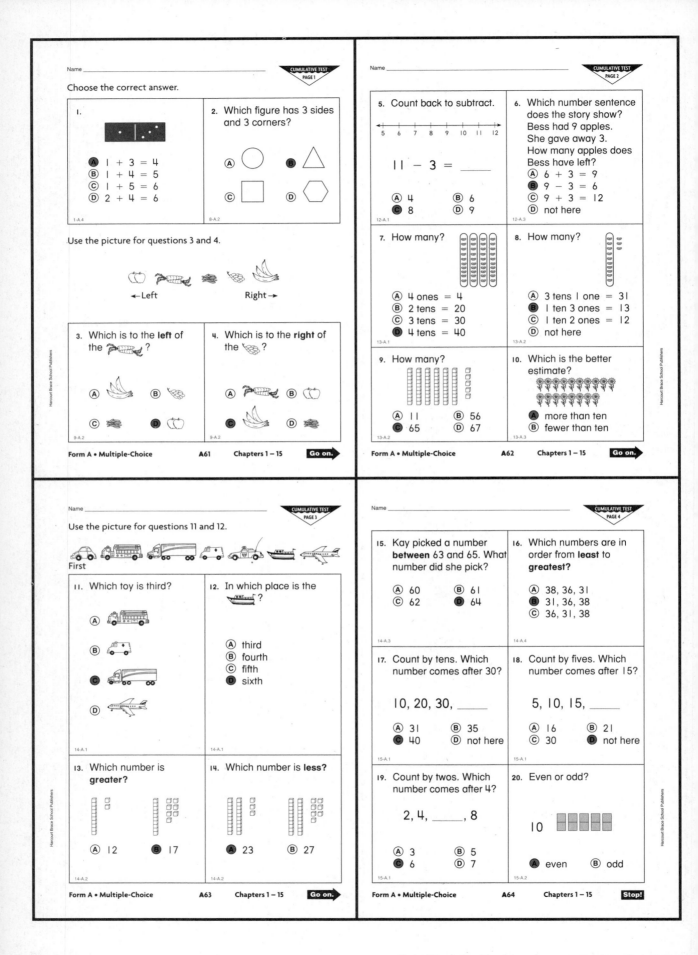

Name _____

Choose the correct answer.

1.

- (A) $1 + 3 = 4$
- (B) $1 + 4 = 5$
- (C) $1 + 5 = 6$
- (D) $2 + 4 = 6$

1-A.4

2. Which figure has 3 sides and 3 corners?

- (A) ○
- (B) △
- (C) ▢
- (D) ⬡

8-A.2

Use the picture for questions 3 and 4.

← Left   Right →

3. Which is to the **left** of the 🥕?

- (A)
- (B)
- (C)
- (D)

9-A.2

4. Which is to the **right** of the 🍇?

- (A)
- (B)
- (C)
- (D)

9-A.2

Form A • Multiple-Choice   A61   Chapters 1 – 15   **Go on.**

Name _____

5. Count back to subtract.

$$11 - 3 = \_\_\_\_$$

- (A) 4
- (B) 6
- (C) 8
- (D) 9

12-A.1

6. Which number sentence does the story show?
Bess had 9 apples.
She gave away 3.
How many apples does Bess have left?

- (A) $6 + 3 = 9$
- (B) $9 - 3 = 6$
- (C) $9 + 3 = 12$
- (D) not here

12-A.3

7. How many?

- (A) 4 ones = 4
- (B) 2 tens = 20
- (C) 3 tens = 30
- (D) 4 tens = 40

13-A.1

8. How many?

- (A) 3 tens 1 one = 31
- (B) 1 ten 3 ones = 13
- (C) 1 ten 2 ones = 12
- (D) not here

13-A.2

9. How many?

- (A) 11
- (B) 56
- (C) 65
- (D) 67

13-A.2

10. Which is the better estimate?

- (A) more than ten
- (B) fewer than ten

13-A.3

Form A • Multiple-Choice   A62   Chapters 1 – 15   **Go on.**

Name _____

Use the picture for questions 11 and 12.

First

11. Which toy is third?

- (A)
- (B)
- (C)
- (D)

14-A.1

12. In which place is the 🚤?

- (A) third
- (B) fourth
- (C) fifth
- (D) sixth

14-A.1

13. Which number is **greater**?

- (A) 12
- (B) 17

14-A.2

14. Which number is **less**?

- (A) 23
- (B) 27

14-A.2

Form A • Multiple-Choice   A63   Chapters 1 – 15   **Go on.**

Name _____

15. Kay picked a number **between** 63 and 65. What number did she pick?

- (A) 60
- (B) 61
- (C) 62
- (D) 64

14-A.3

16. Which numbers are in order from **least** to **greatest**?

- (A) 38, 36, 31
- (B) 31, 36, 38
- (C) 36, 31, 38

14-A.4

17. Count by tens. Which number comes after 30?

$$10, 20, 30, \_\_\_\_$$

- (A) 31
- (B) 35
- (C) 40
- (D) not here

15-A.1

18. Count by fives. Which number comes after 15?

$$5, 10, 15, \_\_\_\_$$

- (A) 16
- (B) 21
- (C) 30
- (D) not here

15-A.1

19. Count by twos. Which number comes after 4?

$$2, 4, \_\_\_\_, 8$$

- (A) 3
- (B) 5
- (C) 6
- (D) 7

15-A.1

20. Even or odd?

10

- (A) even
- (B) odd

15-A.2

Form A • Multiple-Choice   A64   Chapters 1 – 15   **Stop!**

Multiple-Choice Format • Test Answers

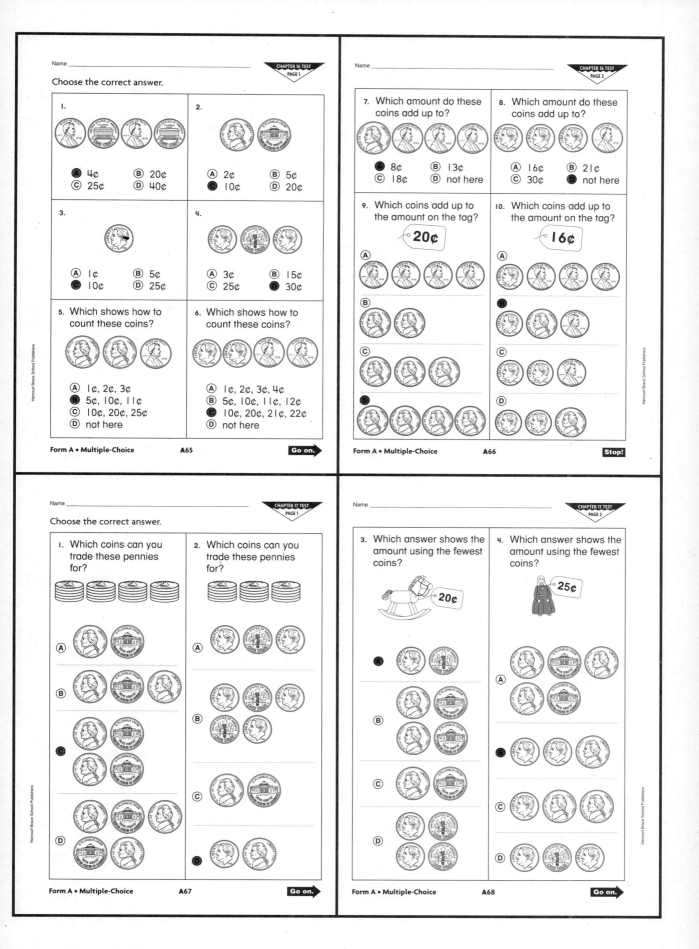

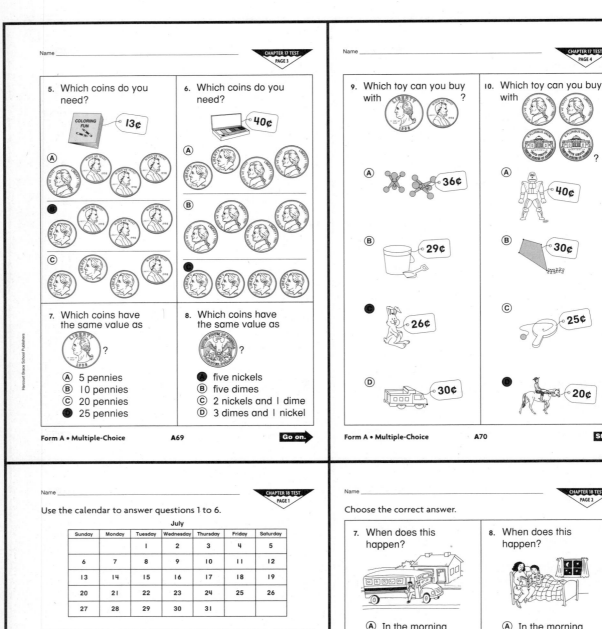

5. Which coins do you need?

COLORING FUN   13¢

Ⓐ

Ⓑ

Ⓒ

6. Which coins do you need?

40¢

Ⓐ

Ⓑ

Ⓒ

7. Which coins have the same value as ☺ ?

Ⓐ 5 pennies
Ⓑ 10 pennies
Ⓒ 20 pennies
Ⓓ 25 pennies

8. Which coins have the same value as ☺ ?

Ⓐ five nickels
Ⓑ five dimes
Ⓒ 2 nickels and 1 dime
Ⓓ 3 dimes and 1 nickel

9. Which toy can you buy with 🪙🪙 ?

Ⓐ 36¢

Ⓑ 29¢

Ⓒ 26¢

Ⓓ 30¢

10. Which toy can you buy with 🪙🪙🪙🪙 ?

Ⓐ 40¢

Ⓑ 30¢

Ⓒ 25¢

Ⓓ 20¢

Use the calendar to answer questions 1 to 6.

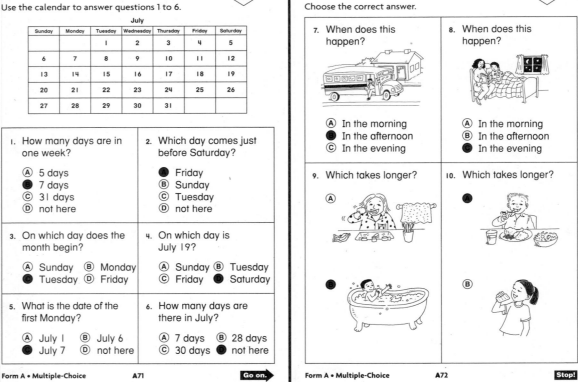

July

Sunday	Monday	Tuesday	Wednesday	Thursday	Friday	Saturday
		1	2	3	4	5
6	7	8	9	10	11	12
13	14	15	16	17	18	19
20	21	22	23	24	25	26
27	28	29	30	31		

1. How many days are in one week?

Ⓐ 5 days
Ⓑ 7 days
Ⓒ 31 days
Ⓓ not here

2. Which day comes just before Saturday?

Ⓐ Friday
Ⓑ Sunday
Ⓒ Tuesday
Ⓓ not here

3. On which day does the month begin?

Ⓐ Sunday   Ⓑ Monday
Ⓒ Tuesday   Ⓓ Friday

4. On which day is July 19?

Ⓐ Sunday   Ⓑ Tuesday
Ⓒ Friday   Ⓓ Saturday

5. What is the date of the first Monday?

Ⓐ July 1   Ⓑ July 6
Ⓒ July 7   Ⓓ not here

6. How many days are there in July?

Ⓐ 7 days   Ⓑ 28 days
Ⓒ 30 days   Ⓓ not here

Choose the correct answer.

7. When does this happen?

Ⓐ In the morning
Ⓑ In the afternoon
Ⓒ In the evening

8. When does this happen?

Ⓐ In the morning
Ⓑ In the afternoon
Ⓒ In the evening

9. Which takes longer?

Ⓐ

Ⓑ

10. Which takes longer?

Ⓐ

Ⓑ

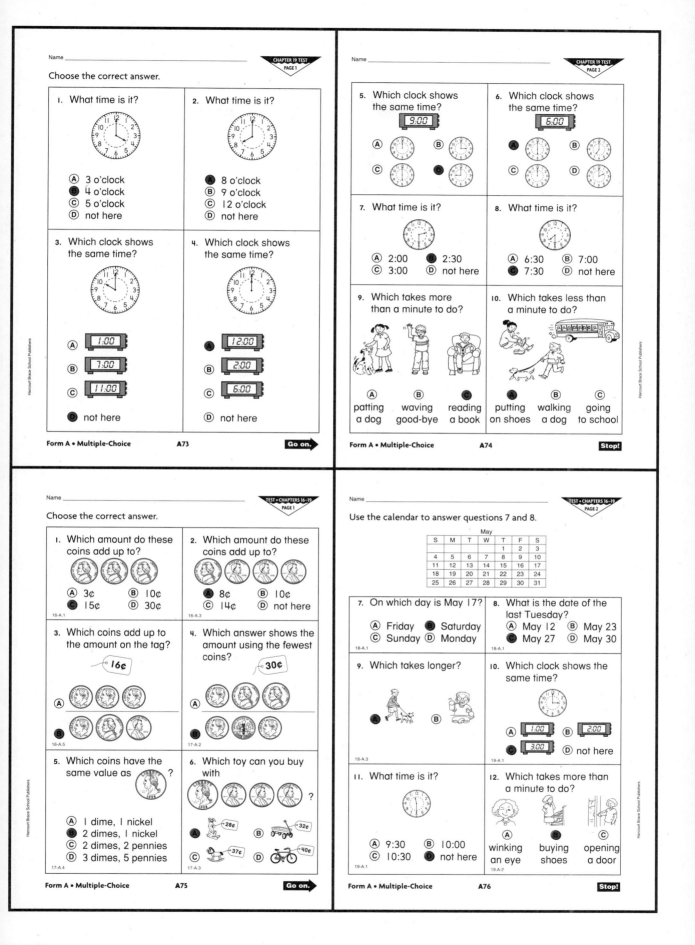

Choose the correct answer.

1.
$$\begin{array}{r} 3 \\ + 5 \\ \hline \end{array}$$
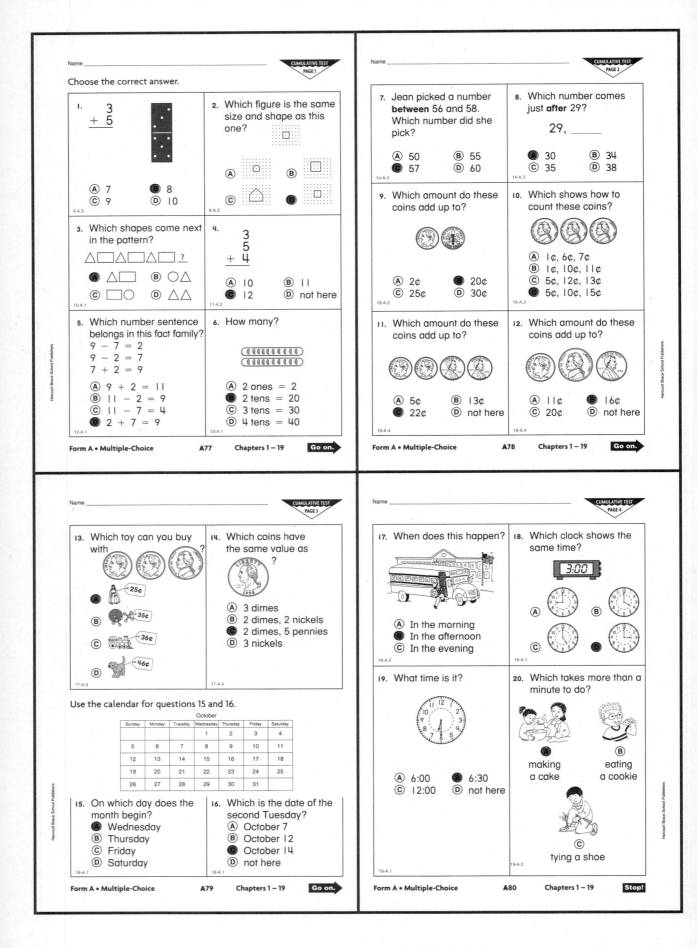
Ⓐ 7 ● 8
Ⓒ 9 Ⓓ 10
3-A.3

2. Which figure is the same size and shape as this one?
Ⓐ Ⓑ
Ⓒ ● Ⓓ
8-A.3

3. Which shapes come next in the pattern?
△□△□△□ ?
● Ⓐ △△ Ⓑ ○△
Ⓒ □○ Ⓓ △△
10-A.1

4.
$$\begin{array}{r} 3 \\ 5 \\ + 4 \\ \hline \end{array}$$
Ⓐ 10 Ⓑ 11
● Ⓒ 12 Ⓓ not here
11-A.2

5. Which number sentence belongs in this fact family?
9 − 7 = 2
9 − 2 = 7
7 + 2 = 9
Ⓐ 9 + 2 = 11
Ⓑ 11 − 2 = 9
Ⓒ 11 − 7 = 4
● Ⓓ 2 + 7 = 9
12-A.1

6. How many?
Ⓐ 2 ones = 2
● Ⓑ 2 tens = 20
Ⓒ 3 tens = 30
Ⓓ 4 tens = 40
13-A.1

7. Jean picked a number **between** 56 and 58. Which number did she pick?
Ⓐ 50 Ⓑ 55
● Ⓒ 57 Ⓓ 60
14-A.3

8. Which number comes just **after** 29?
29, ____
● Ⓐ 30 Ⓑ 34
Ⓒ 35 Ⓓ 38
14-A.3

9. Which amount do these coins add up to?
Ⓐ 2¢ ● Ⓑ 20¢
Ⓒ 25¢ Ⓓ 30¢
16-A.2

10. Which shows how to count these coins?
Ⓐ 1¢, 6¢, 7¢
Ⓑ 1¢, 10¢, 11¢
Ⓒ 5¢, 12¢, 13¢
● Ⓓ 5¢, 10¢, 15¢
16-A.3

11. Which amount do these coins add up to?
Ⓐ 5¢ Ⓑ 13¢
● Ⓒ 22¢ Ⓓ not here
16-A.4

12. Which amount do these coins add up to?
Ⓐ 11¢ ● Ⓑ 16¢
Ⓒ 20¢ Ⓓ not here
16-A.4

13. Which toy can you buy with ?
● Ⓐ —25¢
Ⓑ —35¢
Ⓒ —36¢
Ⓓ —46¢
17-A.3

14. Which coins have the same value as ?
Ⓐ 3 dimes
Ⓑ 2 dimes, 2 nickels
● Ⓒ 2 dimes, 5 pennies
Ⓓ 3 nickels
17-A.4

Use the calendar for questions 15 and 16.

October

Sunday	Monday	Tuesday	Wednesday	Thursday	Friday	Saturday
			1	2	3	4
5	6	7	8	9	10	11
12	13	14	15	16	17	18
19	20	21	22	23	24	25
26	27	28	29	30	31	

15. On which day does the month begin?
● Ⓐ Wednesday
Ⓑ Thursday
Ⓒ Friday
Ⓓ Saturday
18-A.1

16. Which is the date of the second Tuesday?
Ⓐ October 7
Ⓑ October 12
● Ⓒ October 14
Ⓓ not here
18-A.1

17. When does this happen?
Ⓐ In the morning
● Ⓑ In the afternoon
Ⓒ In the evening
18-A.2

18. Which clock shows the same time?
3:00
Ⓐ Ⓑ
Ⓒ ● Ⓓ
19-A.1

19. What time is it?
Ⓐ 6:00 ● Ⓑ 6:30
Ⓒ 12:00 Ⓓ not here
19-A.1

20. Which takes more than a minute to do?
● Ⓐ making a cake
Ⓑ eating a cookie
Ⓒ tying a shoe
19-A.2

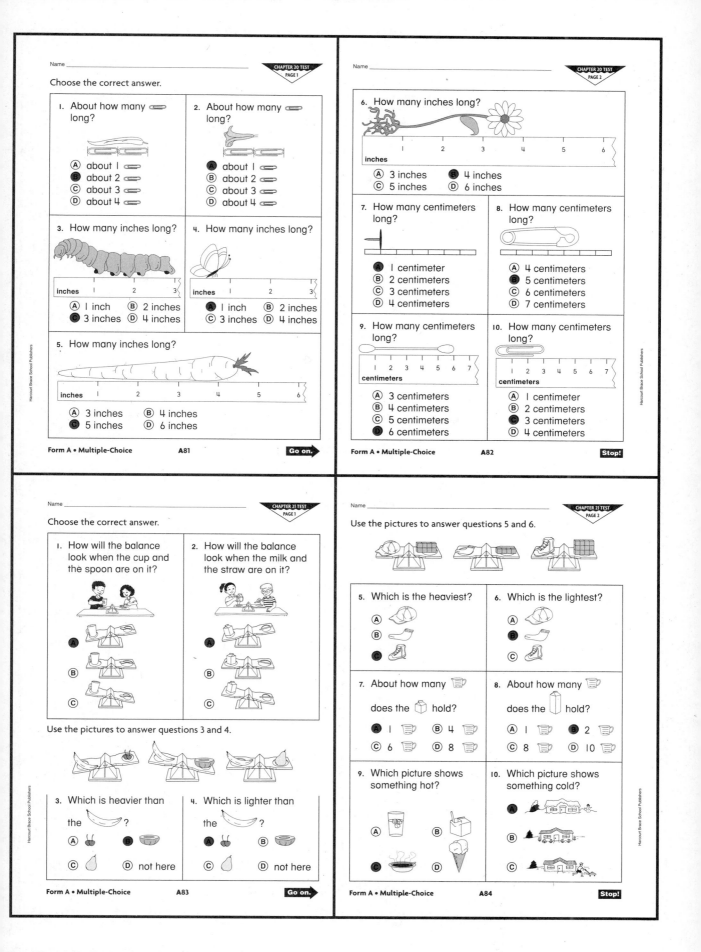

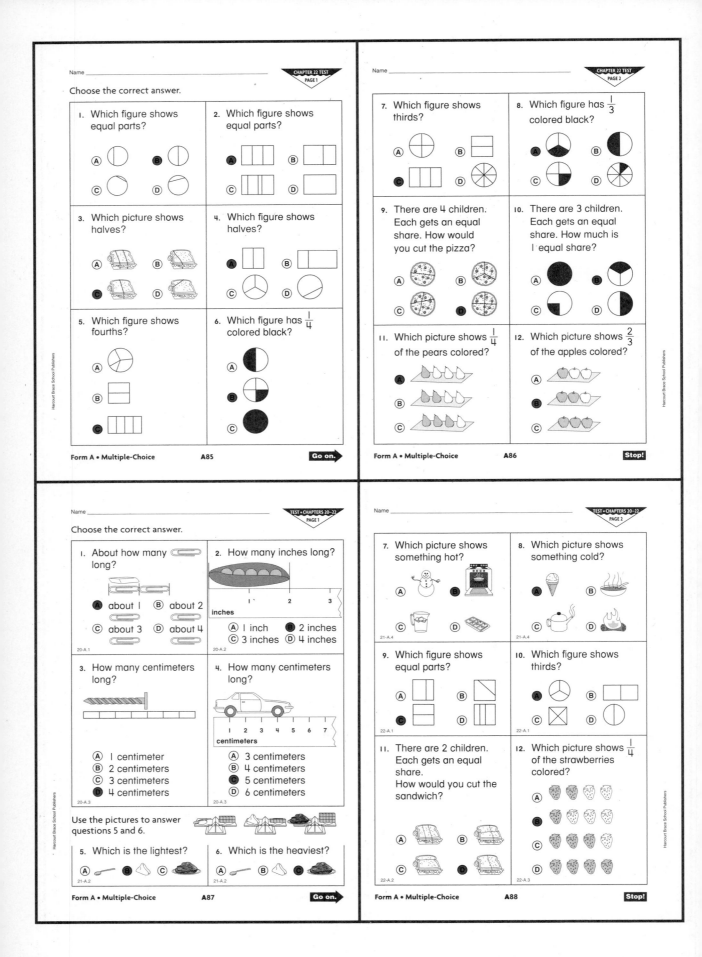

Multiple-Choice Format • Test Answers

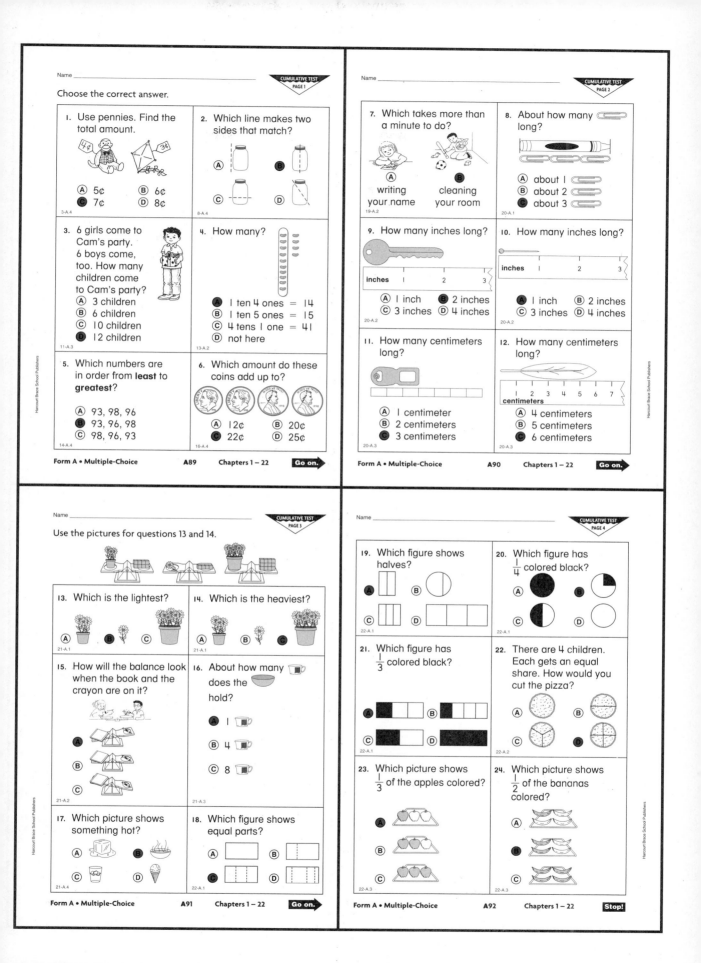

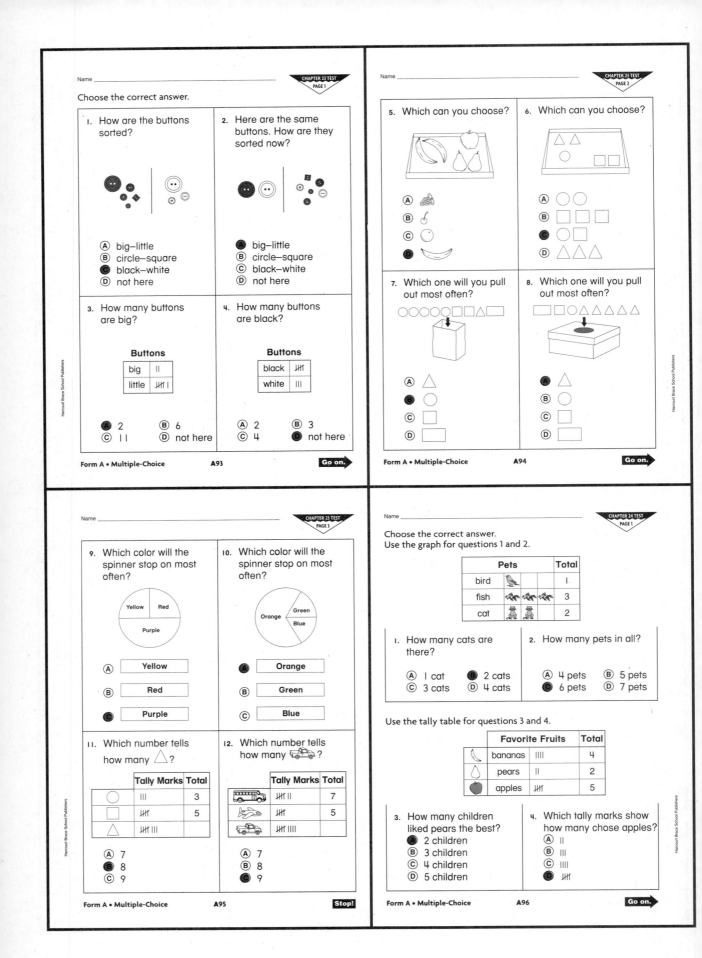

Name _____

Choose the correct answer.

1. How are the buttons sorted?

Ⓐ big–little
Ⓑ circle–square
● black–white
Ⓓ not here

2. Here are the same buttons. How are they sorted now?

● big–little
Ⓑ circle–square
Ⓒ black–white
Ⓓ not here

3. How many buttons are big?

Buttons

| big | II |
| little | IIII I |

● 2   Ⓑ 6
Ⓒ II   Ⓓ not here

4. How many buttons are black?

Buttons

| black | IIII |
| white | III |

Ⓐ 2   Ⓑ 3
Ⓒ 4   ● not here

Form A • Multiple-Choice   A93   Go on.

Name _____

5. Which can you choose?

Ⓐ
Ⓑ
Ⓒ
●

6. Which can you choose?

Ⓐ
Ⓑ
●
Ⓓ

7. Which one will you pull out most often?

Ⓐ △
● ●
Ⓒ □
Ⓓ ▭

8. Which one will you pull out most often?

● △
Ⓑ ●
Ⓒ □
Ⓓ ▭

Form A • Multiple-Choice   A94   Go on.

Name _____

9. Which color will the spinner stop on most often?

Ⓐ Yellow
Ⓑ Red
● Purple

10. Which color will the spinner stop on most often?

● Orange
Ⓑ Green
Ⓒ Blue

11. Which number tells how many △?

	Tally Marks	Total
○	III	3
□	IIII	5
△	IIII III	

Ⓐ 7
● 8
Ⓒ 9

12. Which number tells how many 🚙?

	Tally Marks	Total
🚌	IIII II	7
✈	IIII	5
🚙	IIII IIII	

Ⓐ 7
Ⓑ 8
● 9

Form A • Multiple-Choice   A95   Stop!

Name _____

Choose the correct answer.
Use the graph for questions 1 and 2.

Pets		Total
bird		1
fish		3
cat		2

1. How many cats are there?

Ⓐ 1 cat   ● 2 cats
Ⓒ 3 cats   Ⓓ 4 cats

2. How many pets in all?

Ⓐ 4 pets   Ⓑ 5 pets
● 6 pets   Ⓓ 7 pets

Use the tally table for questions 3 and 4.

	Favorite Fruits		Total
	bananas	IIII	4
	pears	II	2
	apples	IIII	5

3. How many children liked pears the best?
● 2 children
Ⓑ 3 children
Ⓒ 4 children
Ⓓ 5 children

4. Which tally marks show how many chose apples?
Ⓐ II
Ⓑ III
Ⓒ IIII
● IIII

Form A • Multiple-Choice   A96   Go on.

Use the graph for questions 5 and 6.

Favorite Fruits

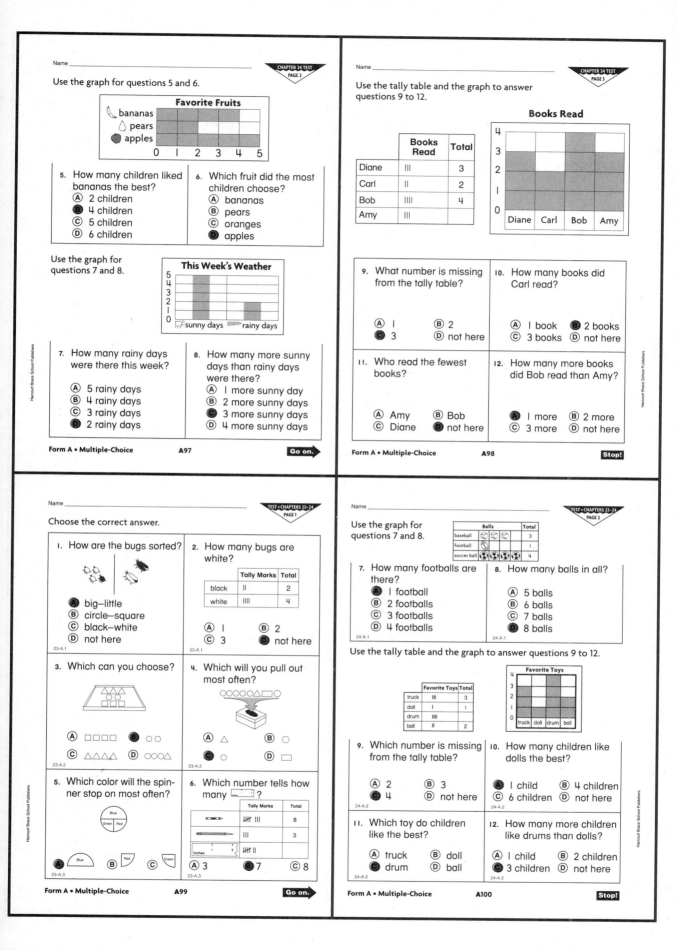

bananas
pears
apples

0 1 2 3 4 5

5. How many children liked bananas the best?
- Ⓐ 2 children
- Ⓑ 4 children
- Ⓒ 5 children
- Ⓓ 6 children

6. Which fruit did the most children choose?
- Ⓐ bananas
- Ⓑ pears
- Ⓒ oranges
- Ⓓ apples

Use the graph for questions 7 and 8.

This Week's Weather

5
4
3
2
1
0
   sunny days   rainy days

7. How many rainy days were there this week?
- Ⓐ 5 rainy days
- Ⓑ 4 rainy days
- Ⓒ 3 rainy days
- Ⓓ 2 rainy days

8. How many more sunny days than rainy days were there?
- Ⓐ 1 more sunny day
- Ⓑ 2 more sunny days
- Ⓒ 3 more sunny days
- Ⓓ 4 more sunny days

Use the tally table and the graph to answer questions 9 to 12.

Books Read

	Books Read	Total
Diane	III	3
Carl	II	2
Bob	IIII	4
Amy	III	

4
3
2
1
0
   Diane   Carl   Bob   Amy

9. What number is missing from the tally table?
- Ⓐ 1
- Ⓑ 2
- Ⓒ 3
- Ⓓ not here

10. How many books did Carl read?
- Ⓐ 1 book
- Ⓑ 2 books
- Ⓒ 3 books
- Ⓓ not here

11. Who read the fewest books?
- Ⓐ Amy
- Ⓑ Bob
- Ⓒ Diane
- Ⓓ not here

12. How many more books did Bob read than Amy?
- Ⓐ 1 more
- Ⓑ 2 more
- Ⓒ 3 more
- Ⓓ not here

Choose the correct answer.

1. How are the bugs sorted?
- Ⓐ big–little
- Ⓑ circle–square
- Ⓒ black–white
- Ⓓ not here

23-A.1

2. How many bugs are white?

	Tally Marks	Total
black	II	2
white	IIII	4

- Ⓐ 1
- Ⓑ 2
- Ⓒ 3
- Ⓓ not here

23-A.1

3. Which can you choose?

- Ⓐ ☐☐☐☐
- Ⓑ ○○
- Ⓒ △△△△
- Ⓓ ○○○△

23-A.2

4. Which will you pull out most often?

- Ⓐ △
- Ⓑ ⬡
- Ⓒ ○
- Ⓓ ☐

23-A.2

5. Which color will the spinner stop on most often?

Blue
Green Red

- Ⓐ Blue
- Ⓑ Red
- Ⓒ Green

23-A.3

6. Which number tells how many ✏ ?

	Tally Marks	Total
	LHT III	8
	III	3
inches	LHT II	

- Ⓐ 3
- Ⓑ 7
- Ⓒ 8

23-A.3

Use the graph for questions 7 and 8.

	Balls	Total
baseball		3
football		1
soccer ball		4

7. How many footballs are there?
- Ⓐ 1 football
- Ⓑ 2 footballs
- Ⓒ 3 footballs
- Ⓓ 4 footballs

24-A.1

8. How many balls in all?
- Ⓐ 5 balls
- Ⓑ 6 balls
- Ⓒ 7 balls
- Ⓓ 8 balls

24-A.1

Use the tally table and the graph to answer questions 9 to 12.

	Favorite Toys	Total
truck	III	3
doll	I	1
drum	IIII	
ball	II	2

Favorite Toys

4
3
2
1
0
   truck doll drum ball

9. Which number is missing from the tally table?
- Ⓐ 2
- Ⓑ 3
- Ⓒ 4
- Ⓓ not here

24-A.2

10. How many children like dolls the best?
- Ⓐ 1 child
- Ⓑ 4 children
- Ⓒ 6 children
- Ⓓ not here

24-A.2

11. Which toy do children like the best?
- Ⓐ truck
- Ⓑ doll
- Ⓒ drum
- Ⓓ ball

24-A.2

12. How many more children like drums than dolls?
- Ⓐ 1 child
- Ⓑ 2 children
- Ⓒ 3 children
- Ⓓ not here

24-A.2

Multiple-Choice Format • Test Answers

149

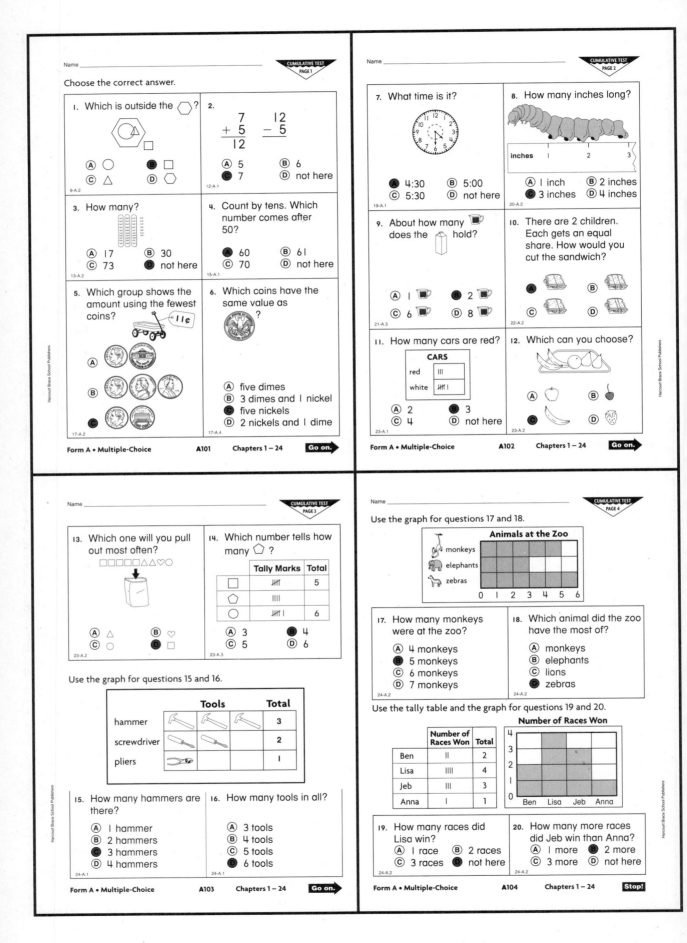

Name _____

Choose the correct answer.

1. Which is outside the ⬡?

Ⓐ ○ Ⓑ □
Ⓒ △ Ⓓ ⬡

9-A.2

2.

$$\begin{array}{r} 7 \\ + 5 \\ \hline 12 \end{array} \qquad \begin{array}{r} 12 \\ - 5 \\ \hline \end{array}$$

Ⓐ 5 Ⓑ 6
Ⓒ 7 Ⓓ not here

12-A.1

3. How many?

Ⓐ 17 Ⓑ 30
Ⓒ 73 Ⓓ not here

13-A.2

4. Count by tens. Which number comes after 50?

Ⓐ 60 Ⓑ 61
Ⓒ 70 Ⓓ not here

15-A.1

5. Which group shows the amount using the fewest coins?

11¢

Ⓐ
Ⓑ
Ⓒ

17-A.2

6. Which coins have the same value as ?

Ⓐ five dimes
Ⓑ 3 dimes and 1 nickel
Ⓒ five nickels
Ⓓ 2 nickels and 1 dime

17-A.4

Form A • Multiple-Choice   A101   Chapters 1 – 24   Go on.

Name _____

7. What time is it?

Ⓐ 4:30 Ⓑ 5:00
Ⓒ 5:30 Ⓓ not here

19-A.1

8. How many inches long?

inches 1   2   3

Ⓐ 1 inch Ⓑ 2 inches
Ⓒ 3 inches Ⓓ 4 inches

20-A.2

9. About how many 🥤 does the 🥛 hold?

Ⓐ 1 Ⓑ 2
Ⓒ 6 Ⓓ 8

21-A.3

10. There are 2 children. Each gets an equal share. How would you cut the sandwich?

Ⓐ Ⓑ
Ⓒ Ⓓ

22-A.2

11. How many cars are red?

CARS	
red	III
white	IIII I

Ⓐ 2 Ⓑ 3
Ⓒ 4 Ⓓ not here

23-A.1

12. Which can you choose?

Ⓐ Ⓑ
Ⓒ Ⓓ

23-A.2

Form A • Multiple-Choice   A102   Chapters 1 – 24   Go on.

Name _____

13. Which one will you pull out most often?

□□□□□△△♡○

Ⓐ △ Ⓑ ♡
Ⓒ ○ Ⓓ □

23-A.2

14. Which number tells how many ⬠?

	Tally Marks	Total
□	IIII	5
⬠	IIII	
○	IIII I	6

Ⓐ 3 Ⓑ 4
Ⓒ 5 Ⓓ 6

23-A.3

Use the graph for questions 15 and 16.

	Tools			Total
hammer				3
screwdriver				2
pliers				1

15. How many hammers are there?

Ⓐ 1 hammer
Ⓑ 2 hammers
Ⓒ 3 hammers
Ⓓ 4 hammers

24-A.1

16. How many tools in all?

Ⓐ 3 tools
Ⓑ 4 tools
Ⓒ 5 tools
Ⓓ 6 tools

24-A.1

Form A • Multiple-Choice   A103   Chapters 1 – 24   Go on.

Name _____

Use the graph for questions 17 and 18.

Animals at the Zoo

monkeys
elephants
zebras
0 1 2 3 4 5 6

17. How many monkeys were at the zoo?

Ⓐ 4 monkeys
Ⓑ 5 monkeys
Ⓒ 6 monkeys
Ⓓ 7 monkeys

24-A.2

18. Which animal did the zoo have the most of?

Ⓐ monkeys
Ⓑ elephants
Ⓒ lions
Ⓓ zebras

24-A.2

Use the tally table and the graph for questions 19 and 20.

	Number of Races Won	Total
Ben	II	2
Lisa	IIII	4
Jeb	III	3
Anna	I	1

Number of Races Won

4
3
2
1
0
Ben Lisa Jeb Anna

19. How many races did Lisa win?

Ⓐ 1 race Ⓑ 2 races
Ⓒ 3 races Ⓓ not here

24-A.2

20. How many more races did Jeb win than Anna?

Ⓐ 1 more Ⓑ 2 more
Ⓒ 3 more Ⓓ not here

24-A.2

Form A • Multiple-Choice   A104   Chapters 1 – 24   Stop!

Name _____

Choose the correct answer.

1.
$$\begin{array}{r} 7 \\ +7 \\ \hline 14 \end{array} \qquad \begin{array}{r} 7 \\ +8 \\ \hline \end{array}$$

Ⓐ 15 Ⓑ 16
Ⓒ 17 Ⓓ 18

2.
$5 + 5 = 10$
$5 + 6 = \underline{\hspace{1cm}}$

Ⓐ 9 Ⓑ 10
● 11 Ⓓ 12

3.
$3 + 3 = 6$
$3 + 2 = \underline{\hspace{1cm}}$

Ⓐ 4 ● 5
Ⓒ 6 Ⓓ 7

4.
$$\begin{array}{r} 9 \\ +9 \\ \hline 18 \end{array} \qquad \begin{array}{r} 9 \\ +8 \\ \hline \end{array}$$

Ⓐ 15 Ⓑ 16
● 17 Ⓓ 18

5.
$7 + 6 = \underline{\hspace{1cm}}$

● 13 Ⓑ 14
Ⓒ 15 Ⓓ not here

6.
$6 + 5 = \underline{\hspace{1cm}}$

Ⓐ 9 Ⓑ 10
● 11 Ⓓ not here

7.
$4 + 5 = \underline{\hspace{1cm}}$

Ⓐ 8 ● 9
Ⓒ 10 Ⓓ not here

8.
$8 + 7 = \underline{\hspace{1cm}}$

Ⓐ 16 Ⓑ 17
Ⓒ 18 ● not here

Form A • Multiple-Choice   A105   Go on.

Name _____

9.
$6 + 6 = 12$

$12 - 6 = \underline{\hspace{1cm}}$

Ⓐ 4 Ⓑ 5
● 6 Ⓓ 7

10.
$8 - 4 = 4$
$4 + 4 = \underline{\hspace{1cm}}$

Ⓐ 7 ● 8
Ⓒ 9 Ⓓ 10

11.
$9 + 9 = 18$
$18 - 9 = \underline{\hspace{1cm}}$

Ⓐ 8 ● 9
Ⓒ 10 Ⓓ not here

12.
$8 + 8 = 16$
$16 - 8 = \underline{\hspace{1cm}}$

Ⓐ 5 Ⓑ 6
Ⓒ 7 ● not here

13. Jan has 7 dolls.
Sue has 2 more than Jan.

How many dolls do they have in all?

Ⓐ 13 dolls Ⓑ 14 dolls
Ⓒ 15 dolls ● 16 dolls

14. Tina had some cars.
Luis gave her 7 more.
Now she has 14.

How many cars did she have to start?

Ⓐ 6 cars ● 7 cars
Ⓒ 8 cars Ⓓ 9 cars

Form A • Multiple-Choice   A106   Stop!

Name _____

Choose the correct answer.

1. Make a 10. Then add.
$$\begin{array}{r} 9 \\ +4 \\ \hline \end{array}$$

Ⓐ 12 ● 13
Ⓒ 14 Ⓓ 15

2. Make a 10. Then add.
$$\begin{array}{r} 8 \\ +7 \\ \hline \end{array}$$

Ⓐ 13 Ⓑ 14
● 15 Ⓓ 16

3.
$$\begin{array}{r} 7 \\ +4 \\ \hline \end{array}$$

● 11 Ⓑ 12
Ⓒ 13 Ⓓ not here

4.
$$\begin{array}{r} 9 \\ +7 \\ \hline \end{array}$$

Ⓐ 13 Ⓑ 14
Ⓒ 15 ● not here

5.
$$\begin{array}{r} 8 \\ 2 \\ +4 \\ \hline \end{array}$$

● 14 Ⓑ 15
Ⓒ 16 Ⓓ 17

6.
$$\begin{array}{r} 3 \\ 4 \\ +3 \\ \hline \end{array}$$

Ⓐ 8 Ⓑ 9
● 10 Ⓓ 11

7.
$$\begin{array}{r} 9 \\ 1 \\ +2 \\ \hline \end{array}$$

Ⓐ 9 Ⓑ 10
Ⓒ 11 ● 12

8.
$$\begin{array}{r} 5 \\ 5 \\ +3 \\ \hline \end{array}$$

Ⓐ 12 ● 13
Ⓒ 14 Ⓓ 15

Form A • Multiple-Choice   A107   Go on.

Name _____

9.
$$\begin{array}{r} 9 \\ +2 \\ \hline 11 \end{array} \qquad \begin{array}{r} 11 \\ -2 \\ \hline \end{array}$$

Ⓐ 6 Ⓑ 7
Ⓒ 8 ● 9

10.
$$\begin{array}{r} 6 \\ +7 \\ \hline 13 \end{array} \qquad \begin{array}{r} 13 \\ -7 \\ \hline \end{array}$$

Ⓐ 4 Ⓑ 5
● 6 Ⓓ 7

11.
$$\begin{array}{r} 8 \\ +8 \\ \hline 16 \end{array} \qquad \begin{array}{r} 16 \\ -8 \\ \hline \end{array}$$

● 8 Ⓑ 9
Ⓒ 10 Ⓓ 11

12.
$$\begin{array}{r} 9 \\ +8 \\ \hline 17 \end{array} \qquad \begin{array}{r} 17 \\ -8 \\ \hline \end{array}$$

Ⓐ 6 Ⓑ 7
Ⓒ 8 ● 9

13.
$$\begin{array}{r} 5 \\ +9 \\ \hline 14 \end{array} \qquad \begin{array}{r} 14 \\ -9 \\ \hline \end{array}$$

Ⓐ 4 ● 5
Ⓒ 6 Ⓓ not here

14.
$$\begin{array}{r} 9 \\ +9 \\ \hline 18 \end{array} \qquad \begin{array}{r} 18 \\ -9 \\ \hline \end{array}$$

Ⓐ 6 Ⓑ 7
Ⓒ 8 ● not here

15.
$$\begin{array}{r} 9 \\ +3 \\ \hline 12 \end{array} \qquad \begin{array}{r} 12 \\ -3 \\ \hline \end{array}$$

Ⓐ 3 Ⓑ 6
● 9 Ⓓ not here

16.
$$\begin{array}{r} 6 \\ +9 \\ \hline 15 \end{array} \qquad \begin{array}{r} 15 \\ -9 \\ \hline \end{array}$$

Ⓐ 5 ● 6
Ⓒ 7 Ⓓ not here

Form A • Multiple-Choice   A108   Stop!

Multiple-Choice Format • Test Answers

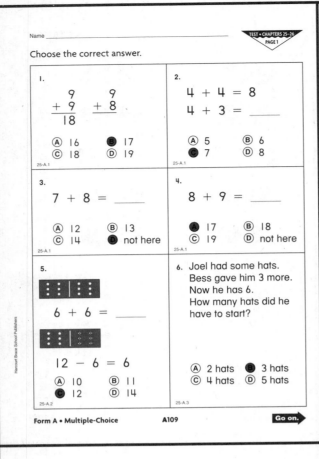

Choose the correct answer.

1.

$$+\ \begin{matrix}9\\9\end{matrix} \quad +\ \begin{matrix}9\\8\end{matrix}$$
$$\overline{18}$$

(A) 16　　(B) 17
(C) 18　　(D) 19

25-A.1

2.

$4 + 4 = 8$
$4 + 3 = $ _____

(A) 5　　(B) 6
(C) 7　　(D) 8

25-A.1

3.

$7 + 8 = $ _____

(A) 12　　(B) 13
(C) 14　　(D) not here

25-A.1

4.

$8 + 9 = $ _____

(A) 17　　(B) 18
(C) 19　　(D) not here

25-A.1

5.

$6 + 6 = $ _____

$12 - 6 = 6$

(A) 10　　(B) 11
(C) 12　　(D) 14

25-A.2

6. Joel had some hats. Bess gave him 3 more. Now he has 6. How many hats did he have to start?

(A) 2 hats　　(B) 3 hats
(C) 4 hats　　(D) 5 hats

25-A.3

Form A • Multiple-Choice　　A109　　`Go on.`

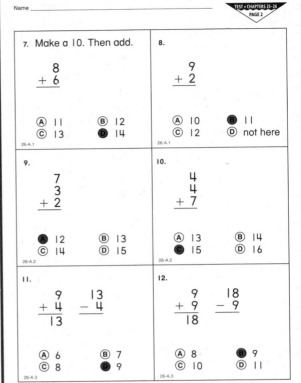

7. Make a 10. Then add.

$$+\ \begin{matrix}8\\6\end{matrix}$$

(A) 11　　(B) 12
(C) 13　　(D) 14

26-A.1

8.

$$+\ \begin{matrix}9\\2\end{matrix}$$

(A) 10　　(B) 11
(C) 12　　(D) not here

26-A.1

9.

$$\begin{matrix}7\\3\\+\ 2\end{matrix}$$

(A) 12　　(B) 13
(C) 14　　(D) 15

26-A.2

10.

$$\begin{matrix}4\\4\\+\ 7\end{matrix}$$

(A) 13　　(B) 14
(C) 15　　(D) 16

26-A.2

11.

$$+\ \begin{matrix}9\\4\end{matrix} \quad -\ \begin{matrix}13\\4\end{matrix}$$
$$\overline{13}$$

(A) 6　　(B) 7
(C) 8　　(D) 9

26-A.3

12.

$$+\ \begin{matrix}9\\9\end{matrix} \quad -\ \begin{matrix}18\\9\end{matrix}$$
$$\overline{18}$$

(A) 8　　(B) 9
(C) 10　　(D) 11

26-A.3

Form A • Multiple-Choice　　A110　　`Stop!`

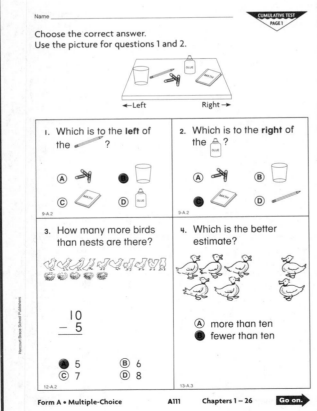

Choose the correct answer.
Use the picture for questions 1 and 2.

←Left　　Right→

1. Which is to the **left** of the ✏ ?

(A)　　(B)
(C)　　(D)

9-A.2

2. Which is to the **right** of the 🍶 ?

(A)　　(B)
(C)　　(D)

9-A.2

3. How many more birds than nests are there?

$$\begin{matrix}10\\-\ 5\end{matrix}$$

(A) 5　　(B) 6
(C) 7　　(D) 8

12-A.2

4. Which is the better estimate?

(A) more than ten
(B) fewer than ten

13-A.3

Form A • Multiple-Choice　　A111　　Chapters 1 – 26　　`Go on.`

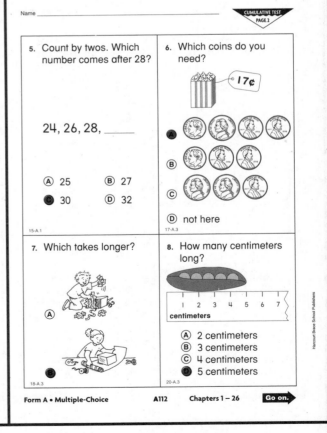

5. Count by twos. Which number comes after 28?

$$24, 26, 28, \rule{1cm}{0.4pt}$$

(A) 25　　(B) 27
(C) 30　　(D) 32

15-A.1

6. Which coins do you need?

17¢

(A)
(B)
(C)
(D) not here

17-A.3

7. Which takes longer?

(A)
(B)

18-A.3

8. How many centimeters long?

centimeters

(A) 2 centimeters
(B) 3 centimeters
(C) 4 centimeters
(D) 5 centimeters

20-A.3

Form A • Multiple-Choice　　A112　　Chapters 1 – 26　　`Go on.`

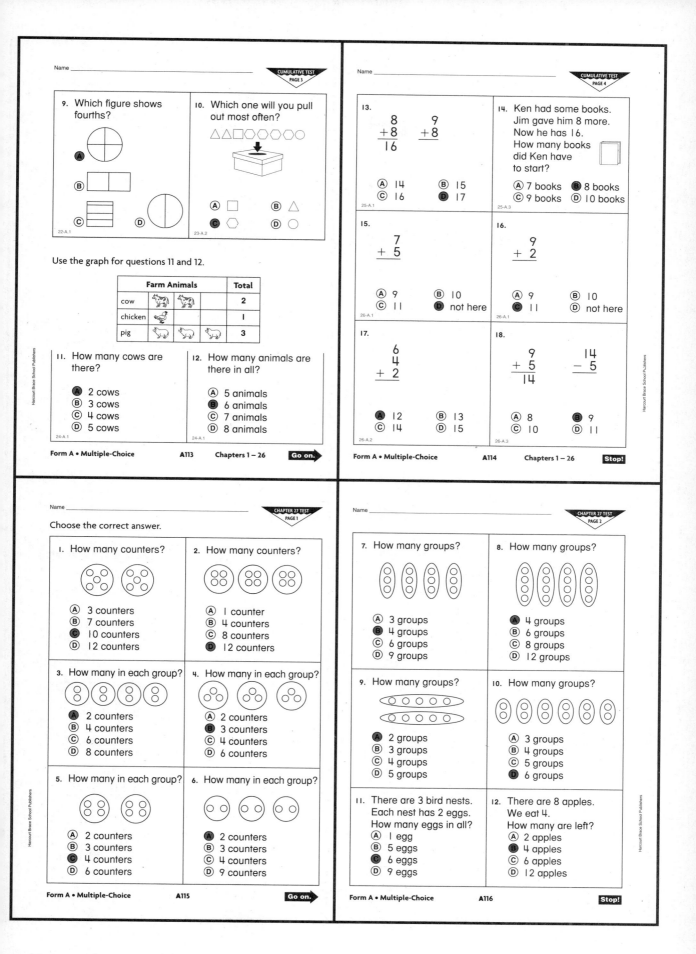

CUMULATIVE TEST PAGE 3

9. Which figure shows fourths?

Ⓐ (circle divided in quarters)

Ⓑ (rectangle divided in two)

Ⓒ (rectangle divided in rows)

Ⓓ (circle divided in half)

22-A.1

10. Which one will you pull out most often?

△ △ ▢ ◯ ◯ ⬡ ◯

Ⓐ ▢   Ⓑ △
Ⓒ ⬡   Ⓓ ◯

23-A.2

Use the graph for questions 11 and 12.

Farm Animals				Total
cow	🐄	🐄		2
chicken	🐓			1
pig	🐖	🐖	🐖	3

11. How many cows are there?

Ⓐ 2 cows
Ⓑ 3 cows
Ⓒ 4 cows
Ⓓ 5 cows

24-A.1

12. How many animals are there in all?

Ⓐ 5 animals
Ⓑ 6 animals
Ⓒ 7 animals
Ⓓ 8 animals

24-A.1

CUMULATIVE TEST PAGE 4

13.
$$8 \atop +8 \over 16$$ $$9 \atop +8$$

Ⓐ 14   Ⓑ 15
Ⓒ 16   Ⓓ 17

25-A.1

14. Ken had some books. Jim gave him 8 more. Now he has 16. How many books did Ken have to start?

Ⓐ 7 books   Ⓑ 8 books
Ⓒ 9 books   Ⓓ 10 books

25-A.3

15.
$$7 \atop +5$$

Ⓐ 9   Ⓑ 10
Ⓒ 11   Ⓓ not here

26-A.1

16.
$$9 \atop +2$$

Ⓐ 9   Ⓑ 10
Ⓒ 11   Ⓓ not here

26-A.1

17.
$$6 \atop 4 \atop +2$$

Ⓐ 12   Ⓑ 13
Ⓒ 14   Ⓓ 15

26-A.2

18.
$$9 \atop +5 \over 14$$ $$14 \atop -5$$

Ⓐ 8   Ⓑ 9
Ⓒ 10   Ⓓ 11

26-A.3

CHAPTER 27 TEST PAGE 1

Choose the correct answer.

1. How many counters?

Ⓐ 3 counters
Ⓑ 7 counters
Ⓒ 10 counters
Ⓓ 12 counters

2. How many counters?

Ⓐ 1 counter
Ⓑ 4 counters
Ⓒ 8 counters
Ⓓ 12 counters

3. How many in each group?

Ⓐ 2 counters
Ⓑ 4 counters
Ⓒ 6 counters
Ⓓ 8 counters

4. How many in each group?

Ⓐ 2 counters
Ⓑ 3 counters
Ⓒ 4 counters
Ⓓ 6 counters

5. How many in each group?

Ⓐ 2 counters
Ⓑ 3 counters
Ⓒ 4 counters
Ⓓ 6 counters

6. How many in each group?

Ⓐ 2 counters
Ⓑ 3 counters
Ⓒ 4 counters
Ⓓ 9 counters

CHAPTER 27 TEST PAGE 2

7. How many groups?

Ⓐ 3 groups
Ⓑ 4 groups
Ⓒ 6 groups
Ⓓ 9 groups

8. How many groups?

Ⓐ 4 groups
Ⓑ 6 groups
Ⓒ 8 groups
Ⓓ 12 groups

9. How many groups?

Ⓐ 2 groups
Ⓑ 3 groups
Ⓒ 4 groups
Ⓓ 5 groups

10. How many groups?

Ⓐ 3 groups
Ⓑ 4 groups
Ⓒ 5 groups
Ⓓ 6 groups

11. There are 3 bird nests. Each nest has 2 eggs. How many eggs in all?

Ⓐ 1 egg
Ⓑ 5 eggs
Ⓒ 6 eggs
Ⓓ 9 eggs

12. There are 8 apples. We eat 4. How many are left?

Ⓐ 2 apples
Ⓑ 4 apples
Ⓒ 6 apples
Ⓓ 12 apples

Multiple-Choice Format • Test Answers

153

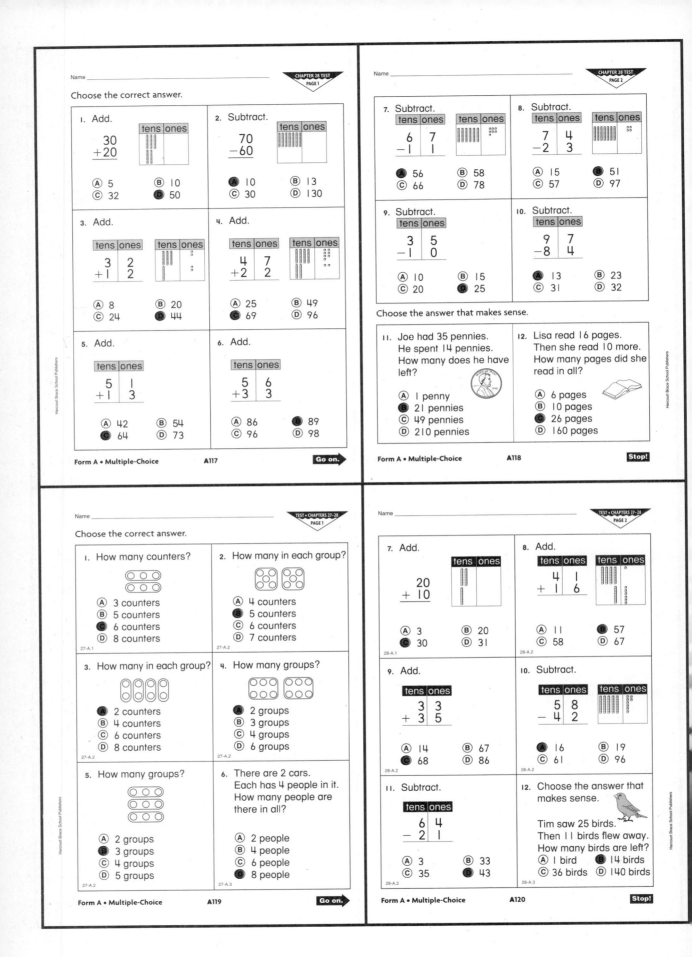

Multiple-Choice Format • Test Answers

Choose the correct answer.

1. Which number sentence belongs in this fact family?

$9 + 3 = 12$
$3 + 9 = 12$
$12 - 9 = 3$

Ⓐ $3 + 3 = 6$
Ⓑ $12 - 4 = 8$
Ⓒ $6 + 3 = 9$
● $12 - 3 = 9$

12-A.1

2. How many?

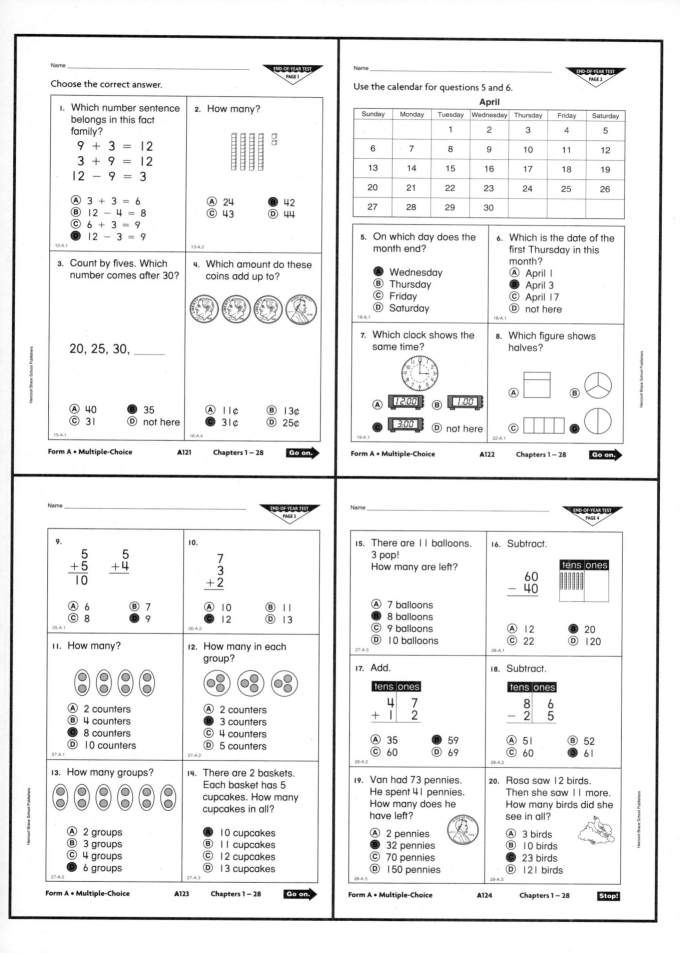

Ⓐ 24   ● 42
Ⓒ 43   Ⓓ 44

13-A.2

3. Count by fives. Which number comes after 30?

20, 25, 30, _____

Ⓐ 40   ● 35
Ⓒ 31   Ⓓ not here

15-A.1

4. Which amount do these coins add up to?

Ⓐ 11¢   Ⓑ 13¢
● 31¢   Ⓓ 25¢

16-A.4

Use the calendar for questions 5 and 6.

April

Sunday	Monday	Tuesday	Wednesday	Thursday	Friday	Saturday
		1	2	3	4	5
6	7	8	9	10	11	12
13	14	15	16	17	18	19
20	21	22	23	24	25	26
27	28	29	30			

5. On which day does the month end?

● Wednesday
Ⓑ Thursday
Ⓒ Friday
Ⓓ Saturday

18-A.1

6. Which is the date of the first Thursday in this month?

Ⓐ April 1
● April 3
Ⓒ April 17
Ⓓ not here

18-A.1

7. Which clock shows the same time?

Ⓐ 12:00   Ⓑ 1:00
Ⓒ 3:00   Ⓓ not here

19-A.1

8. Which figure shows halves?

Ⓐ
Ⓑ
Ⓒ
●

22-A.1

9.

$\begin{array}{r} 5 \\ +5 \\ \hline 10 \end{array}$ $\begin{array}{r} 5 \\ +4 \\ \hline \end{array}$

Ⓐ 6   Ⓑ 7
Ⓒ 8   ● 9

25-A.1

10.

$\begin{array}{r} 7 \\ 3 \\ +2 \\ \hline \end{array}$

Ⓐ 10   Ⓑ 11
Ⓒ 12   ● 13

26-A.2

11. How many?

Ⓐ 2 counters
Ⓑ 4 counters
● 8 counters
Ⓓ 10 counters

27-A.1

12. How many in each group?

Ⓐ 2 counters
● 3 counters
Ⓒ 4 counters
Ⓓ 5 counters

27-A.2

13. How many groups?

Ⓐ 2 groups
Ⓑ 3 groups
Ⓒ 4 groups
● 6 groups

27-A.2

14. There are 2 baskets. Each basket has 5 cupcakes. How many cupcakes in all?

● 10 cupcakes
Ⓑ 11 cupcakes
Ⓒ 12 cupcakes
Ⓓ 13 cupcakes

27-A.3

15. There are 11 balloons. 3 pop! How many are left?

Ⓐ 7 balloons
● 8 balloons
Ⓒ 9 balloons
Ⓓ 10 balloons

27-A.3

16. Subtract.

tens	ones

$\begin{array}{r} 60 \\ -40 \\ \hline \end{array}$

Ⓐ 12   ● 20
Ⓒ 22   Ⓓ 120

28-A.1

17. Add.

tens	ones
4	7
+1	2

Ⓐ 35   ● 59
Ⓒ 60   Ⓓ 69

28-A.2

18. Subtract.

tens	ones
8	6
-2	5

Ⓐ 51   Ⓑ 52
Ⓒ 60   ● 61

28-A.2

19. Van had 73 pennies. He spent 41 pennies. How many does he have left?

Ⓐ 2 pennies
● 32 pennies
Ⓒ 70 pennies
Ⓓ 150 pennies

28-A.3

20. Rosa saw 12 birds. Then she saw 11 more. How many birds did she see in all?

Ⓐ 3 birds
Ⓑ 10 birds
● 23 birds
Ⓓ 121 birds

28-A.3

Multiple-Choice Format • Test Answers

Free-Response Format Tests

The free-response format tests are useful as diagnostic tools. The work the student performs provides information about what the student understands about the concepts and/or procedures so that appropriate reteaching can be chosen from the many options in the program.

There is an Inventory Test which tests the learning goals from the previous grade level. This can be used at the beginning of the year or as a placement test when a new student enters your class.

There is a Chapter Test for each chapter and a Multi-Chapter Test to be used as review after several chapters in a content cluster. Also, there are Cumulative Tests at the same point as the Multi-Chapter Tests. The Cumulative Test reviews content from Chapter 1 through the current chapter.

Math Advantage also provides multiple-choice format tests that parallel the free-response format tests. You may wish to use one form as a pretest and one form as a posttest.

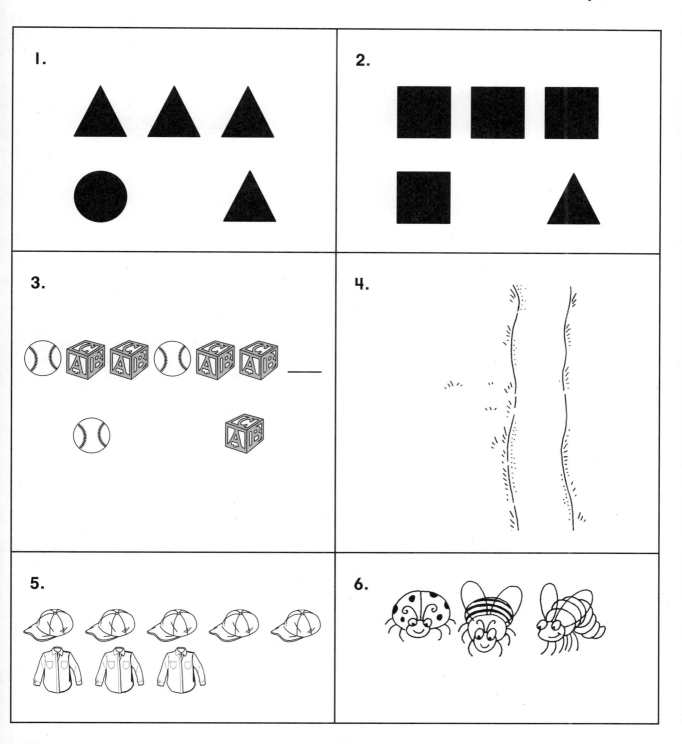

(1, 2) Circle the shape that belongs in the group. (3) Circle the toy that comes next in the pattern. (4) Draw a puppy to the left of the path. (5) Circle the group that has fewer. (6) Draw a group that has one more.

Name ______________________________

7.

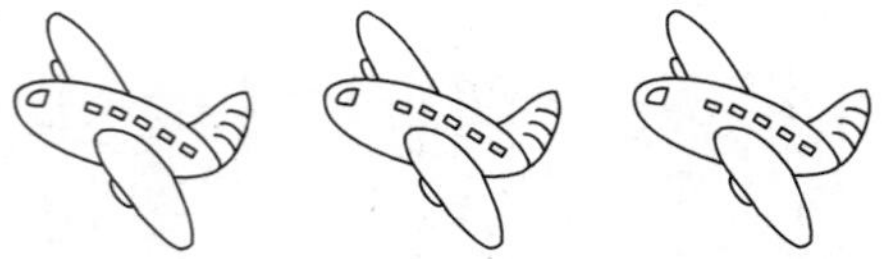

______

8.

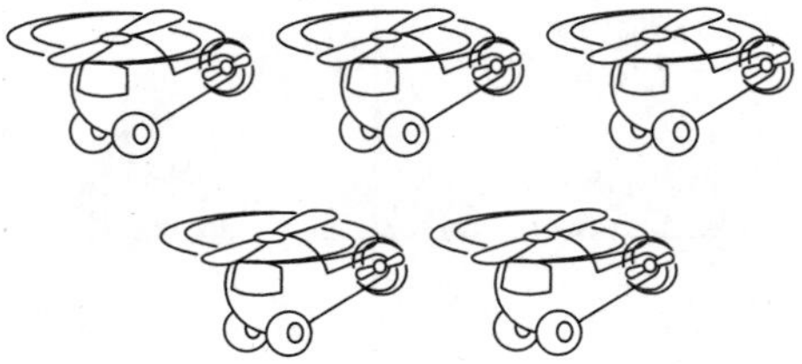

______

9.

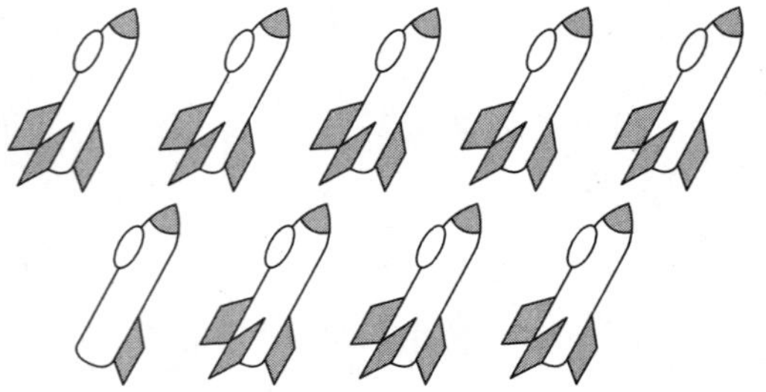

______

10.

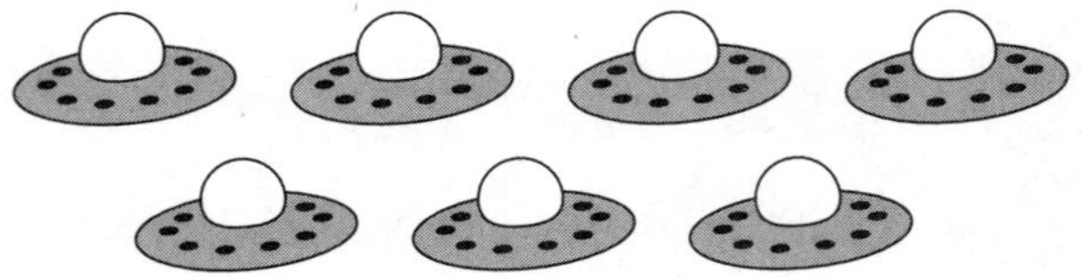

______

11.

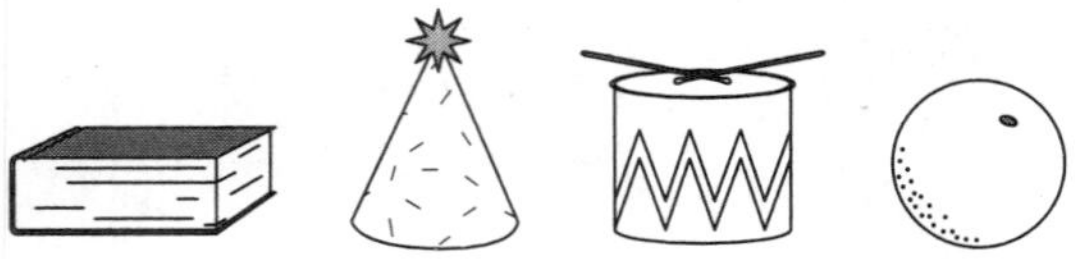

12.

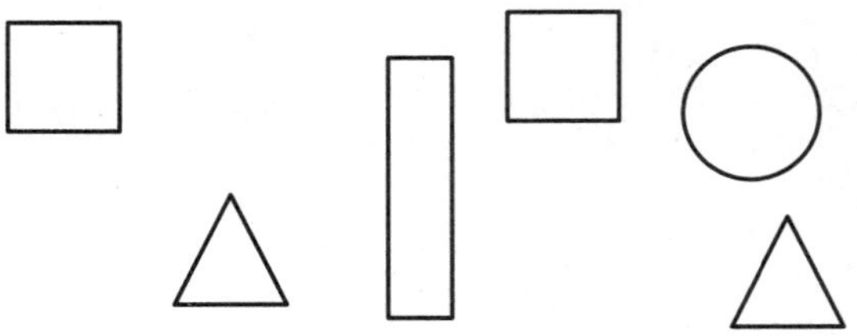

(7–10) Write the number that tells how many things are in the group. (11) Circle the object that is shaped like a cone. (12) Color the triangles blue. Color the squares red.

Name _____

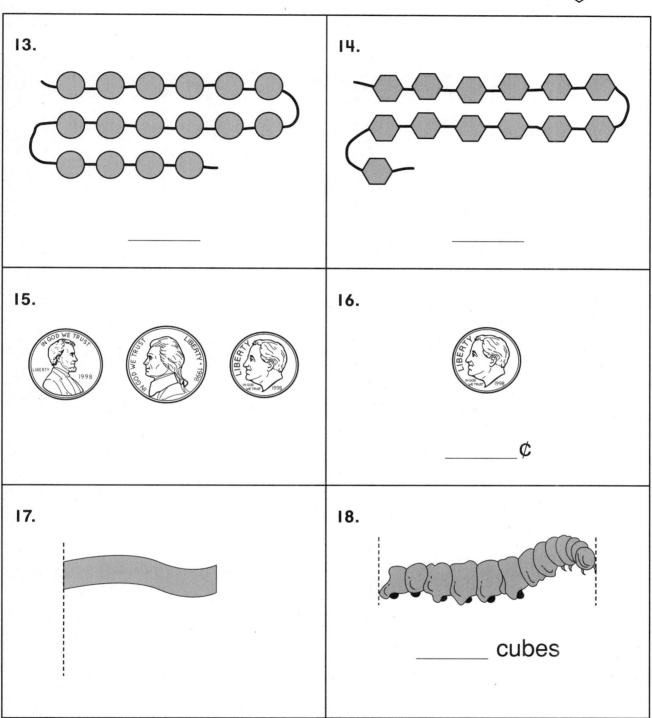

13. _____

14. _____

15.

16. _____ ¢

17.

18. _____ cubes

(13, 14) Write the number that tells how many beads there are. (15) Circle the penny. (16) Write how many cents the coin is worth. (17) Draw a ribbon that is longer than the one you see. (18) Write how many connecting cubes long the caterpillar is.

19.

20.

_____ o'clock

21.

_____ + _____ = _____

22.

_____ − _____ = _____

(19) Circle the child who is third in line. (20) Write the number that tells the hour. (21) Tell a story about the picture. Write the addition sentence that tells the story. (22) Tell a story about the picture. Write the subtraction sentence that tells the story.

Write the correct answer.

1.

2 boys play.
1 boy runs.

WORKMAT

How many in all?

 _____ boys

2.

2 girls swing.
2 girls run.

WORKMAT

How many in all?

_____ girls

3.

$1 + 1 = $ _____

4.

$4 + 1 = $ _____

5.

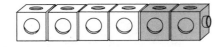

$4 + 2 = $ _____

6.

$1 + 2 = $ _____

7.

$5 + 1 = \underline{\qquad}$

8.

$1 + 3 = \underline{\qquad}$

9. Write the addition sentence.

$\underline{\qquad} + \underline{\qquad} = \underline{\qquad}$

10. Write the addition sentence.

$\underline{\qquad} + \underline{\qquad} = \underline{\qquad}$

11. Write the addition sentence.

$\underline{\qquad} + \underline{\qquad} = \underline{\qquad}$

12. Write the addition sentence.

$\underline{\qquad} + \underline{\qquad} = \underline{\qquad}$

Name _____

Write the correct answer.

1.

4 birds.
2 fly away.

WORKMAT

How many are left?

_____ birds

2.

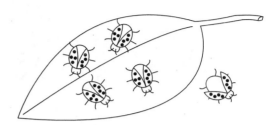

5 bugs.
1 flies away.

WORKMAT

How many are left?

_____ bugs

3.

$6 - 1 = $ _____

4.

$4 - 1 = $ _____

5.

$3 - 2 = $ _____

6.

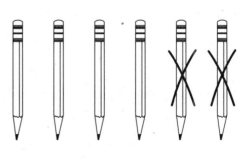

$6 - 2 = $ _____

7. Write the subtraction sentence.

___ − ___ = ___

8. Write the subtraction sentence.

___ − ___ = ___

9. Write the subtraction sentence.

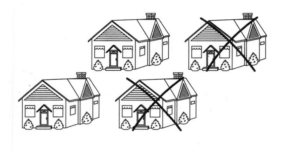

___ − ___ = ___

10. Write the subtraction sentence.

___ − ___ = ___

11. Add or subtract. Use counters.

4 bees are in a tree.
2 more come.

How many in all?

_____ bees

12. Add or subtract. Use counters.

5 sheep eat grass.
1 goes away.

How many are left?

_____ sheep

Form B • Free-Response   **B166**   **Stop!**

Write the correct answer.

1.

2 boys swing.
1 boy runs.

How many in all?

_____ boys

2.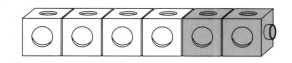

$4 + 2 =$ _____

3.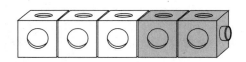

$3 + 2 =$ _____

4.

$3 + 1 =$ _____

5. Write the addition
sentence.

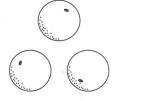

____ $+$ ____ $=$ ____

6. Write the addition
sentence.

____ $+$ ____ $=$ ____

7.

3 birds are in
a tree.
2 fly away.

WORKMAT

How many are left?

_____ birds

8.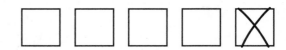

$5 - 1 = $ _____

9. Write the subtraction
sentence.

____ — ____ = ____

10. Write the subtraction
sentence.

____ — ____ = ____

11. Add or subtract.
Use counters.

5 flowers grow.
1 more grows.

How many in all?

_____ flowers

12. Add or subtract.
Use counters.

4 kites are in the sky.
2 blow away.

How many are left?

_____ kites

Write the correct answer.

1.

I dog sleeps.
I dog eats.

How many in all?

_____ dogs

2.

4 ducks walk.
2 ducks swim.

How many in all?

_____ ducks

3.

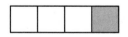

3 + 1 = _____

4.

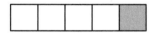

4 + 1 = _____

5.

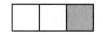

2 + 1 = _____

6.

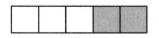

3 + 2 = _____

7.

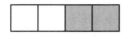

$2 + 2 =$ _____

8.

$4 + 1 =$ _____

9.

$3 + 3 =$ _____

10.

$2 + 3 =$ _____

11. Write the addition sentence.

___ $+$ ___ $=$ ___

12. Write the addition sentence.

___ $+$ ___ $=$ ___

13.

2 butterflies rest.
1 flies away.

How many are left?
_____ butterfly

14.

5 cats drink.
2 walk away.

How many are left?
_____ cats

15.

4 − 1 = _____

16.

4 − 3 = _____

17.

6 − 1 = _____

18.

3 − 2 = _____

19.

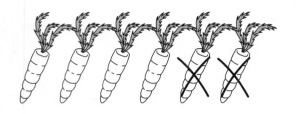

6 − 2 = _____

20.

4 − 2 = _____

21. Write the subtraction sentence.

_____ − _____ = _____

22. Write the subtraction sentence.

_____ − _____ = _____

23. Add or subtract. Use counters.

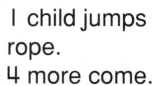

1 child jumps rope.
4 more come.

How many in all?
_____ children

24. Add or subtract. Use counters.

5 pigs eat corn.
3 go away.

How many are left?
_____ pigs

Name _____

Write the correct answer.

1.

$$3 + 2 = 5$$

$$2 + 3 = \underline{\hspace{2cm}}$$

2.

$$2 + 4 = 6$$

$$4 + 2 = \underline{\hspace{2cm}}$$

3. Use cubes. What is a way to make 8?

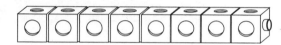

_____

4. Use cubes. What is a way to make 7?

_____

5. Use cubes. What is a way to make 9?

_____

6. Use cubes. What is a way to make 10?

_____

7.

4 + 4 = _____

8.

4 + 3 = _____

9.

$$\begin{array}{r} 2 \\ +3 \\ \hline \end{array}$$

10.

$$\begin{array}{r} 6 \\ +4 \\ \hline \end{array}$$

11. Use pennies. Find the total amount.

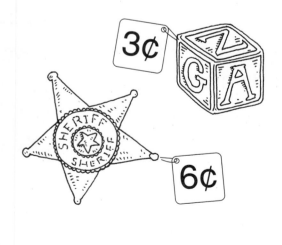

_____ ¢

12. Use pennies. Find the total amount.

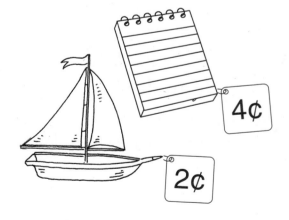

_____ ¢

Name _____

Write the correct answer.

1.

$4 + 1 = $ _____

2.

$5 + 2 = $ _____

3.

$6 + 3 = $ _____

4.

$5 + 3 = $ _____

5.

$$\begin{array}{r} 4 \\ +2 \\ \hline \end{array}$$

6.

$$\begin{array}{r} 7 \\ +3 \\ \hline \end{array}$$

7. Write the doubles fact.

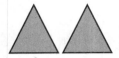 

___ + ___ = ___

8. Write the doubles fact.

___ + ___ = ___

9.

$$\begin{array}{r} 3 \\ +2 \\ \hline \end{array}$$

10.

$$\begin{array}{r} 6 \\ +4 \\ \hline \end{array}$$

11. Add or subtract.

I walk 4 dogs.
2 get away.

How many are left?

_____ dogs

12. Add or subtract.

I have 4 kittens.
3 more come.
How many do I have
in all?

_____ kittens

Name _____

Write the correct answer.

1.

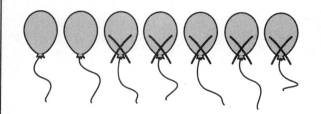

$7 - 5 =$ _____

2.

$8 - 2 =$ _____

3.

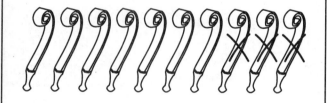

$10 - 3 =$ _____

4.

$9 - 6 =$ _____

5.

$$\begin{array}{r} 9 \\ -\ 4 \\ \hline \end{array}$$

6.

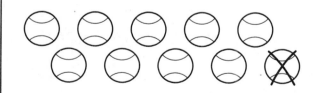

$$\begin{array}{r} 10 \\ -\ 1 \\ \hline \end{array}$$

7.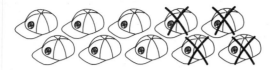

$$\begin{array}{r} 10 \\ -4 \\ \hline \end{array}$$

8.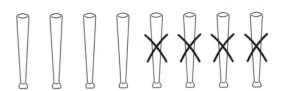

$$\begin{array}{r} 8 \\ -4 \\ \hline \end{array}$$

9. Complete the fact family.

$$3 + 5 = 8$$
$$8 - 5 = 3$$
$$5 + 3 = 8$$
$$8 - 3 = \underline{\qquad}$$

10. Complete the fact family.

$$\begin{array}{r} 4 \\ +2 \\ \hline 6 \end{array} \qquad \begin{array}{r} 2 \\ +4 \\ \hline 6 \end{array} \qquad \begin{array}{r} 6 \\ -2 \\ \hline 4 \end{array} \qquad \begin{array}{r} 6 \\ -4 \\ \hline \end{array}$$

11. How many more ?

$$7 - 4 = \underline{\qquad}$$

_____ more 🏐

12. How many more 🐕?

$$9 - 2 = \underline{\qquad}$$

_____ more 🐕

Name _____

Write the correct answer.

1.

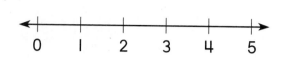

$$3 - 1 = \underline{\quad}$$

2.

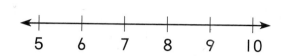

$$10 - 2 = \underline{\quad}$$

3.

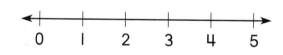

$$4 - 3 = \underline{\quad}$$

4.

$$8 - 3 = \underline{\quad}$$

5.

$$\begin{array}{r} 8 \\ -1 \\ \hline \end{array}$$

6.

$$\begin{array}{r} 7 \\ -3 \\ \hline \end{array}$$

7.

$$\begin{array}{r} 7 \\ -7 \\ \hline \end{array}$$

8.

$$\begin{array}{r} 5 \\ -0 \\ \hline \end{array}$$

9.

$$\begin{array}{r} 9 \\ -3 \\ \hline \end{array}$$

10.

$$\begin{array}{r} 7 \\ +2 \\ \hline \end{array}$$

11.

6 frogs are by a pond.
3 hop away.
How many now?

_____ frogs

12.

4 birds are on a tree.
3 more come.
How many now?

_____ birds

Write the correct answer.

1. Find the missing sum.

$5 + 1 = 6$

$1 + 5 = $ _____

2. Use counters.
   What is a way to
   make 8?

   _____

3.

$4 + 3 = $ _____

4. Count on to add.

$8 + 1 = $ _____

5. Write the doubles fact
   that goes with the
   picture.

   _____ + _____ = _____

6.

Bill has 7 pups.
2 more come to him.
How many pups does
he have now?

_____ pups

7.

$$\begin{array}{r} 7 \\ -6 \\ \hline \end{array}$$

8.

$$8 + 2 = 10$$
$$2 + 8 = 10$$
$$10 - 2 = 8$$
$$10 - 8 = \underline{\quad}$$

9. How many more  ?

$$6 - 2 = \underline{\quad}$$

_____ more

10.

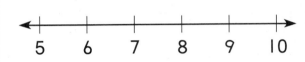

$$8 - 3 = \underline{\quad}$$

11.

$$\begin{array}{r} 2 \\ -2 \\ \hline \end{array}$$

12.

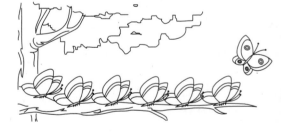

7 butterflies are on
a tree.
1 flies away.

How many butterflies
are there now?

_____ butterflies

Name _____

Write the correct answer.

1.

3 girls play.
1 girl jumps.

How many in all?
_____ girls

2.

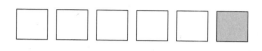

$5 + 1 =$ _____

3.

$3 + 2 =$ _____

4.

$5 - 1 =$ _____

5.

$3 - 2 =$ _____

6. Add or subtract. Use counters.

2 boats are sailing.
1 goes away.

How many are left?
_____ boat

7.

$5 + 2 = 7$

$2 + 5 = \underline{\hphantom{000}}$

8. Use cubes.
What is a way to
make 8?

_____

9. Use cubes.
What is a way to
make 10?

_____

10.

$4 + 5 = \underline{\hphantom{000}}$

11. Use pennies. Find the
total amount.

4¢   **3¢**

_____ ¢

12.

$8 + 1 = \underline{\hphantom{000}}$

13.

$5 + 3 =$ _____

14. Write the doubles fact.

_____ $+$ _____ $=$ _____

15.

$$\begin{array}{r} 7 \\ + 3 \\ \hline \end{array}$$

16. Add or subtract.

There are 6 rabbits.
I more comes.

How many are there
in all?

_____ rabbits

17.

$7 - 3 =$ _____

18.

$10 - 2 =$ _____

19.

$$- \begin{array}{r} 8 \\ 3 \end{array}$$

20. How many more ?

$$9 - 5 = \underline{\hspace{1.5cm}}$$

21.

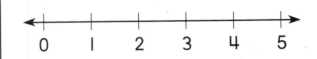

$$4 - 2 = \underline{\hspace{1.5cm}}$$

22.

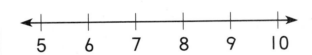

$$9 - 3 = \underline{\hspace{1.5cm}}$$

23.

$$- \begin{array}{r} 7 \\ 1 \end{array}$$

24.

5 mice are eating.
1 runs away.

How many now?
_____ mice

Name _____

Write the correct answer.

1. Circle the object that has the same shape.

2. Circle the object that has the same shape.

3. Circle the object that has the same shape.

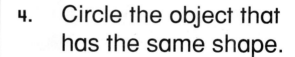

4. Circle the object that has the same shape.

5. Circle the object that has the same shape.

6. Circle the object that has the same shape.

7. Circle the figure that will stack.

8. Circle the figure that will roll.

9. Circle the figure that has all flat faces.

10. Write how many cubes.

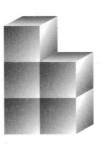

_____ cubes

Write the correct answer.

1. Circle the plane figure that matches the face of the solid figure.

2. Circle the plane figure that matches the face of the solid figure.

3. Circle the plane figure that matches the face of the solid figure.

4. Circle the plane figure that matches the face of the solid figure.

5. Write how many sides this figure has.

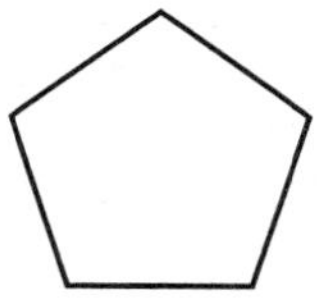

_____ sides

6. Write how many corners this figure has.

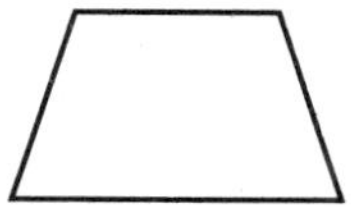

_____ corners

7. Circle the figure that has 0 sides and 0 corners.

8. Circle the figure that has 5 sides and 5 corners.

9. Circle the figure that is the same size and shape as this one.

10. Circle the figure that is the same size and shape as this one.

11. Circle the picture that shows two sides that match.

12. Circle the picture that shows two sides that match.

Name _____

Write the correct answer.

1. Circle the open figure.

2. Circle the closed figure.

3. Color the figure outside the ☐.

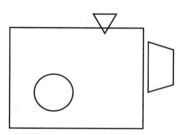

4. Color the figure inside the ☐.

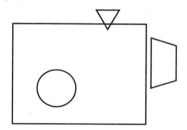

Use the grid to answer questions 5 and 6.

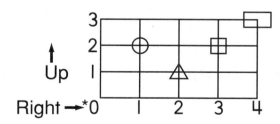

5. Start at *. Go right 1. Go up 2. Circle the shape that is there.

6. Start at *. Go right 4. Go up 3. Circle the shape that is there.

Use the picture to answer questions 7 to 10.

← Left   Right →

7. Circle the animal to the **right** of the .

8. Circle the animal to the **left** of the .

9. Circle the object to the **left** of the .

10. Circle the object to the **right** of the .

Write the correct answer.

1. Circle the pattern.

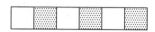

2. Circle the pattern.

3. Circle the shape that comes next in the pattern.

4. Circle the shape that comes next in the pattern.

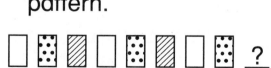

5. Circle the shapes that come next in the pattern.

□ △ ○ □ △ ○ □ _?_ _?_

△ △   □ △

○ □   △ ○

6. Circle the shapes that come next in the pattern.

⬮ ⬯ ⬰ ⬮ ⬯ ⬰ ⬮ ⬯ ⬰ _?_ _?_

⬮ ○   ⬮ ⬯

⬮ ⬮   ○ ⬯

7. Circle the different pattern that uses the same shapes as this one.

△ △ ○ △ △ ○ △ △ ○

△ ○ ○ △ ○ ○

○ □ ○ □ ○ □

△ △ □ △ △ □

8. Circle the different pattern that uses the same shapes as this one.

□ ○ ○ □ ○ ○ □ ○ ○

◇ ○ □ ◇ ○ □

○ □ ○ □ ○ □

△ ◇ ○ △ ◇ ○

9. Mark an X on the shape that is a mistake in the pattern.

○ △ ○ △ ○ ◇ ○ △

10. Circle the shape that fixes this mistake in the pattern.

□ □ ○ □ □ ○ □ △̶ ○

△   ◇   □   ○

Write the correct answer.

1. Circle the object that has the same shape.

2. Circle the object that has the same shape.

3. Circle the solid figure that will roll.

4. Circle the plane figure that matches the face of the solid figure.

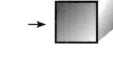

5. Circle the figure that has 3 sides and 3 corners.

6. Circle the picture that shows two sides that match.

Use the grid to answer questions 7 and 8.

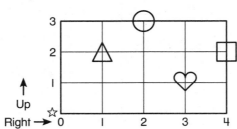

| 7. | Start at ☆. Go right 3. Go up 1. Draw the shape that is there. | 8. | Start at ☆. Go right 2. Go up 3. Draw the shape that is there. |

7. Start at ☆. Go right 3. Go up 1. Draw the shape that is there.

8. Start at ☆. Go right 2. Go up 3. Draw the shape that is there.

9. Circle the closed figure.

10. Circle the squares that continue the pattern.

11. Circle a different pattern that uses the same shapes as this one.

12. Circle the shape that is a mistake in the pattern.

○

□

△

Write the correct answer.

1.

$$3 + 2 = \underline{\hspace{1.5cm}}$$

2. Write the addition sentence.

$$\underline{\hspace{1cm}} + \underline{\hspace{1cm}} = \underline{\hspace{1cm}}$$

3.

6 ducks sit by the pond.
2 swim away.

How many are left?
_____ ducks

4. Write the subtraction sentence.

$$\underline{\hspace{1cm}} - \underline{\hspace{1cm}} = \underline{\hspace{1cm}}$$

5.

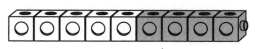

$$5 + 4 = 9$$

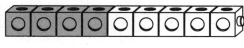

$$4 + 5 = \underline{\hspace{1.5cm}}$$

6.

$$\begin{array}{r} 8 \\ -\ 4 \\ \hline \end{array}$$

7. Complete the fact family.

4 + 3 = 7   7 − 3 = 4

3 + 4 = 7   7 − 4 = ___

8.

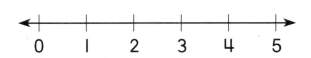

0   1   2   3   4   5

5 − 3 = _____

9. Circle the object that has the same shape.

10. Circle the object that has the same shape.

11. Circle the figure that will roll.

12. Circle the figure that has no flat faces.

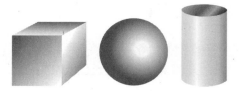

13. Circle the plane figure that matches the face of the solid figure.

14. Circle the figure that is the same size and shape as this one.

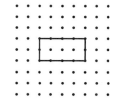

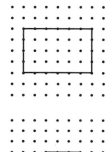

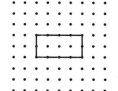

15. Circle the picture that shows two sides that match.

16. Circle the open figure.

17. Color the figure on the ◯.

◯   ▭

▢   △

18. Start at ☆. Go right 2. Go up 1. Circle the shape that is there.

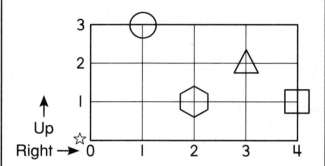

▢   ◯

△   ⬡

19. Circle the shapes that come next in the pattern.

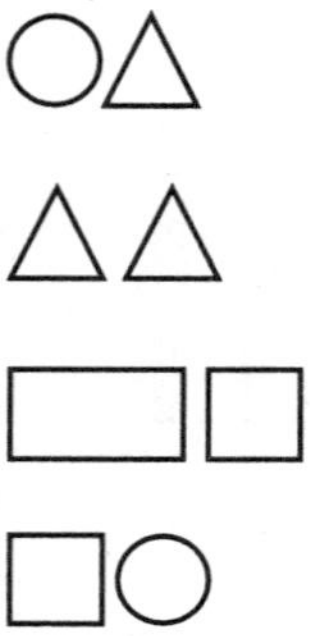

◯△▢◯△▢◯△▢ _?_ _?_

◯△

△△

▭▭

▢◯

20. Mark an X on the shape that is a mistake in the pattern.

▭◯△▭◯▢▭◯△

Name _____

Write the correct answer.

1. Count on to add.

$$6 + 3 = \underline{\qquad}$$

2. Count on to add.

$$5 + 2 = \underline{\qquad}$$

3. Count on to add.

$$5 + 3 = \underline{\qquad}$$

4. Count on to add.

$$7 + 1 = \underline{\qquad}$$

5.

$$\begin{array}{r} 2 \\ +2 \\ \hline \end{array}$$

6.

$$\begin{array}{r} 4 \\ +4 \\ \hline \end{array}$$

7.

Jan spent 9¢.
Tom spent 3¢.

How much did they
spend in all?

_____¢

8.

Van saved 5¢.
Mary saved 5¢.

How much did they
save in all?

_____¢

Go on.

9.

$$\begin{array}{r} 2 \\ 4 \\ +5 \\ \hline \end{array}$$

10.

$$\begin{array}{r} 4 \\ 0 \\ +8 \\ \hline \end{array}$$

11.

$$\begin{array}{r} 5 \\ +4 \\ \hline \end{array}$$

12.

$$\begin{array}{r} 9 \\ +1 \\ \hline \end{array}$$

13.

$3 + 8 = $ _____

14.

$5 + 7 = $ _____

15. 6 cats play in the yard.
4 more cats come to play.
How many cats play in the yard?

_____ cats

16. 7 sheep are eating grass.
2 more come to eat.
How many sheep are eating grass?

_____ sheep

Write the correct answer.

1.

$6 + 3 = 9$

$9 - 3 =$ _____

2.

$8 + 3 = 11$

$11 - 3 =$ _____

3.

$$\begin{array}{r} 4 \\ +6 \\ \hline 10 \end{array} \qquad \begin{array}{r} 10 \\ -6 \\ \hline \end{array}$$

4.

$$\begin{array}{r} 7 \\ +\ 5 \\ \hline 12 \end{array} \qquad \begin{array}{r} 12 \\ -\ 5 \\ \hline \end{array}$$

5. Count back to subtract.

$9 - 2 =$ _____

6. Count back to subtract.

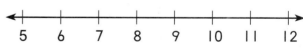

$10 - 1 =$ _____

7. How many more apples than pears are there?

$$\begin{array}{r} 12 \\ -4 \\ \hline \end{array}$$

8. How many fewer plums than bananas are there?

$$\begin{array}{r} 11 \\ -9 \\ \hline \end{array}$$

9. Circle the number sentence that belongs in this fact family.

3 + 9 = 12
9 + 3 = 12
12 − 3 = 9
- - - - - - - - - - - - - - - - - -
3 + 3 = 6
12 − 9 = 3
9 − 3 = 6

10. Circle the number sentence that belongs in this fact family.

10 − 3 = 7
10 − 7 = 3
3 + 7 = 10
- - - - - - - - - - - - - - - - - -
7 + 3 = 10
4 + 3 = 7
10 − 6 = 4

11. Write the number sentence the story shows.
Sam had 11 balls.
He gave away 7.
How many balls does Sam have left?

_____ ◯ _____ = _____

_____ balls

12. Write the number sentence the story shows.
I had 8 pennies.
I found 4 more.
How many pennies do I have now?

_____ ◯ _____ = _____

_____ pennies

Write the correct answer.

1.

$$7 + 3 = \underline{\hspace{1cm}}$$

2.

$$\begin{array}{r} 6 \\ +6 \\ \hline \end{array}$$

3.

$$\begin{array}{r} 3 \\ 5 \\ +3 \\ \hline \end{array}$$

4.

$$\begin{array}{r} 1 \\ 2 \\ +7 \\ \hline \end{array}$$

5. Lee spent 6¢.

Rosa spent 5¢.

How much did they spend in all?

_____ ¢

6. 8 cats are drinking milk.

1 more cat comes to drink.

How many cats are drinking milk?

_____ cats

7.

$$9 + 2 \over 11$$

$$11 - 2$$

8.

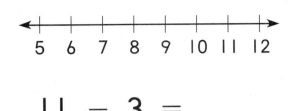

5 6 7 8 9 10 11 12

$$11 - 3 = \underline{\hspace{1cm}}$$

9. How many more oranges than apples are there?

$$10 - 6$$

10. Write the number sentence that belongs in this fact family.

$$9 + 3 = 12$$
$$3 + 9 = 12$$
$$12 - 9 = 3$$

$$\underline{\hspace{1cm}} \bigcirc \underline{\hspace{1cm}} = \underline{\hspace{1cm}}$$

11. Write the number sentence the story shows.

Ray had 10 toys.
He gave 5 away.
How many toys does Ray have left?

$$\underline{\hspace{1cm}} \bigcirc \underline{\hspace{1cm}} = \underline{\hspace{1cm}}$$

12. Write the number sentence the story shows.

I have 4 pennies.
I find 7 more.
How many pennies do I have now?

$$\underline{\hspace{1cm}} \bigcirc \underline{\hspace{1cm}} = \underline{\hspace{1cm}}$$

Name _____

Write the correct answer.

1.

2 girls read.
2 girls play.
How many in all?

_____ girls

2.

3 skunks smell flowers.
1 walks away.
How many are left?

_____ skunks

3. Use cubes. What is a way to make 7?

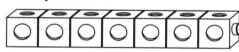

_____

4. Circle the object that has the same shape.

5. Circle the plane figure that matches the face of the solid figure.

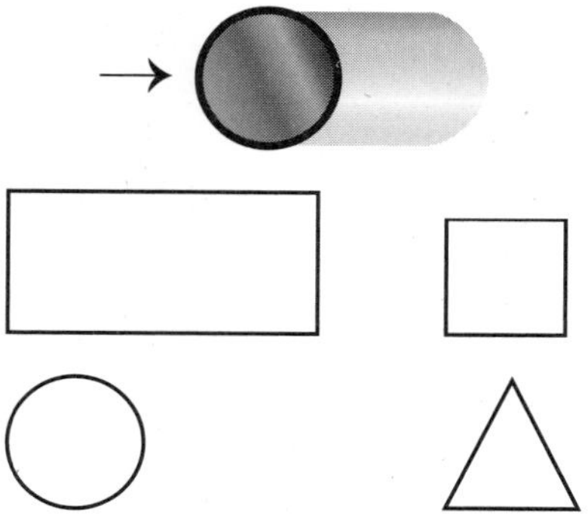

6. Circle the closed figure.

7. Circle the shape that comes next in the pattern.

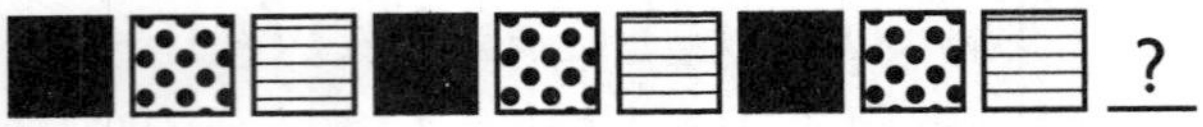

8. Circle the different pattern that uses the same shapes as this one.

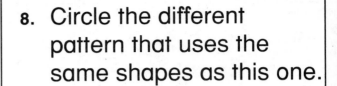

9. Count on to add.

$$7 + 1 = \underline{\qquad}$$

10. Count on to add.

$$8 + 3 = \underline{\qquad}$$

11.

$$\begin{array}{r} 4 \\ + 4 \\ \hline \end{array}$$

12.

$$\begin{array}{r} 7 \\ + 2 \\ \hline \end{array}$$

13.

$$\begin{array}{r} 6 \\ + \ 4 \\ \hline \end{array}$$

14.

$$\begin{array}{r} 5 \\ 4 \\ + \ 3 \\ \hline \end{array}$$

15. 6 turtles swim in a pond.

3 more turtles come to swim.

How many turtles are in the pond?

_____ turtles

16. 3 girls are reading.

2 more come to read.

How many girls are reading?

_____ girls

17.

$$\begin{array}{r} 2 \\ + \ 6 \\ \hline 8 \end{array} \qquad \begin{array}{r} 8 \\ - \ 6 \\ \hline \end{array}$$

18. Count back to subtract.

5 6 7 8 9 10 11 12

$$11 - 3 = \underline{\hspace{1.5cm}}$$

19. Circle the number sentence that belongs in this fact family.

$$8 + 4 = 12$$
$$4 + 8 = 12$$
$$12 - 8 = 4$$

- -

$$12 - 4 = 8$$
$$11 - 3 = 8$$
$$8 - 4 = 4$$

20. How many more spoons than forks are there?

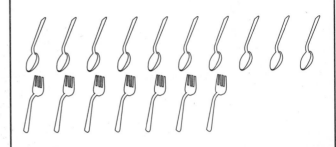

$$\begin{array}{r} 10 \\ -\ 7 \\ \hline \end{array}$$

21. Write the number sentence the story shows.

Suzy had 11 balloons. She gave 6 away.

How many balloons does Suzy have left?

____ ◯ ____ = ____

_____ balloons

22. Write the number sentence the story shows.

I had 9 pencils. I found 3 more.

How many pencils do I have now?

____ ◯ ____ = ____

_____ pencils

Name _____

Write the correct answer.

1. How many?

   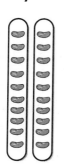

   2 tens = _____

2. How many?

   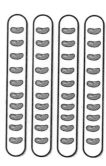

   4 tens = _____

3. How many?

   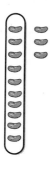

   1 ten 3 ones = _____

4. How many?

   1 ten 7 ones = _____

5. How many?

   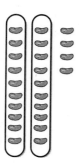

   _____

6. How many?

   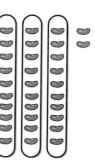

   _____

7. How many?

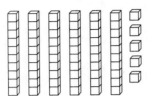

_____

8. How many?

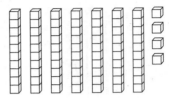

_____

9. How many?

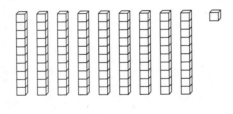

_____

10. How many?

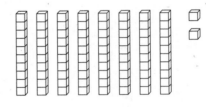

_____

11. Circle the better estimate.

more than 10

fewer than 10

12. Circle the better estimate.

more than 10

fewer than 10

Name _____

Write the correct answer.
Use this picture to answer questions 1 and 2.

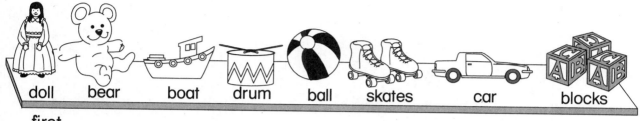

| doll | bear | boat | drum | ball | skates | car | blocks |

first

1. Write the name of the **third** toy.

    _____

2. Write the name of the **seventh** toy.

    _____

3. Circle the number that is **greater.**

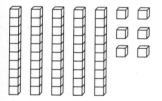

56   42

4. Circle the number that is **greater.**

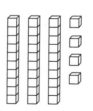 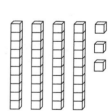

34   43

5. Circle the number that is **less**.

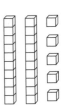

25   19

6. Circle the number that is **less**.

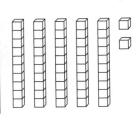

52   55

7. Write the number that comes just **before** 68.

_____, 68

8. Write the number that comes just **after** 68.

68, _____

9. Write the number that comes **between** 81 and 83.

81, _____, 83

10. Ann picked a number **between** 36 and 38. Write the number that she picked.

36, _____, 38

11. Write these numbers in order from **least** to **greatest**.

79, 73, 77

_____, _____, _____

12. Write these numbers in order from **least** to **greatest**.

98, 51, 62, 29

_____, _____, _____, _____

Name _____

Write the correct answer.
Use the art to answer questions 1 and 2.

10   20   30   ____   50   60   ____ coins

---

1. Count by tens. Write the number that comes after 30.

   _____

2. Count by tens. Write the number that comes after 60.

   _____

Use the table to answer questions 3 and 4.

Sunday	Monday	Tuesday	Wednesday	Thursday	Friday	Saturday
10	20					

---

3. Hazel's hens lay 10 eggs each day. Hazel has 10 eggs on Sunday. Write how many eggs she has on Thursday.

   _____ eggs

4. Write how many eggs Hazel has on Saturday.

   _____ eggs

Form B • Free-Response   B215   Go on.

Use the pictures to answer questions 5 and 6.

5   10   15   ____   25   30   ____ stars

5. Count by fives. Write the number that comes after 15. _____	6. Count by fives. Write the number that comes after 30. _____

Use the pictures to answer questions 7 and 8.

2   4   ____   8   10   ____   14 cherries

7. Count by twos. Write the number that comes after 4. _____	8. Count by twos. Write the number that comes after 10. _____
9. Circle **even** or **odd**. 4  even odd	10. Circle **even** or **odd**. 13  even odd

Write the correct answer.

1. How many?

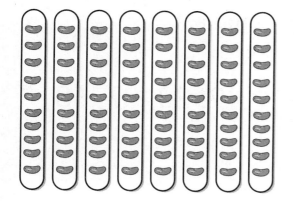

8 tens = _____

2. How many?

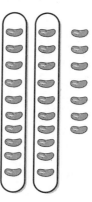

_____

3. How many?

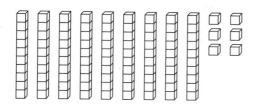

_____

4. Circle the better estimate.

more than 10
fewer than 10

5. Circle the number that is **greater.**

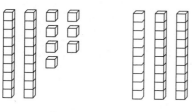

27   32

6. Write the number that comes just **after** 32.

32, _____

7. Ben picked a number **between** 72 and 74. Write the number he picked.

72, _____, 74

8. Write these numbers in order from **least** to **greatest.**

49, 20, 87, 68

_____, _____, _____, _____

9. Count by tens. Write the number that comes **after** 40.

_____

10. Count by fives. Write the number that comes **after** 25.

_____

11. Count by twos. Write the number that comes after 8.

_____

12. Circle **even** or **odd.**

5

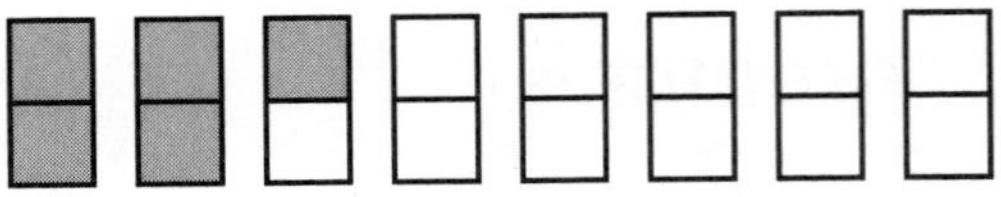

even   odd

Write the correct answer.

1.

___ + ___ = ___

2. Circle the figure that has 4 sides and 4 corners.

Use the picture to answer questions 3 and 4.

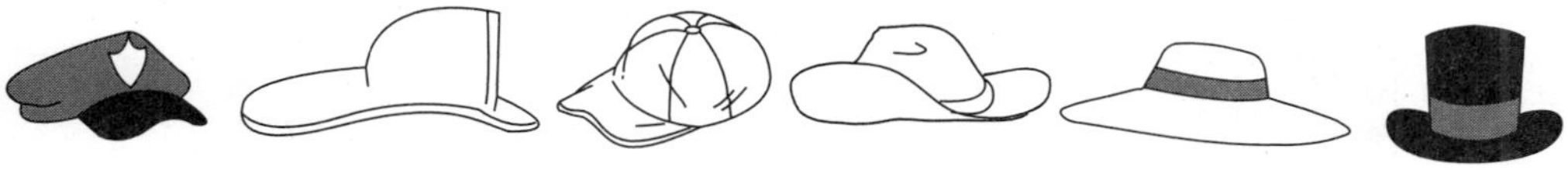

← Left   Right →

3. Circle the hat to the **right** of the .

4. Circle the hat to the **left** of the .

_____   _____

5. Count back to subtract.

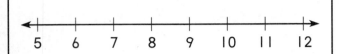

$11 - 2 =$ _____

6. Write the number sentence the story shows.

Pat had 12 toys. She gave away 5. How many toys does Pat have left?

_____ ◯ _____ = _____

_____ toys

7. How many?

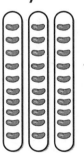

3 tens = _____

8. How many?

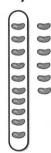

1 ten 6 ones = _____

9. How many?

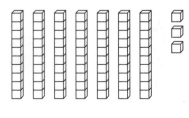

_____

10. Circle the better estimate.

more than 10
fewer than 10.

Use the picture to answer questions 11 and 12 .

First

---

11. Write the name of the **fifth** animal.

_____

12. Write the name of the **first** animal.

_____

---

13. Circle the number that is **greater.**

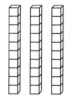   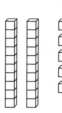

32   29

14. Circle the number that is **less.**

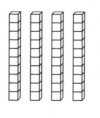   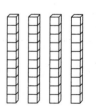

46   42

---

15. Jon picked a number **between** 47 and 49. Write the number that he picked.

47, _____, 49

16. Write these numbers in order from **least** to **greatest.**

65, 62, 68

_____, _____, _____

17. Count by tens. Write the number that comes after 20.

10, 20, _____, 40

_____

18. Count by fives. Write the number that comes after 10.

5, 10, _____, 20

_____

19. Count by twos. Write the number that comes after 6.

2, 4, 6, _____

_____

20. Circle **even** or **odd.**

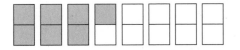

even   odd

1. Write the amount.

_____ ¢

2. Write the amount.

_____ ¢

3. Write the amount.

_____ ¢

4. Write the amount.

_____ ¢

5. Count. Write the amount.

_____ ¢, _____ ¢, _____ ¢, _____ ¢

6. Count. Write the amount.

_____ ¢, _____ ¢, _____ ¢, _____ ¢

7. Write the amount.

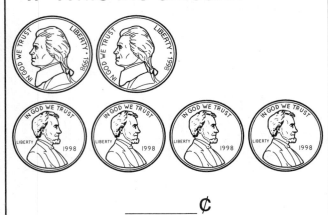

_____ ¢

8. Write the amount.

_____ ¢

9. Which two groups add up to the amount on the tag? Color them.

10. Which two groups add up to the amount on the tag? Color them.

Write the correct answer.

1. Circle the group of coins you can trade these pennies for.

2. Circle the group of coins you can trade these pennies for.

3. Circle the group that uses the fewest coins to show the amount.

4. Circle the group that uses the fewest coins to show the amount.

Circle the group of coins you need.

5.

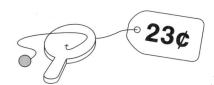

6.

7. Write how many pennies

equal a .

_____ pennies

8. Circle coins that equal 25¢.

9. Circle what you could buy with

17¢

32¢

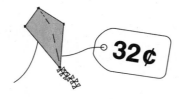
36¢

49¢

10. Circle what you could buy with

53¢

42¢

50¢

40¢

Name _____

Write the correct answer.
Use the calendar to answer questions 1 to 6.

January						
Sunday	Monday	Tuesday	Wednesday	Thursday	Friday	Saturday
			1	2	3	4
5	6	7	8	9	10	11
12	13	14	15	16	17	18
19	20	21	22	23	24	25
26	27	28	29	30	31	

1. How many months are in one year?

    _____months

2. Which day comes just after Sunday?

    _____

3. On which day does this month begin?

    _____

4. On which day is January 28?

    _____

5. What is the date of the first Saturday in this month?

    January _____

6. How many days are in this month?

    _____days

7. Does this happen in the morning, in the afternoon, or in the evening?

in the _____

8. Does this happen in the morning, in the afternoon, or in the evening?

in the _____

9. Circle the one that takes longer to do.

write your name

write a story

10. Circle the one that takes longer to do.

carry the ball

throw the ball

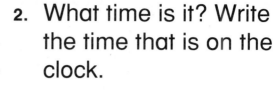

Write the correct answer.

1. What time is it? Write the time that is on the clock.

_____ o'clock

2. What time is it? Write the time that is on the clock.

_____ o'clock

3. Read the clock. Write the time.

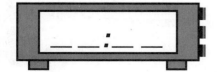

4. Read the clock. Write the time.

5. Draw the hour hand and the minute hand to show the time.

6. Draw the hour hand and the minute hand to show the time.

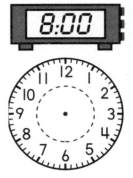

7. Write the time.

_____

8. Write the time.

_____

9. Does it take **more** than a minute or **less** than a minute to turn on a light?

_____ than a minute

10. Does it take **more** than a minute or **less** than a minute to ride to school?

_____ than a minute

Name _____

Write the correct answer.

1. Write the amount.

_____ ¢

2. Write the amount.

_____ ¢

3. Circle the coins that show the amount on the tag. 13¢

4. Circle the answer that shows the amount using the fewest coins. 21¢

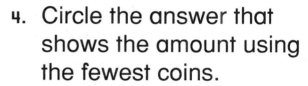

5. Circle the coins that equal a  .

6. Circle what you could buy with

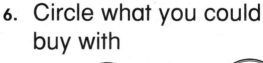

 53¢   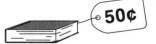 50¢

 49¢    45¢

Use the calendar to answer questions 7 and 8.

February

S	M	T	W	T	F	S
						1
2	3	4	5	6	7	8
9	10	11	12	13	14	15
16	17	18	19	20	21	22
23	24	25	26	27	28	

7. On what day is February 14?

_____

8. What is the date of the first Tuesday in this month?

February _____

9. Which takes longer?

10. Write the time.

 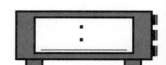

11. What time is it?

: _____

12. Which takes less than a minute to do?

Write the correct answer.

1.

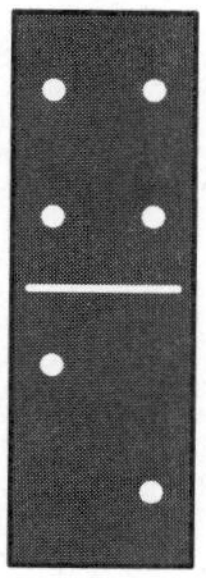

$$\begin{array}{r} 4 \\ + \ 2 \\ \hline \end{array}$$

2. Circle the figure that is the same size and shape as this one.

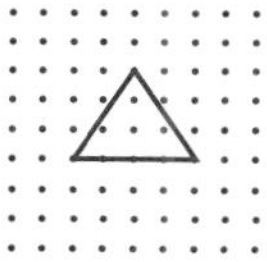

3. Circle the shapes that come next in the pattern.

○○△○○△○ ? ?

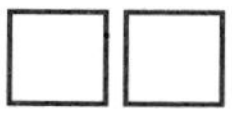

□△   ○△

△△   □□

4.

$$\begin{array}{r} 5 \\ 3 \\ + \ 2 \\ \hline \end{array}$$

5. Circle the number sentence that belongs in this fact family.

11 − 6 = 5
11 − 5 = 6
6 + 5 = 11
----
11 − 1 = 10
5 + 6 = 11
11 + 1 = 12

6. How many?

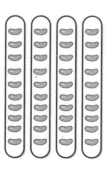

4 tens = _____

7. Paul picked a number **between** 72 and 74. Write the number that he picked.

72, _____, 74

8. Write the number that comes just **before** 48.

_____, 48

9. Write the amount.

_____ ¢

10. Count. Write the amount.

_____ ¢, _____ ¢, _____ ¢, _____ ¢

11. Write the amount.

_____ ¢

12. Write the amount.

_____ ¢

Name _____

13. Circle what you could buy with 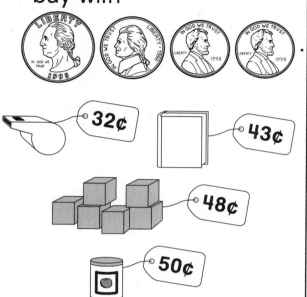 .

14. Write how many nickels equal a  .

32¢

43¢

48¢

50¢

_____ nickels

Use the calendar to answer questions 15 and 16.

December

Sunday	Monday	Tuesday	Wednesday	Thursday	Friday	Saturday
	1	2	3	4	5	6
7	8	9	10	11	12	13
14	15	16	17	18	19	20
21	22	23	24	25	26	27
28	29	30	31			

15. On which day is December 20?

_____

16. What is the date of the first Tuesday in the month?

December _____

17. Does this happen in the morning, in the afternoon, or in the evening?

In the _____

18. Draw the hour hand and the minute hand to show the time.

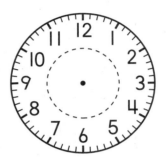

19. Write the time.

_____

20. Does it take **more** than a minute or **less** than a minute to close a door?

_____ than a minute

Write the correct answer.

1. About how many  long is the leaf?

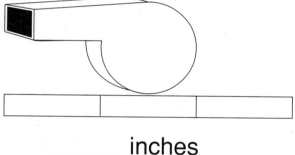

About _____

2. About how many  long is the flower?

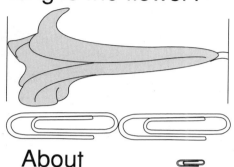

About _____

3. How many inches long.

_____ inches

4. How many inches long.

_____ inch

5. Write how many inches long.

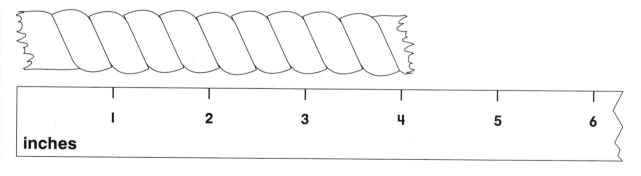

_____ inches

6. How many inches long.

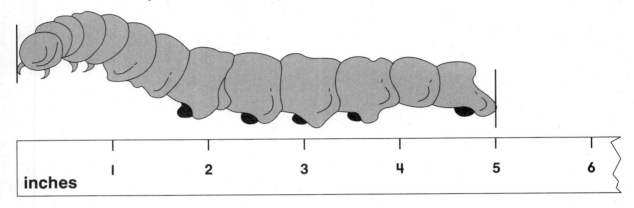

_____ inches.

7. How many centimeters long.

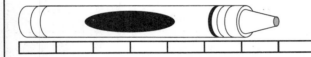

_____ centimeters

8. How many centimeters long.

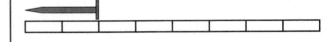

_____ centimeters

9. How many centimeters long.

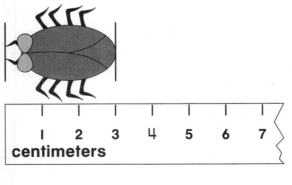

_____ centimeters

10. How many centimeters long.

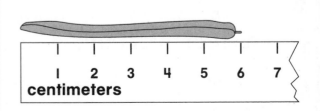

_____ centimeters

Name _____

Write the correct answer.

1. How will the balance look when the book and the paper clip are on it? Circle the answer.

2. How will the balance look when the scissors and the rubber band are on it? Circle the answer.

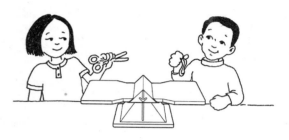

Use the pictures to answer questions 3 and 4.

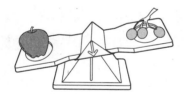 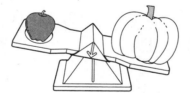 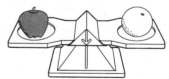

3. Circle the one that is heavier than the .

4. Circle the one that is lighter than the .

Use the pictures to answer questions 5 and 6.

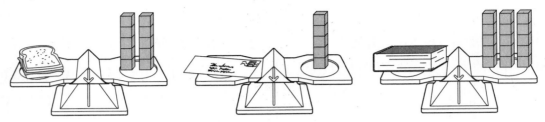

5. Circle the one that is the heaviest.

6. Circle the one that is the lightest.

7. About how many 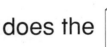 does the hold?

about _____

8. About how many does the  hold?

about _____

9. Circle the picture that shows something cold.

10. Circle the picture that shows something hot.

Circle the correct answer.

1. Circle the figure that shows equal parts.

2. Circle the figure that shows equal parts.

3. Circle the picture that shows halves.

4. Circle the figure that shows halves.

5. Circle the figure that shows fourths.

6. Circle the figure that has $\frac{1}{4}$ colored black.

7. Circle the figure that shows thirds.

8. Circle the figure that has $\frac{1}{3}$ colored black.

9. There are 2 children. Each gets an equal share.

How should you cut the sandwich? Circle your answer.

10. There are 4 children. Each gets an equal share.

How should you cut the pie? Circle your answer.

11. Circle the group that shows $\frac{1}{4}$ of the pears colored.

12. Circle the group that shows $\frac{1}{3}$ of the strawberries colored.

Name _____

Write the correct answer.

1. About how many long?

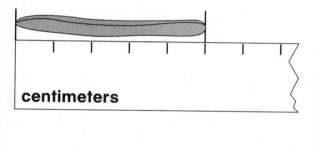

about _____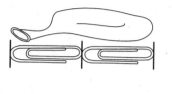

2. How many inches long?

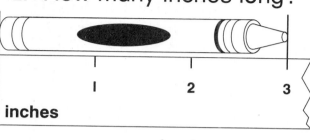

inches

_____ inches

3. How many centimeters long?

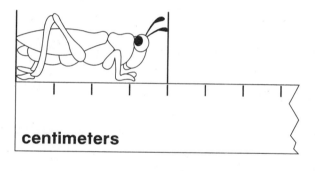

centimeters

_____ centimeters

4. How many centimeters long?

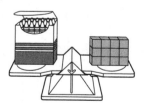

centimeters

_____ centimeters

Use the pictures to answer questions 5 and 6.

5. Draw the one that is lightest.

6. Draw the one that is heaviest.

7. Circle the picture that shows something cold.

8. Circle the picture that shows something hot.

MILK

9. Show two equal parts.

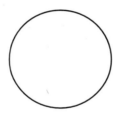

10. Show three equal parts.

11. There are 4 children. Each gets an equal share. How would you cut the pizza? Draw lines to show.

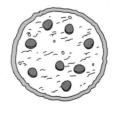

12. Color $\frac{1}{2}$ of the apples.

Write the correct answer.

1. Use pennies. Find the total amount.

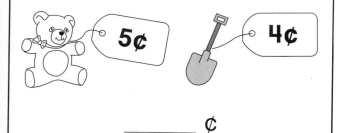

_____ ¢

2. Circle the picture that shows two sides that match.

3. 7 mice eat nuts.
4 more mice come to eat.
How many mice eat nuts?

_____ mice

4. How many?

1 ten 7 ones = _____

5. Write these numbers in order from **least** to **greatest.**

88, 82, 85

_____ , _____ , _____

6. Which two groups add up to the amount on the tag? Color them.

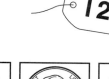

12¢

7. Does it take **more** than a minute or **less** than a minute to plant a garden?

_____ than a minute

8. About how many 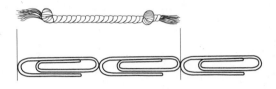 long is the yarn?

about _____

9. How many inches long?

_____ inches

10. How many inches long?

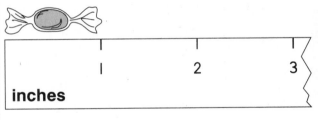

_____ inch

11. How many centimeters long?

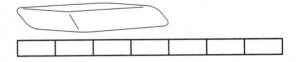

_____ centimeters

12. How many centimeters long?

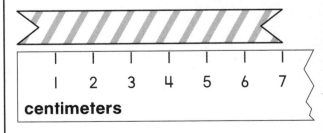

_____ centimeters

Name _____

Use the pictures for questions 13 and 14.

---

13. Circle the one that is the lightest.

14. Circle the one that is the heaviest.

15. How will the balance look when the plate and the feather are on it? Circle the answer.

16. About how many does the

hold?

about _____

17. Circle the picture that shows something cold.

18. Circle the figure that shows equal parts.

---

19. Circle the figure that shows halves.

20. Circle the figure that has $\frac{1}{4}$ colored black.

21. Circle the figure that has $\frac{1}{3}$ colored black.

22. There are 3 children. Each gets an equal share. How should you cut the pizza? Circle the answer.

23. Circle the picture that shows $\frac{1}{2}$ of the pears colored.

24. Circle the picture that shows $\frac{1}{4}$ of the strawberries colored.

Write the correct answer.

1. Circle the words that tell how the shirts are sorted.

big–little   black–white

2. Here are the same shirts. Circle the words that tell how the shirts are sorted now.

big–little   black–white

3. Write how many shirts are big.

Shirts	
big	III
little	卅 I

_____ are big.

4. Write how many shirts are black.

Shirts	
white	IIII
black	卅

_____ are black.

5. Circle the things you could choose from the tray.

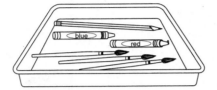

6. Circle the things you could choose from the tray.

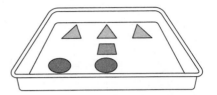

   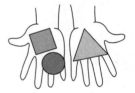

7. Circle the shape you will pull out of the bag most often.

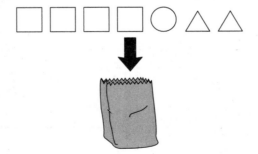

8. Circle the shape you will pull out of the box most often.

9. Write the color the spinner will stop on more often.

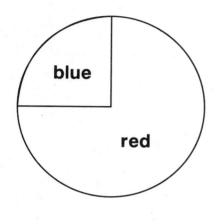

_____

10. Write the color the spinner will stop on most often.

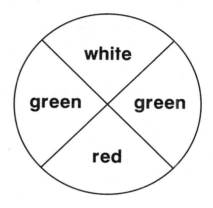

_____

11. Write the number that tells how many 🐷 .

	Tally Marks	Total
🐷	ⵌ II	
🦆	ⵌ I	6
🐟	ⵌ III	8

_____ pigs

12. Write the number that tells how many 🥁 .

	Tally Marks	Total
🧍	III	3
🥁	ⵌ IIII	
🧸	ⵌ I	6

_____ drums

Use the graph to answer questions 1 and 2.

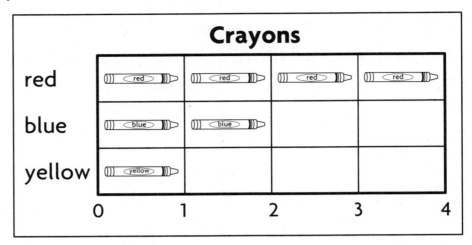

Crayons

1. Write how many red crayons there are.

_____ red crayons

2. Write how many crayons there are in all.

_____ crayons

Use the tally table to answer questions 3 and 4.

Favorite Games		Total
tag	⊥⊥⊥⊥	5
hopscotch	I	I
kickball		3

3. Write how many children like tag the best.

_____ children

4. Write tally marks to show how many like kickball the best.

_____

Use the graph to answer questions 5 and 6.

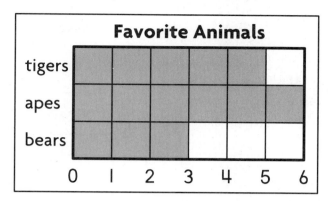

5. Write how many children like bears the best.

_____ children

6. What animal got the most votes?

_____

Use the graph to answer questions 7 and 8.

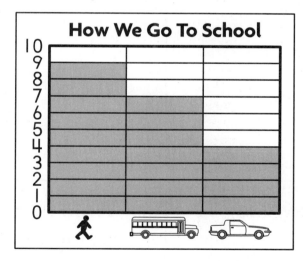

7. Write how many children ride the bus to school.

_____ children

8. Write how many more children walk than ride the bus.

_____ more children

Use the tally table and the graph to answer
questions 9 to 12.

	Pictures We Drew	Total
Al	I	I
Kim	III	3
Sam		2
Jane	IIII	4

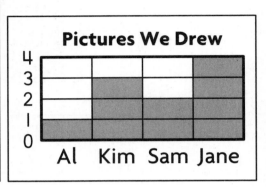

Pictures We Drew

4
3
2
1
0

Al   Kim   Sam   Jane

9. Make tally marks to show how many pictures Sam drew.

_____

10. Write how many pictures Kim drew.

_____ pictures

11. Write who drew the most pictures.

_____

12. Write how many more pictures Kim drew than Al drew.

_____ more pictures

Write the correct answer.

1. Circle the words that tell how the items are sorted.

 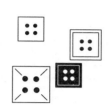

black–white
circle–square

2. How many shapes are square?

Shapes	
triangle	IIII
square	III

_____ are square.

3. Circle the shapes you could choose from the tray.

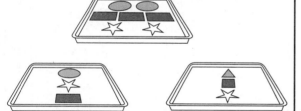

4. Draw the shape you will pull from the bag most often.

5. Which color will the spinner stop on most often?

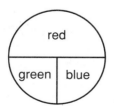

red

green | blue

_____

6. Which number tells how many 🐭 ?

	Tally Marks	Total
🐕	IIII	5
🐈	III	3
🐭	IIII	

_____ 🐭

Use the graph to answer questions 7 and 8.

Animals		Total
ducks	🦆 🦆 🦆	3
pigs	🐖 🐖 🐖 🐖	4
chickens	🐔 🐔 🐔 🐔 🐔	5

7. How many chickens are there?

_____ chickens

8. How many animals are there in all?

_____ animals

Use the tally table and the graph to answer questions 9 to 12.

Favorite Fruits			Total
apple	🍎	I	I
banana	🍌	IIII	4
grapes	🍇		3
pear	🍐	II	2

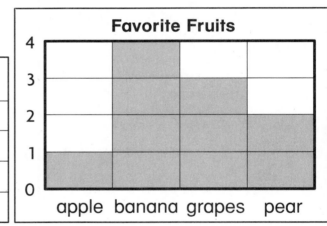

Favorite Fruits

9. Make tally marks for how many like grapes best.

_____

10. How many like pears best?

_____

11. Which fruit do the most people like best?

_____

12. How many more people like grapes best than like apples best?

_____

Name ______________________________

Write the correct answer.

1. Circle the figure on the .

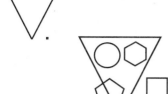

2.

$$\begin{array}{r} 8 \\ +\ 4 \\ \hline 12 \end{array} \qquad \begin{array}{r} 12 \\ -\ 4 \\ \hline \end{array}$$

3. How many?

______

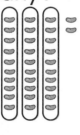

4. Count by tens. Write the number that comes after 80.

______

5. Circle the group that uses the fewest coins to show the amount.

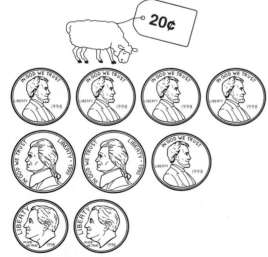

6. Circle coins that equal 25¢.

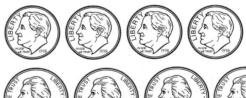

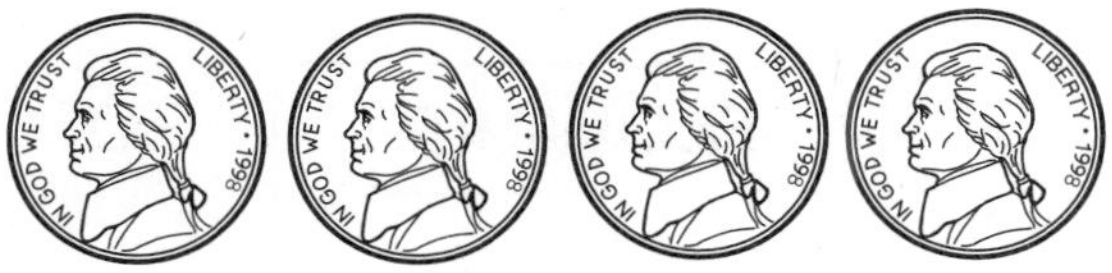

7. Write the time.

_____ : _____

8. How many inches long?

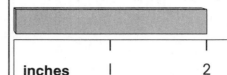

inches

_____ inches

9. About how many does the hold?

about _____

10. There are 3 children. Each gets an equal share. How would you cut the cake? Circle your answer.

11. How many flowers are yellow?

FLOWERS	
red	III
yellow	IIII I

_____ are yellow.

12. Circle the things you could choose from the tray.

13. Circle the shape you will pull out of the bag most often.

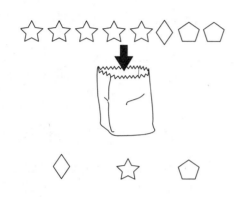

14. Write the number that tells how many .

	Tally Marks	Total
🐕	IIIX III	8
🐈	IIIX	?
🐹	IIII	4

_____ cats

Use the graph for questions 15 and 16.

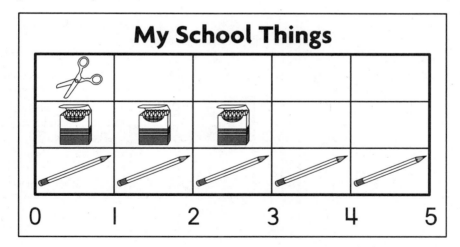

15. How many pencils are there?

_____ pencils

16. How many school things are there in all?

_____ school things

Use the graph for questions 17 and 18.

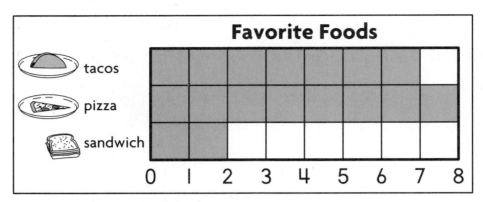

Favorite Foods

| | tacos | pizza | sandwich |
| | 0 1 2 3 4 5 6 7 8 |

---

17. Write how many children like tacos the best.

_____ children

18. Write the food that is liked best by the most children.

_____

Use the tally table and the graph to answer questions 19 and 20.

	Favorite Fruits	Total
banana	IIII	4
orange	II	2
apple	III	3
grapes	I	1

Favorite Fruits

4
3
2
1
0
banana orange apple grapes

---

19. How many children like apples the best?

_____ children

20. How many more children like bananas best than like oranges best?

_____ more children

Write the correct answer.

1.

$$\begin{array}{r} 4 \\ +4 \\ \hline 8 \end{array} \qquad \begin{array}{r} 4 \\ +5 \\ \hline \end{array}$$

2.

$$\begin{array}{r} 8 \\ +8 \\ \hline 16 \end{array} \qquad \begin{array}{r} 8 \\ +9 \\ \hline \end{array}$$

3.

$$\begin{array}{r} 5 \\ +5 \\ \hline 10 \end{array} \qquad \begin{array}{r} 5 \\ +4 \\ \hline \end{array}$$

4.

$$\begin{array}{r} 7 \\ +7 \\ \hline 14 \end{array} \qquad \begin{array}{r} 7 \\ +6 \\ \hline \end{array}$$

5.

$$\begin{array}{r} 7 \\ +8 \\ \hline \end{array}$$

6.

$$\begin{array}{r} 4 \\ +3 \\ \hline \end{array}$$

7.

$$\begin{array}{r} 5 \\ +6 \\ \hline \end{array}$$

8.

$$\begin{array}{r} 9 \\ +8 \\ \hline \end{array}$$

9.

$7 + 7 = 14$

$14 - 7 =$ _____

10.

$8 + 8 = 16$

16

11.

$12 - 6 = 6$

$6 + 6 =$ _____

12.

$18 - 9 = 9$

$9 + 9 =$ _____

13. Lani read 7 books. Bo read 1 more than Lani. Write how many books they read in all.

_____ books

14. Ruth picked some flowers. Pat gave her 3 more. Now she has 6. Write how many flowers Ruth picked herself.

_____ flowers

Write the correct answer.

1.

$$\begin{array}{r} 8 \\ +5 \\ \hline \end{array}$$

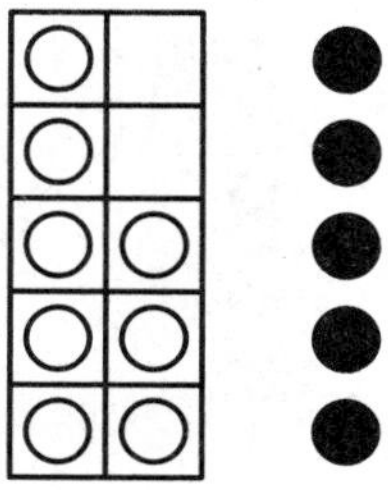

2.

$$\begin{array}{r} 9 \\ +3 \\ \hline \end{array}$$

3.

$$\begin{array}{r} 9 \\ +8 \\ \hline \end{array}$$

4.

$$\begin{array}{r} 7 \\ +5 \\ \hline \end{array}$$

5.

$$\begin{array}{r} 7 \\ 3 \\ +6 \\ \hline \end{array}$$

6.

$$\begin{array}{r} 6 \\ 2 \\ +6 \\ \hline \end{array}$$

7.

$$\begin{array}{r} 1 \\ 5 \\ +9 \\ \hline \end{array}$$

8.

$$\begin{array}{r} 4 \\ 4 \\ +5 \\ \hline \end{array}$$

9.

$$\begin{array}{r} 7 \\ +5 \\ \hline 12 \end{array}$$
$$\begin{array}{r} 12 \\ -5 \\ \hline \end{array}$$

10.

$$\begin{array}{r} 8 \\ +3 \\ \hline 11 \end{array}$$
$$\begin{array}{r} 11 \\ -3 \\ \hline \end{array}$$

11.

$$\begin{array}{r} 6 \\ +8 \\ \hline 14 \end{array}$$
$$\begin{array}{r} 14 \\ -8 \\ \hline \end{array}$$

12.

$$\begin{array}{r} 5 \\ +9 \\ \hline 14 \end{array}$$
$$\begin{array}{r} 14 \\ -9 \\ \hline \end{array}$$

13.

$$\begin{array}{r} 9 \\ +9 \\ \hline 18 \end{array}$$
$$\begin{array}{r} 18 \\ -9 \\ \hline \end{array}$$

14.

$$\begin{array}{r} 7 \\ +6 \\ \hline 13 \end{array}$$
$$\begin{array}{r} 13 \\ -6 \\ \hline \end{array}$$

15.

$$\begin{array}{r} 6 \\ +9 \\ \hline 15 \end{array}$$
$$\begin{array}{r} 15 \\ -9 \\ \hline \end{array}$$

16.

$$\begin{array}{r} 8 \\ +9 \\ \hline 17 \end{array}$$
$$\begin{array}{r} 17 \\ -9 \\ \hline \end{array}$$

Write the correct answer.

1.

$$\begin{array}{r} 3 \\ + 3 \\ \hline 6 \end{array} \qquad \begin{array}{r} 3 \\ + 4 \\ \hline \end{array}$$

2.

$$\begin{array}{r} 8 \\ + 8 \\ \hline 16 \end{array} \qquad \begin{array}{r} 8 \\ + 7 \\ \hline \end{array}$$

3.

$$4 + 4 = \underline{\hspace{2cm}}$$

4.

$$7 + 6 = \underline{\hspace{2cm}}$$

5.

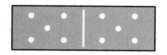

$$5 + 5 = 10$$

$$10 - 5 = \underline{\hspace{2cm}}$$

6. Leah had some pens. Beth gave her 6 more. Now she has 12.

How many pens did she have to start?

_____ pens

Name ______________________________

7.

$$\begin{array}{r} 7 \\ +\ 4 \\ \hline \end{array}$$

8.

$$\begin{array}{r} 9 \\ +\ 6 \\ \hline \end{array}$$

9.

$$\begin{array}{r} 6 \\ 4 \\ +\ 8 \\ \hline \end{array}$$

10.

$$\begin{array}{r} 3 \\ 3 \\ +\ 6 \\ \hline \end{array}$$

11.

$$\begin{array}{r} 6 \\ +\ 3 \\ \hline 9 \end{array} \qquad \begin{array}{r} 9 \\ -\ 3 \\ \hline \end{array}$$

12.

$$\begin{array}{r} 7 \\ +\ 3 \\ \hline 10 \end{array} \qquad \begin{array}{r} 10 \\ -\ 3 \\ \hline \end{array}$$

Name _____

Write the correct answer.
Use the picture for questions 1 and 2.

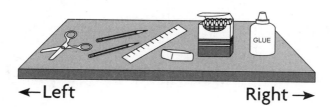

←Left   Right →

---

1. Circle the object to the **right** of the .

2. Circle the object to the **left** of the .

---

3. How many more chickens than ducks are there?

$$\begin{array}{r} 9 \\ -\ 3 \\ \hline \end{array}$$

4. Circle the better estimate.

more than 10

fewer than 10

Form B • Free-Response   **B269**   **Chapters 1 – 26**   **Go on.**

5. Count by twos. What number comes after 46?

42, 44, 46, _____

6. Circle the coins you need.

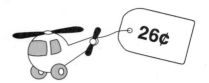

26¢

7. Circle the one that takes longer to do.

8. How many centimeters long?

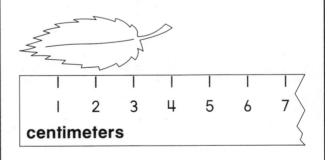

| 1 2 3 4 5 6 7
centimeters

_____ centimeters

9. Circle the figure that shows fourths.

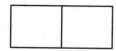

10. Circle the shape you will pull out most often.

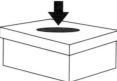

Use the graph for questions 11 and 12.

	Sweets We Like				Total
cookies	🍪	🍪	🍪		3
pie	🥧	🥧	🥧	🥧	4
ice cream	🍦	🍦			2

11. How many children like cookies the best?

_____ children

12. How many fewer children like ice cream than pie?

_____ fewer children

13.

$$
\begin{array}{r}
6 \\
+\ 6 \\
\hline
12
\end{array}
\qquad
\begin{array}{r}
6 \\
+\ 7 \\
\hline
\end{array}
$$

14. Sarah had some rocks. Sam gave her 4 more. Now she has 8. How many rocks did Sarah have to start?

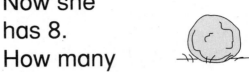

_____ rocks

15.

$$
\begin{array}{r}
7 \\
+\ 4 \\
\hline
\end{array}
$$

16.

$$
\begin{array}{r}
8 \\
+\ 5 \\
\hline
\end{array}
$$

17.

$$
\begin{array}{r}
8 \\
2 \\
+\ 5 \\
\hline
\end{array}
$$

18.

$$
\begin{array}{r}
8 \\
+\ 6 \\
\hline
14
\end{array}
\qquad
\begin{array}{r}
14 \\
-\ 6 \\
\hline
\end{array}
$$

Name _____

Write the correct answer.

1. Here are 3 groups. Each group has 3 counters.

OOO   OOO   OOO

Write how many in all.

_____ counters

2. Here are 4 groups. Each group has 2 counters.

OO   OO   OO   OO

Write how many in all.

_____ counters

3. Here are 5 equal groups.

OO OO OO OO OO

How many counters are in each group?

_____ counters

4. Here are 2 equal groups.

OOO   OOO

How many counters are in each group?

_____ counters

5. Circle counters to make 2 equal groups.

O O O O O O
O O O O O O

How many counters are in each group?

_____ counters

6. Circle counters to make 3 equal groups.

O O O O
O O O O
O O O O

How many counters are in each group?

_____ counters

7. Circle groups. Put 2
counters in each group.

○ ○ ○ ○ ○ ○
○ ○ ○ ○ ○ ○

Write how many groups.

_____ groups

8. Circle groups. Put 5
counters in each group.

○ ○ ○ ○ ○
○ ○ ○ ○ ○

Write how many groups.

_____ groups

9. Circle groups. Put 3
counters in each group.

○ ○ ○ ○
○ ○ ○ ○
○ ○ ○ ○

Write how many groups.

_____ groups

10. Circle groups. Put 2
counters in each group.

○ ○ ○
○ ○ ○

Write how many groups.

_____ groups

11. There are 2 ponds.
Each pond has 4 fish.

How many fish are there
in all?

_____ fish

12. There are 10 birds.
Then 5 birds fly away.

How many birds are
left?

_____ birds

Name _____

Write the correct answer.

1. Add.

$$\begin{array}{r} 40 \\ +10 \\ \hline \end{array}$$

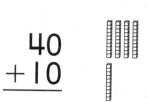

2. Subtract.

$$\begin{array}{r} 60 \\ -30 \\ \hline \end{array}$$

3. Add.

tens	ones
2	5
+1	3

tens	ones

4. Add.

tens	ones
5	4
+1	1

tens	ones

5. Add.

tens	ones
3	4
+2	2

tens	ones

6. Add.

tens	ones
4	5
+4	2

tens	ones

7. Subtract.

tens	ones
7	3
−1	2

tens	ones

8. Subtract.

tens	ones
5	4
−2	1

tens	ones

9. Subtract.

tens	ones
4	9
−1	0

tens	ones

10. Subtract.

tens	ones
8	5
−6	4

tens	ones

Circle the answer that makes sense.

11. Jan had 43 pennies. Then she saved 10 more. How many does she have in all?

33 pennies
43 pennies
53 pennies

12. Alex had 34 shells. Then he gave away 13. How many shells does he have left?

21 shells
34 shells
47 shells

Name _____

Write the correct answer.

1. How many counters?

_____ counters

2. How many counters in each group?

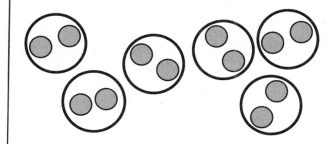

_____ counters

3. How many counters in each group?

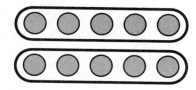

_____ counters

4. How many groups?

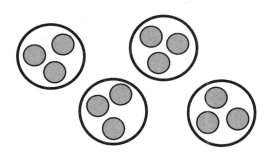

_____ groups

5. How many groups?

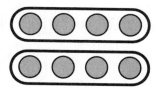

_____ groups

6. There are 3 bags.
Each bag has 2 cookies.

How many cookies are there in all?

_____ cookies

7. Add.

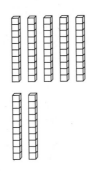

$$
\begin{array}{r}
50 \\
+\ 20 \\
\hline
\end{array}
$$

8. Add.

tens	ones
3	1
+ 1	7

9. Add.

tens	ones
2	4
+ 1	2

10. Subtract.

tens	ones
9	5
− 3	1

11. Subtract.

tens	ones
7	8
− 2	6

12. Circle the answer that makes sense.
Hannah read 14 pages. Then she read 13 more. How many pages did she read in all?

13 pages
27 pages
270 pages

Write the correct answer.

1. Circle the number sentence that belongs in this fact family.

$9 + 2 = 11$

$2 + 9 = 11$

$11 - 2 = 9$

$11 - 9 = 2$

$9 - 2 = 7$

$7 + 2 = 9$

2. How many?

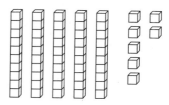

_____

3. Count by fives. Write the number that comes after 35.

25	30	35	___

25, 30, 35, _____

4. Write the amount.

_____ ¢

Use the calendar for questions 5 and 6.

May

Sunday	Monday	Tuesday	Wednesday	Thursday	Friday	Saturday
				1	2	3
4	5	6	7	8	9	10
11	12	13	14	15	16	17
18	19	20	21	22	23	24
25	26	27	28	29	30	31

5. On which day does this month begin?

_____

6. What is the date of the last Friday in this month?

May _____

7. Read the clock. Write the time.

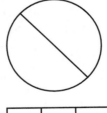

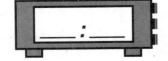

8. Circle the picture that shows halves.

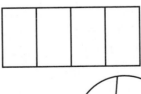

9.

$$\begin{array}{r} 8 \\ +\ 8 \\ \hline 16 \end{array} \qquad \begin{array}{r} 8 \\ +\ 7 \\ \hline \end{array}$$

10.

$$\begin{array}{r} 4 \\ 3 \\ +\ 4 \\ \hline \end{array}$$

11. How many counters?

_____ counters

12. How many in each group?

_____ counters

13. How many groups?

_____ groups

14. There are 6 pens. Each pen has 2 pigs. How many pigs are there in all?

_____ pigs

15. Bo sees 9 deer.
Then 2 deer run away.
How many deer are left?

_____ deer

16. Subtract.

$$\begin{array}{r} 50 \\ -\ 40 \\ \hline \end{array}$$

17. Add.

tens	ones
2	5
+ 1	4

18. Subtract.

tens	ones
9	4
− 5	1

19. Meg had 31 pennies.
Then she saved 25 more.
How many does she
have in all?

6 pennies
56 pennies
130 pennies

20. Lee had 26 cards.
Then he gave away 14.
How many cards does
he have left?

2 cards
12 cards
40 cards

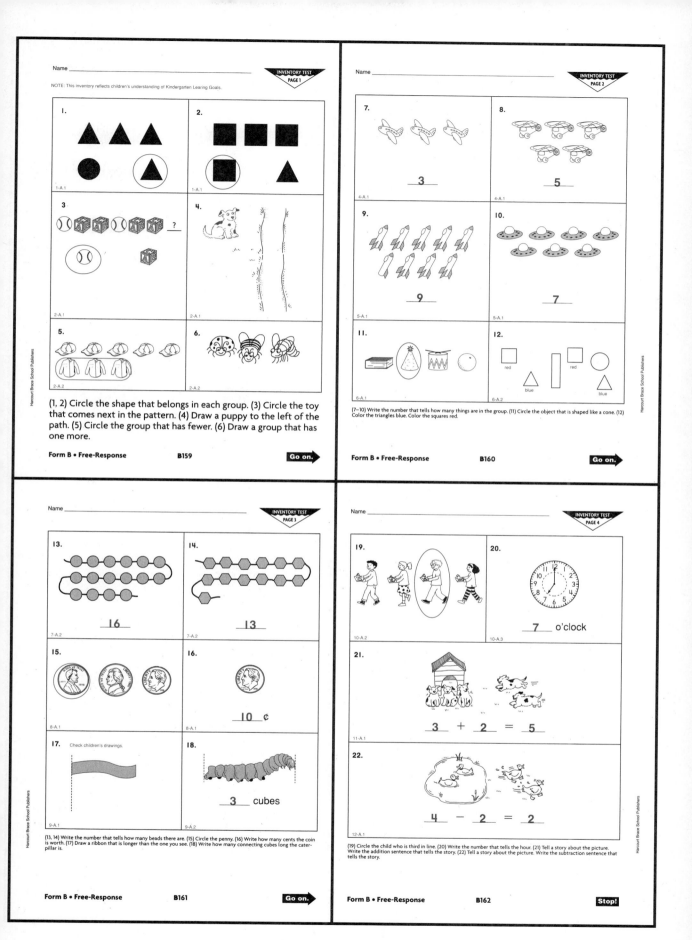

Name _____

INVENTORY TEST
PAGE 1

NOTE: This inventory reflects children's understanding of Kindergarten Learing Goals.

1.

1-A.1

2.

1-A.1

3

?

2-A.1

4.

2-A.1

5.

2-A.2

6.

2-A.2

(1, 2) Circle the shape that belongs in each group. (3) Circle the toy that comes next in the pattern. (4) Draw a puppy to the left of the path. (5) Circle the group that has fewer. (6) Draw a group that has one more.

Form B • Free-Response   **B159**   **Go on.**

7.

_3_

4-A.1

8.

_5_

4-A.1

9.

_9_

5-A.1

10.

_7_

5-A.1

11.

6-A.1

12.

red   red

blue   blue

6-A.2

(7–10) Write the number that tells how many things are in the group. (11) Circle the object that is shaped like a cone. (12) Color the triangles blue. Color the squares red.

Form B • Free-Response   **B160**   **Go on.**

13.

_16_

7-A.2

14.

_13_

7-A.2

15.

8-A.1

16.

_10_ ¢

8-A.1

17. Check children's drawings.

9-A.1

18.

_3_ cubes

9-A.2

(13, 14) Write the number that tells how many beads there are. (15) Circle the penny. (16) Write how many cents the coin is worth. (17) Draw a ribbon that is longer than the one you see. (18) Write how many connecting cubes long the caterpillar is.

Form B • Free-Response   **B161**   **Go on.**

19.

10-A.2

20.

_7_ o'clock

10-A.3

21.

_3_ + _2_ = _5_

11-A.1

22.

_4_ − _2_ = _2_

12-A.1

(19) Circle the child who is third in line. (20) Write the number that tells the hour. (21) Tell a story about the picture. Write the addition sentence that tells the story. (22) Tell a story about the picture. Write the subtraction sentence that tells the story.

Form B • Free-Response   **B162**   **Stop!**

Free-Response Format • Test Answers

Harcourt Brace School Publishers

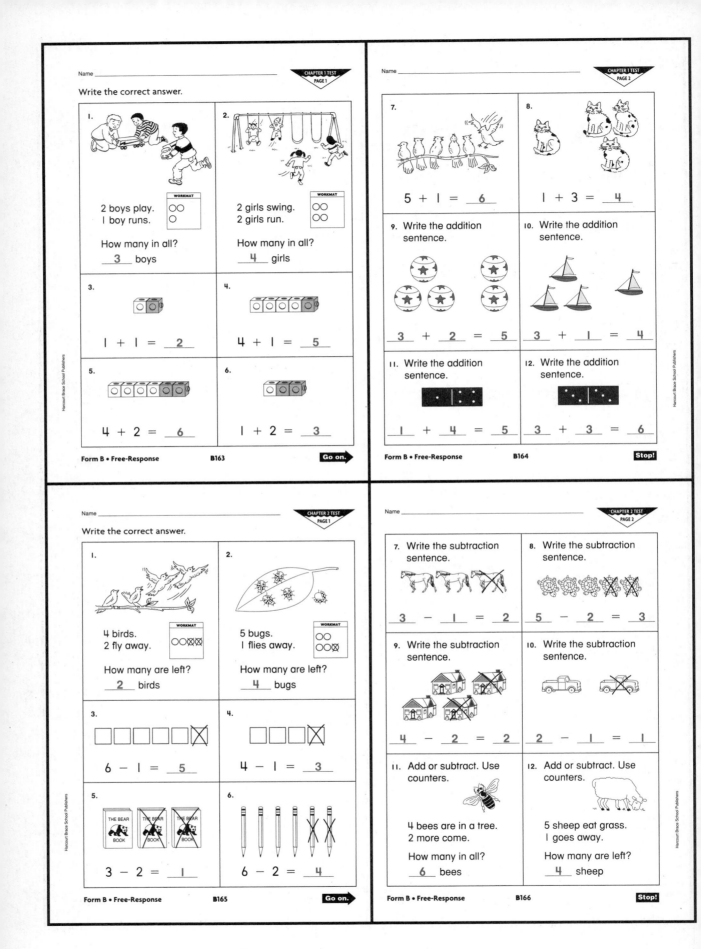

Write the correct answer.

1.

2 boys play.
1 boy runs.

How many in all?
___3___ boys

2.

2 girls swing.
2 girls run.

How many in all?
___4___ girls

3.

1 + 1 = __2__

4.

4 + 1 = __5__

5.

4 + 2 = __6__

6.

1 + 2 = __3__

7.

5 + 1 = __6__

8.

1 + 3 = __4__

9. Write the addition sentence.

__3__ + __2__ = __5__

10. Write the addition sentence.

__3__ + __1__ = __4__

11. Write the addition sentence.

__1__ + __4__ = __5__

12. Write the addition sentence.

__3__ + __3__ = __6__

Write the correct answer.

1.

4 birds.
2 fly away.

How many are left?
___2___ birds

2.

5 bugs.
1 flies away.

How many are left?
___4___ bugs

3.

6 − 1 = __5__

4.

4 − 1 = __3__

5.

3 − 2 = __1__

6.

6 − 2 = __4__

7. Write the subtraction sentence.

__3__ − __1__ = __2__

8. Write the subtraction sentence.

__5__ − __2__ = __3__

9. Write the subtraction sentence.

__4__ − __2__ = __2__

10. Write the subtraction sentence.

__2__ − __1__ = __1__

11. Add or subtract. Use counters.

4 bees are in a tree.
2 more come.

How many in all?
___6___ bees

12. Add or subtract. Use counters.

5 sheep eat grass.
1 goes away.

How many are left?
___4___ sheep

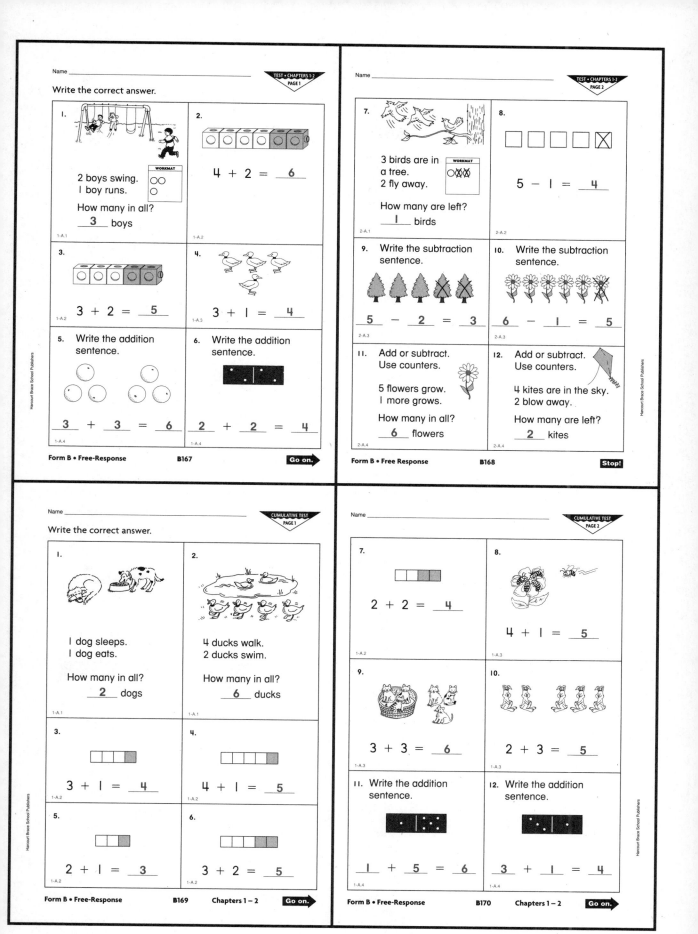

Write the correct answer.

1.
2 boys swing.
1 boy runs.

How many in all?
___3___ boys

1-A.1

2.
$4 + 2 =$ ___6___

1-A.2

3.
$3 + 2 =$ ___5___

1-A.2

4.
$3 + 1 =$ ___4___

1-A.3

5. Write the addition sentence.

___3___ $+$ ___3___ $=$ ___6___

1-A.4

6. Write the addition sentence.

___2___ $+$ ___2___ $=$ ___4___

1-A.4

Form B • Free-Response B167 **Go on.**

7.
3 birds are in a tree.
2 fly away.

How many are left?
___1___ birds

2-A.1

8.
$5 - 1 =$ ___4___

2-A.2

9. Write the subtraction sentence.

___5___ $-$ ___2___ $=$ ___3___

2-A.3

10. Write the subtraction sentence.

___6___ $-$ ___1___ $=$ ___5___

2-A.3

11. Add or subtract. Use counters.

5 flowers grow.
1 more grows.

How many in all?
___6___ flowers

2-A.4

12. Add or subtract. Use counters.

4 kites are in the sky.
2 blow away.

How many are left?
___2___ kites

2-A.4

Form B • Free Response B168 **Stop!**

Write the correct answer.

1.
1 dog sleeps.
1 dog eats.

How many in all?
___2___ dogs

1-A.1

2.
4 ducks walk.
2 ducks swim.

How many in all?
___6___ ducks

1-A.1

3.
$3 + 1 =$ ___4___

1-A.2

4.
$4 + 1 =$ ___5___

1-A.2

5.
$2 + 1 =$ ___3___

1-A.2

6.
$3 + 2 =$ ___5___

1-A.2

Form B • Free-Response B169 **Chapters 1 – 2** **Go on.**

7.
$2 + 2 =$ ___4___

1-A.2

8.
$4 + 1 =$ ___5___

1-A.3

9.
$3 + 3 =$ ___6___

1-A.3

10.
$2 + 3 =$ ___5___

1-A.3

11. Write the addition sentence.

___1___ $+$ ___5___ $=$ ___6___

1-A.4

12. Write the addition sentence.

___3___ $+$ ___1___ $=$ ___4___

1-A.4

Form B • Free-Response B170 **Chapters 1 – 2** **Go on.**

Free-Response Format • Test Answers

285

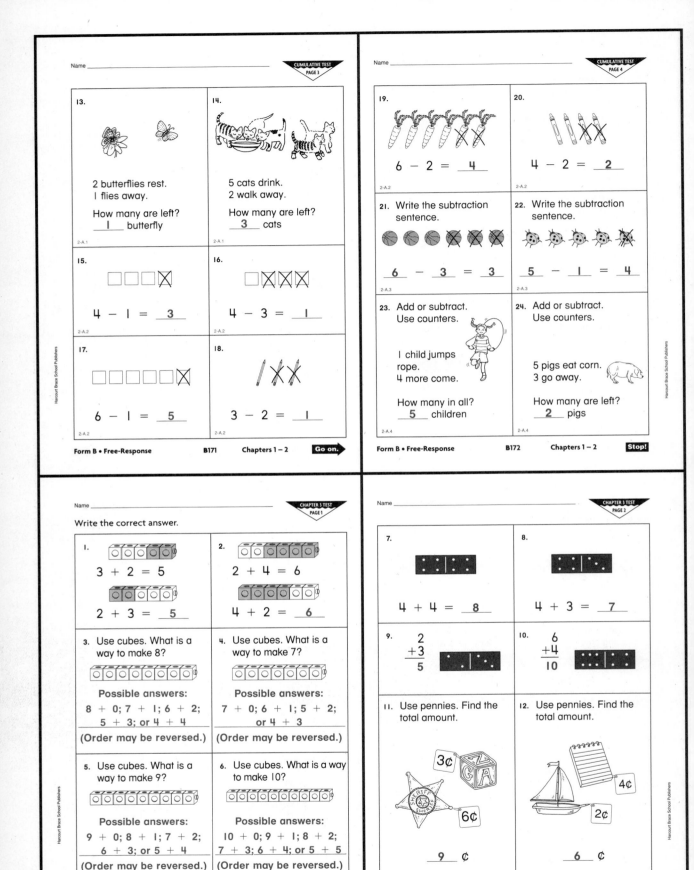

Name _____

13.

2 butterflies rest.
I flies away.

How many are left?
__I__ butterfly

2-A.1

14.

5 cats drink.
2 walk away.

How many are left?
__3__ cats

2-A.1

15.

$4 - 1 = \underline{3}$

2-A.2

16.

$4 - 3 = \underline{1}$

2-A.2

17.

$6 - 1 = \underline{5}$

2-A.2

18.

$3 - 2 = \underline{1}$

2-A.2

Form B • Free-Response   B171   Chapters 1 – 2   Go on.

Name _____

19.

$6 - 2 = \underline{4}$

2-A.2

20.

$4 - 2 = \underline{2}$

2-A.2

21. Write the subtraction
sentence.

$\underline{6} - \underline{3} = \underline{3}$

2-A.3

22. Write the subtraction
sentence.

$\underline{5} - \underline{1} = \underline{4}$

2-A.3

23. Add or subtract.
Use counters.

I child jumps
rope.
4 more come.

How many in all?
__5__ children

2-A.4

24. Add or subtract.
Use counters.

5 pigs eat corn.
3 go away.

How many are left?
__2__ pigs

2-A.4

Form B • Free-Response   B172   Chapters 1 – 2   Stop!

Name _____

Write the correct answer.

I.

$3 + 2 = 5$

$2 + 3 = \underline{5}$

2.

$2 + 4 = 6$

$4 + 2 = \underline{6}$

3. Use cubes. What is a
way to make 8?

Possible answers:
$8 + 0; 7 + 1; 6 + 2;$
$5 + 3; or 4 + 4$
(Order may be reversed.)

4. Use cubes. What is a
way to make 7?

Possible answers:
$7 + 0; 6 + 1; 5 + 2;$
or $4 + 3$
(Order may be reversed.)

5. Use cubes. What is a
way to make 9?

Possible answers:
$9 + 0; 8 + 1; 7 + 2;$
$6 + 3; or 5 + 4$
(Order may be reversed.)

6. Use cubes. What is a way
to make 10?

Possible answers:
$10 + 0; 9 + 1; 8 + 2;$
$7 + 3; 6 + 4; or 5 + 5$
(Order may be reversed.)

Form B • Free-Response   B173   Go on.

Name _____

7.

$4 + 4 = \underline{8}$

8.

$4 + 3 = \underline{7}$

9.
$\begin{array}{r} 2 \\ +3 \\ \hline 5 \end{array}$

10.
$\begin{array}{r} 6 \\ +4 \\ \hline 10 \end{array}$

11. Use pennies. Find the
total amount.

3¢

6¢

__9__ ¢

12. Use pennies. Find the
total amount.

4¢

2¢

__6__ ¢

Form B • Free-Response   B174   Stop!

Free-Response Format • Test Answers

Write the correct answer.

1.
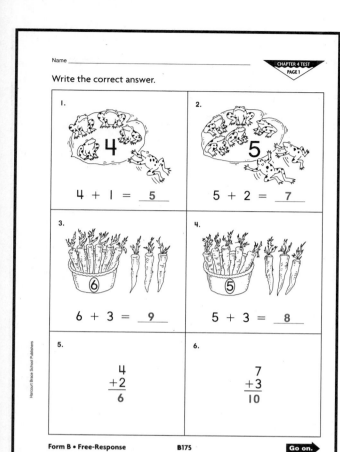
4 + 1 = __5__

2.
5 + 2 = __7__

3.
6 + 3 = __9__

4.
5 + 3 = __8__

5.
$$\begin{array}{r} 4 \\ +2 \\ \hline 6 \end{array}$$

6.
$$\begin{array}{r} 7 \\ +3 \\ \hline 10 \end{array}$$

Form B • Free-Response   B175   Go on. ▶

---

7. Write the doubles fact.
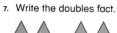
__2__ + __2__ = __4__

8. Write the doubles fact.
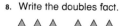
__3__ + __3__ = __6__

9.
$$\begin{array}{r} 3 \\ +2 \\ \hline 5 \end{array}$$

10.
$$\begin{array}{r} 6 \\ +4 \\ \hline 10 \end{array}$$

11. Add or subtract.

I walk 4 dogs.
2 get away.

How many are left?
__2__ dogs

12. Add or subtract.

I have 4 kittens.
3 more come.
How many do I have
in all?
__7__ kittens

Form B • Free-Response   B176   Stop!

Write the correct answer.

1.
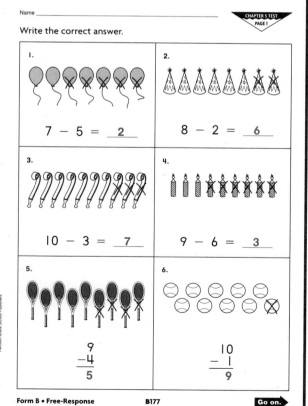
7 − 5 = __2__

2.
8 − 2 = __6__

3.
10 − 3 = __7__

4.
9 − 6 = __3__

5.
$$\begin{array}{r} 9 \\ -4 \\ \hline 5 \end{array}$$

6.
$$\begin{array}{r} 10 \\ -1 \\ \hline 9 \end{array}$$

Form B • Free-Response   B177   Go on. ▶

7.
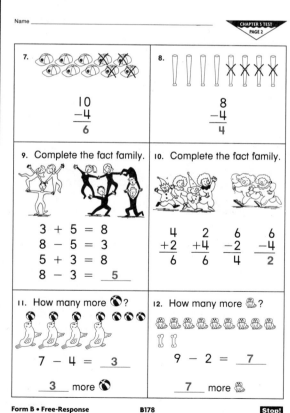
$$\begin{array}{r} 10 \\ -4 \\ \hline 6 \end{array}$$

8.
$$\begin{array}{r} 8 \\ -4 \\ \hline 4 \end{array}$$

9. Complete the fact family.
3 + 5 = 8
8 − 5 = 3
5 + 3 = 8
8 − 3 = __5__

10. Complete the fact family.
$$\begin{array}{r} 4 \\ +2 \\ \hline 6 \end{array} \quad \begin{array}{r} 2 \\ +4 \\ \hline 6 \end{array} \quad \begin{array}{r} 6 \\ -2 \\ \hline 4 \end{array} \quad \begin{array}{r} 6 \\ -4 \\ \hline 2 \end{array}$$

11. How many more ⚽?
7 − 4 = __3__

__3__ more ⚽

12. How many more 🐾?
9 − 2 = __7__

__7__ more 🐾

Form B • Free-Response   B178   Stop!

Free-Response Format • Test Answers

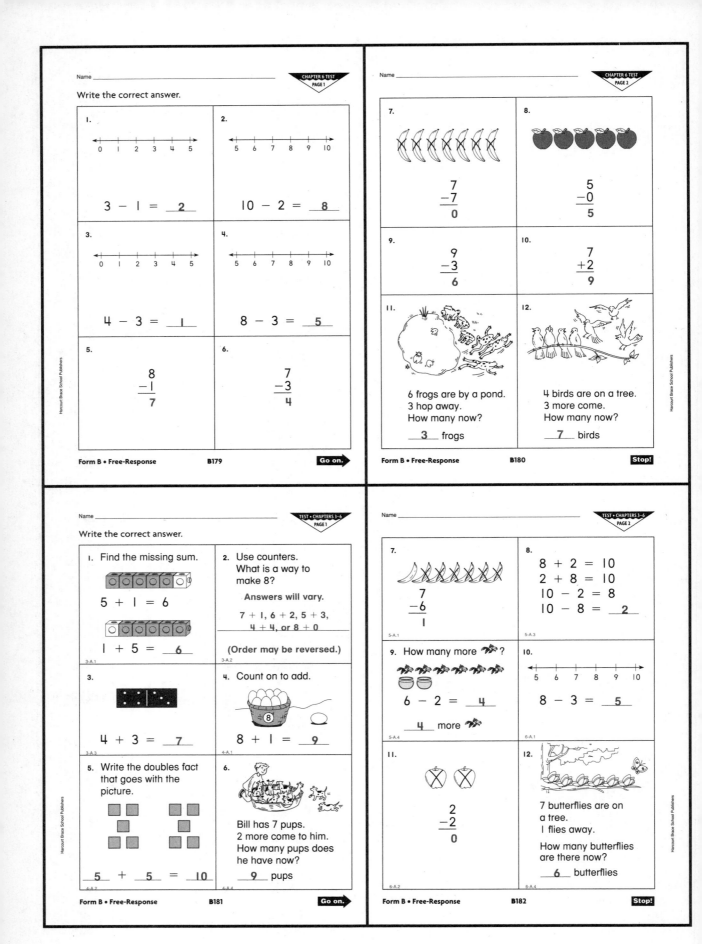

Free-Response Format • Test Answers

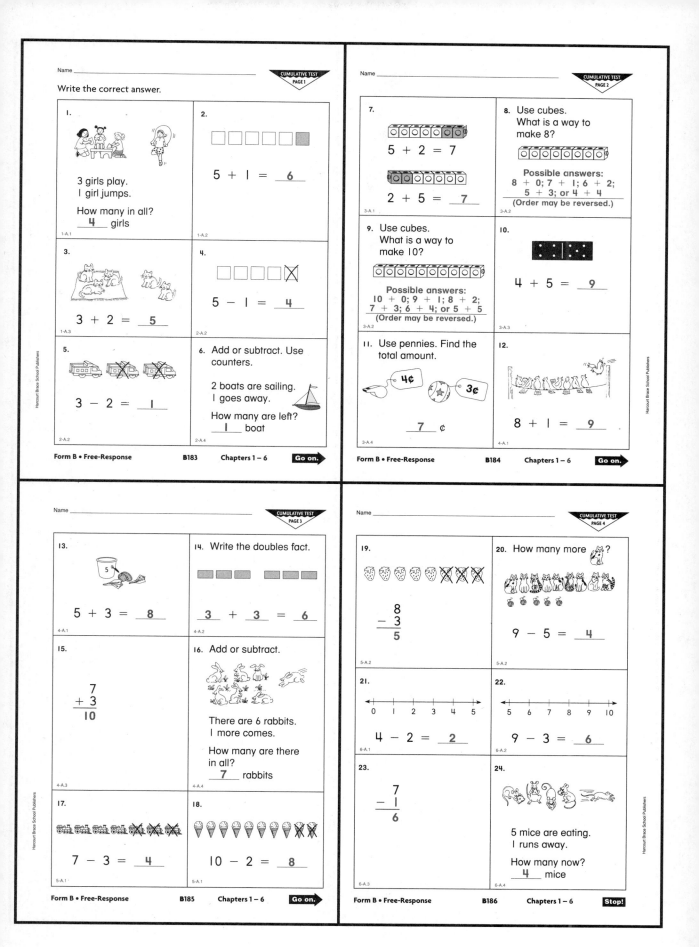

Page 1

Write the correct answer.

1.

3 girls play.
1 girl jumps.

How many in all?
__4__ girls

1-A.1

2.

$5 + 1 = $ __6__

1-A.2

3.

$3 + 2 = $ __5__

1-A.3

4.

$5 - 1 = $ __4__

2-A.2

5.

$3 - 2 = $ __1__

2-A.2

6. Add or subtract. Use counters.

2 boats are sailing.
1 goes away.

How many are left?
__1__ boat

2-A.4

Form B • Free-Response   B183   Chapters 1 – 6   **Go on.**

Page 2

7.

$5 + 2 = $ __7__

$2 + 5 = $ __7__

3-A.1

8. Use cubes.
What is a way to make 8?

Possible answers:
8 + 0; 7 + 1; 6 + 2;
5 + 3; or 4 + 4
(Order may be reversed.)

3-A.2

9. Use cubes.
What is a way to make 10?

Possible answers:
10 + 0; 9 + 1; 8 + 2;
7 + 3; 6 + 4; or 5 + 5
(Order may be reversed.)

3-A.2

10.

$4 + 5 = $ __9__

3-A.3

11. Use pennies. Find the total amount.

4¢   3¢

__7__ ¢

3-A.4

12.

$8 + 1 = $ __9__

4-A.1

Form B • Free-Response   B184   Chapters 1 – 6   **Go on.**

Page 3

13.

$5 + 3 = $ __8__

4-A.1

14. Write the doubles fact.

__3__ + __3__ = __6__

4-A.2

15.

$\begin{array}{r} 7 \\ + 3 \\ \hline 10 \end{array}$

4-A.3

16. Add or subtract.

There are 6 rabbits.
1 more comes.

How many are there in all?
__7__ rabbits

4-A.4

17.

$7 - 3 = $ __4__

5-A.1

18.

$10 - 2 = $ __8__

5-A.1

Form B • Free-Response   B185   Chapters 1 – 6   **Go on.**

Page 4

19.

$\begin{array}{r} 8 \\ - 3 \\ \hline 5 \end{array}$

5-A.2

20. How many more?

$9 - 5 = $ __4__

5-A.2

21.

$4 - 2 = $ __2__

6-A.1

22.

$9 - 3 = $ __6__

6-A.2

23.

$\begin{array}{r} 7 \\ - 1 \\ \hline 6 \end{array}$

6-A.3

24.

5 mice are eating.
1 runs away.

How many now?
__4__ mice

6-A.4

Form B • Free-Response   B186   Chapters 1 – 6   **Stop!**

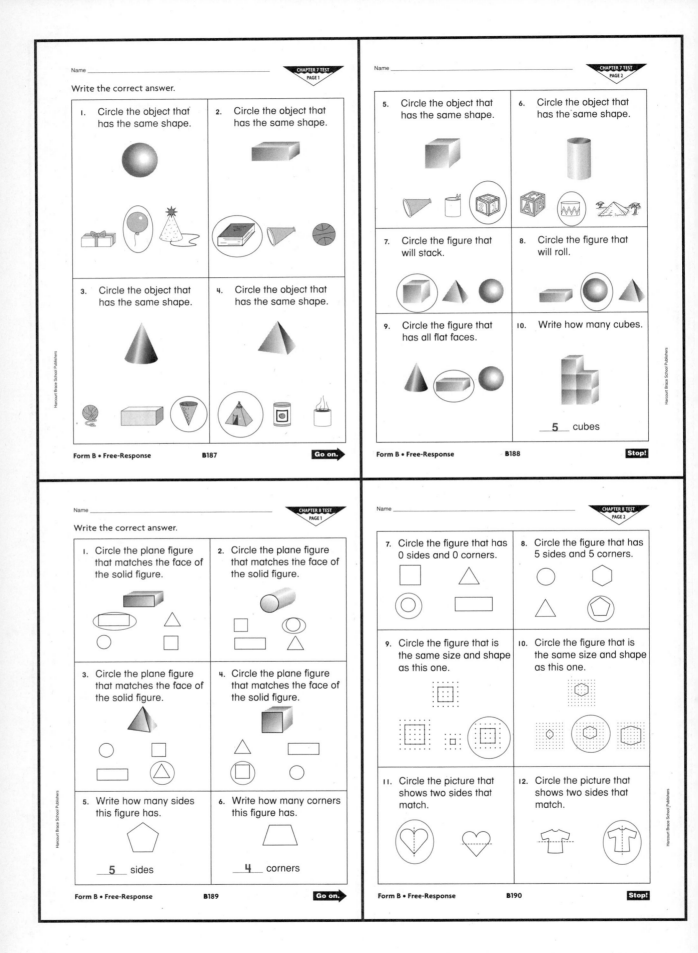

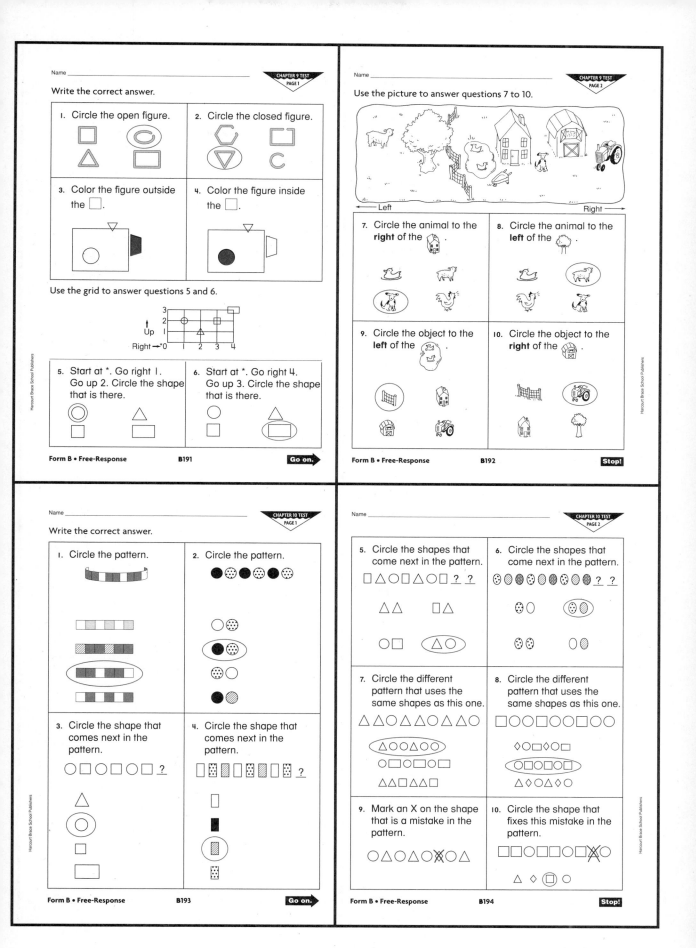

Name _____

Write the correct answer.

1. Circle the open figure.

2. Circle the closed figure.

3. Color the figure outside the ☐.

4. Color the figure inside the ☐.

Use the grid to answer questions 5 and 6.

5. Start at *. Go right 1. Go up 2. Circle the shape that is there.

6. Start at *. Go right 4. Go up 3. Circle the shape that is there.

Form B • Free-Response   B191   Go on.

Name _____

Use the picture to answer questions 7 to 10.

← Left   Right →

7. Circle the animal to the **right** of the 🏠.

8. Circle the animal to the **left** of the tree.

9. Circle the object to the **left** of the bush.

10. Circle the object to the **right** of the barn.

Form B • Free-Response   B192   Stop!

Name _____

Write the correct answer.

1. Circle the pattern.

2. Circle the pattern.

3. Circle the shape that comes next in the pattern.

○☐○☐○☐ ?

4. Circle the shape that comes next in the pattern.

☐▨☐▨☐▨☐ ?

Form B • Free-Response   B193   Go on.

Name _____

5. Circle the shapes that come next in the pattern.

☐△○☐△○ ? ?

6. Circle the shapes that come next in the pattern.

◎◎◎◎◎◎◎◎ ? ?

7. Circle the different pattern that uses the same shapes as this one.

△△○△△○△△○

8. Circle the different pattern that uses the same shapes as this one.

☐○○☐○○☐○○

9. Mark an X on the shape that is a mistake in the pattern.

○△○△○△○○△○△

10. Circle the shape that fixes this mistake in the pattern.

☐☐☐○☐☐☐○☐☐

Form B • Free-Response   B194   Stop!

Free-Response Format • Test Answers

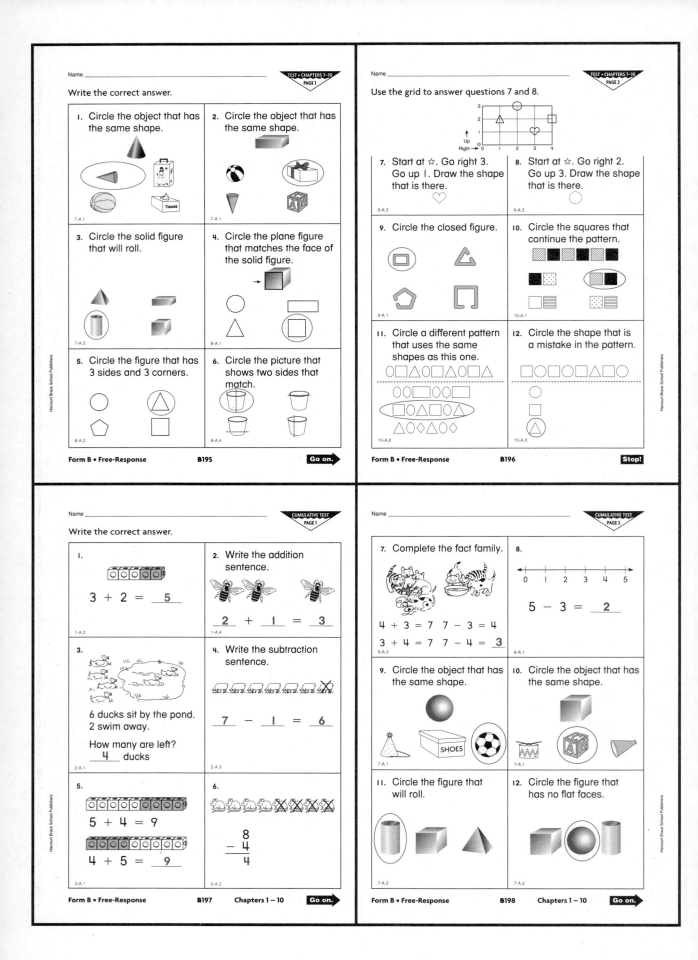

Page 1 (B195)

Write the correct answer.

1. Circle the object that has the same shape.

7-A.1

2. Circle the object that has the same shape.

7-A.1

3. Circle the solid figure that will roll.

7-A.2

4. Circle the plane figure that matches the face of the solid figure.

8-A.1

5. Circle the figure that has 3 sides and 3 corners.

8-A.2

6. Circle the picture that shows two sides that match.

8-A.4

Page 2 (B196)

Use the grid to answer questions 7 and 8.

7. Start at ☆. Go right 3. Go up 1. Draw the shape that is there.

♡

9-A.3

8. Start at ☆. Go right 2. Go up 3. Draw the shape that is there.

○

9-A.3

9. Circle the closed figure.

9-A.1

10. Circle the squares that continue the pattern.

10-A.1

11. Circle a different pattern that uses the same shapes as this one.

10-A.2

12. Circle the shape that is a mistake in the pattern.

10-A.3

Page 3 (B197)

Write the correct answer.

1.

$3 + 2 = \underline{5}$

1-A.2

2. Write the addition sentence.

$\underline{2} + \underline{1} = \underline{3}$

1-A.4

3.

6 ducks sit by the pond. 2 swim away.

How many are left?
$\underline{4}$ ducks

2-A.1

4. Write the subtraction sentence.

$\underline{7} - \underline{1} = \underline{6}$

2-A.3

5.

$5 + 4 = 9$

$4 + 5 = \underline{9}$

3-A.1

6.

$\begin{array}{r} 8 \\ -\ 4 \\ \hline 4 \end{array}$

5-A.2

Page 4 (B198)

7. Complete the fact family.

$4 + 3 = 7 \quad 7 - 3 = 4$
$3 + 4 = 7 \quad 7 - 4 = \underline{3}$

5-A.3

8.

$5 - 3 = \underline{2}$

6-A.1

9. Circle the object that has the same shape.

7-A.1

10. Circle the object that has the same shape.

7-A.1

11. Circle the figure that will roll.

7-A.2

12. Circle the figure that has no flat faces.

7-A.2

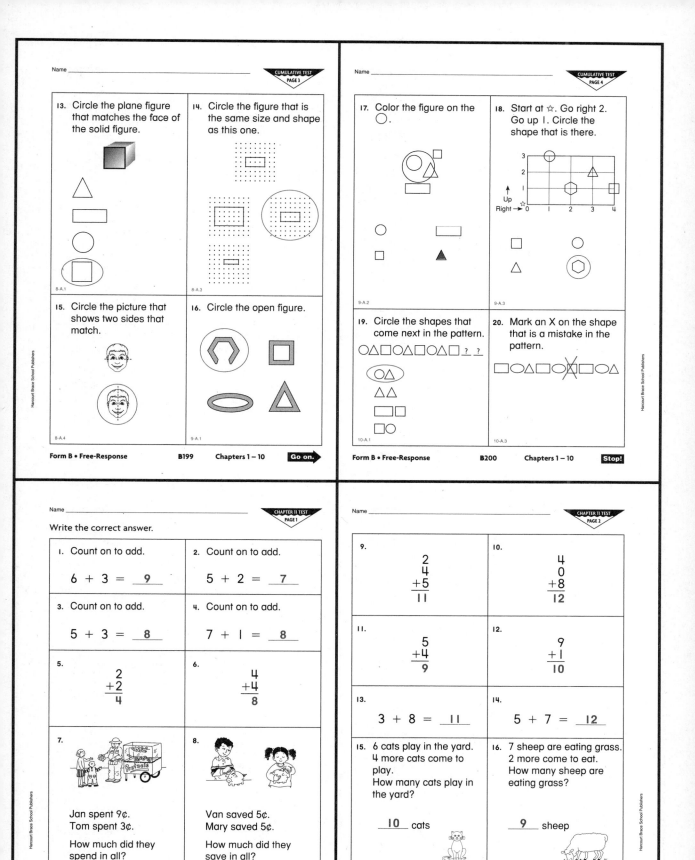

Free-Response Format • Test Answers

Write the correct answer.

1.

$6 + 3 = 9$

$9 - 3 = \underline{}6$

2.

$8 + 3 = 11$

$11 - 3 = \underline{}8$

3.

$\begin{array}{r} 4 \\ +6 \\ \hline 10 \end{array}$ $\quad$ $\begin{array}{r} 10 \\ -6 \\ \hline 4 \end{array}$

4.

$\begin{array}{r} 7 \\ +5 \\ \hline 12 \end{array}$ $\quad$ $\begin{array}{r} 12 \\ -5 \\ \hline 7 \end{array}$

5. Count back to subtract.

5 6 7 8 9 10 11 12

$9 - 2 = \underline{}7$

6. Count back to subtract.

5 6 7 8 9 10 11 12

$10 - 1 = \underline{}9$

---

7. How many more apples than pears are there?

$\begin{array}{r} 12 \\ -4 \\ \hline 8 \end{array}$

8. How many fewer plums than bananas are there?

$\begin{array}{r} 11 \\ -9 \\ \hline 2 \end{array}$

9. Circle the number sentence that belongs in this fact family.

$3 + 9 = 12$
$9 + 3 = 12$
$12 - 3 = 9$
- - - - - - - - - -
$3 + 3 = 6$
$(12 - 9 = 3)$
$9 - 3 = 6$

10. Circle the number sentence that belongs in this fact family.

$10 - 3 = 7$
$10 - 7 = 3$
$3 + 7 = 10$
- - - - - - - - - -
$(7 + 3 = 10)$
$4 + 3 = 7$
$10 - 6 = 4$

11. Write the number sentence the story shows.
Sam had 11 balls.
He gave away 7.
How many balls does Sam have left?

$\underline{11} \ominus \underline{7} = \underline{4}$

$\underline{4}$ balls

12. Write the number sentence the story shows.
I had 8 pennies.
I found 4 more.
How many pennies do I have now?

$\underline{8} \oplus \underline{4} = \underline{12}$

$\underline{12}$ pennies

Write the correct answer.

1.

$7 + 3 = \underline{10}$

11-A.1

2.

$\begin{array}{r} 6 \\ +6 \\ \hline 12 \end{array}$

11-A.1

3.

$\begin{array}{r} 3 \\ 5 \\ +3 \\ \hline 11 \end{array}$

11-A.2

4.

$\begin{array}{r} 1 \\ 2 \\ +7 \\ \hline 10 \end{array}$

11-A.2

5. Lee spent 6¢.
Rosa spent 5¢.
How much did they spend in all?

$\underline{11}$ ¢

11-A.3

6. 8 cats are drinking milk.
1 more cat comes to drink.
How many cats are drinking milk?

$\underline{9}$ cats

11-A.3

7.

$\begin{array}{r} 9 \\ +2 \\ \hline 11 \end{array}$ $\quad$ $\begin{array}{r} 11 \\ -2 \\ \hline 9 \end{array}$

12-A.1

8.

5 6 7 8 9 10 11 12

$11 - 3 = \underline{8}$

12-A.1

9. How many more oranges than apples are there?

$\begin{array}{r} 10 \\ -6 \\ \hline 4 \end{array}$

12-A.2

10. Write the number sentence that belongs in this fact family.

$9 + 3 = 12$
$3 + 9 = 12$
$12 - 9 = 3$

$\underline{12} \ominus \underline{3} = \underline{9}$

12-A.1

11. Write the number sentence the story shows.
Ray had 10 toys.
He gave 5 away.
How many toys does Ray have left?

$\underline{10} \ominus \underline{5} = \underline{5}$

12-A.3

12. Write the number sentence the story shows.
I have 4 pennies.
I find 7 more.
How many pennies do I have now?

$\underline{4} \oplus \underline{7} = \underline{11}$

12-A.3

---

294   **Free-Response Format • Test Answers**

Write the correct answer.

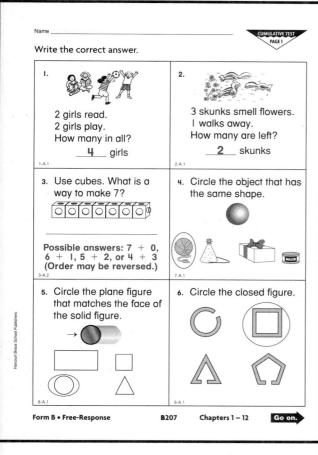

1. 2 girls read.
2 girls play.
How many in all?
___4___ girls

1-A.1

2. 3 skunks smell flowers.
1 walks away.
How many are left?
___2___ skunks

2-A.1

3. Use cubes. What is a way to make 7?

Possible answers: 7 + 0,
6 + 1, 5 + 2, or 4 + 3
(Order may be reversed.)

3-A.2

4. Circle the object that has the same shape.

7-A.1

5. Circle the plane figure that matches the face of the solid figure.

8-A.1

6. Circle the closed figure.

9-A.1

Form B • Free-Response   B207   Chapters 1 – 12   **Go on.**

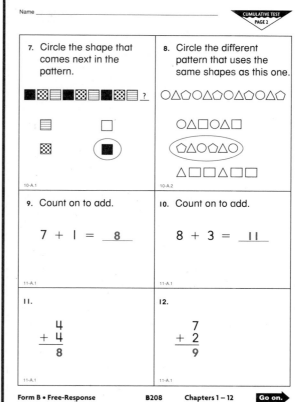

7. Circle the shape that comes next in the pattern.

10-A.1

8. Circle the different pattern that uses the same shapes as this one.

10-A.2

9. Count on to add.

$7 + 1 = $ ___8___

11-A.1

10. Count on to add.

$8 + 3 = $ ___11___

11-A.1

11.
$$\begin{array}{r} 4 \\ + 4 \\ \hline 8 \end{array}$$

11-A.1

12.
$$\begin{array}{r} 7 \\ + 2 \\ \hline 9 \end{array}$$

11-A.1

Form B • Free-Response   B208   Chapters 1 – 12   **Go on.**

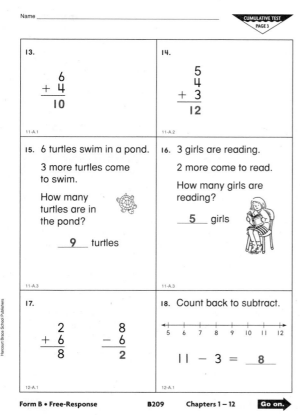

13.
$$\begin{array}{r} 6 \\ + 4 \\ \hline 10 \end{array}$$

11-A.1

14.
$$\begin{array}{r} 5 \\ 4 \\ + 3 \\ \hline 12 \end{array}$$

11-A.2

15. 6 turtles swim in a pond.

3 more turtles come to swim.

How many turtles are in the pond?

___9___ turtles

11-A.3

16. 3 girls are reading.

2 more come to read.

How many girls are reading?

___5___ girls

11-A.3

17.
$$\begin{array}{r} 2 \\ + 6 \\ \hline 8 \end{array} \qquad \begin{array}{r} 8 \\ - 6 \\ \hline 2 \end{array}$$

12-A.1

18. Count back to subtract.

$11 - 3 = $ ___8___

12-A.1

Form B • Free-Response   B209   Chapters 1 – 12   **Go on.**

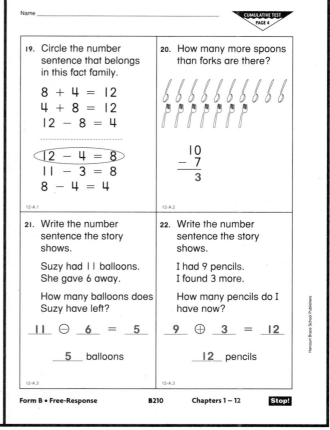

19. Circle the number sentence that belongs in this fact family.

$8 + 4 = 12$
$4 + 8 = 12$
$12 - 8 = 4$

$\boxed{12 - 4 = 8}$
$11 - 3 = 8$
$8 - 4 = 4$

12-A.1

20. How many more spoons than forks are there?

$$\begin{array}{r} 10 \\ - 7 \\ \hline 3 \end{array}$$

12-A.2

21. Write the number sentence the story shows.

Suzy had 11 balloons.
She gave 6 away.

How many balloons does Suzy have left?

___11___ ⊖ ___6___ = ___5___

___5___ balloons

12-A.3

22. Write the number sentence the story shows.

I had 9 pencils.
I found 3 more.

How many pencils do I have now?

___9___ ⊕ ___3___ = ___12___

___12___ pencils

12-A.3

Form B • Free-Response   B210   Chapters 1 – 12   **Stop!**

Free-Response Format • Test Answers

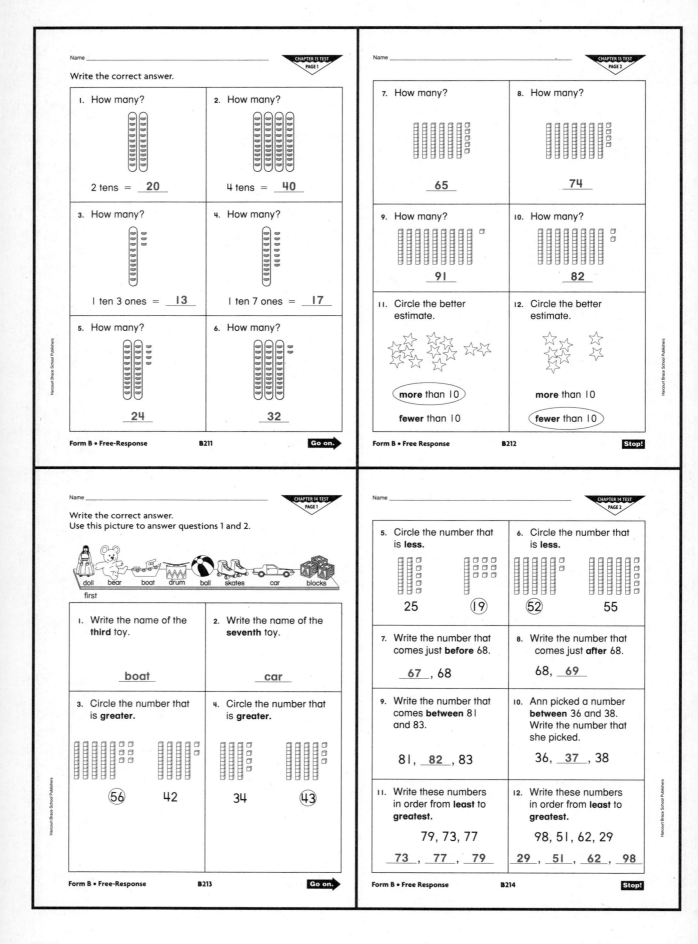

Write the correct answer.

1. How many?

2 tens = __20__

2. How many?

4 tens = __40__

3. How many?

1 ten 3 ones = __13__

4. How many?

1 ten 7 ones = __17__

5. How many?

__24__

6. How many?

__32__

7. How many?

__65__

8. How many?

__74__

9. How many?

__91__

10. How many?

__82__

11. Circle the better estimate.

(more than 10)

fewer than 10

12. Circle the better estimate.

more than 10

(fewer than 10)

Write the correct answer.
Use this picture to answer questions 1 and 2.

doll   bear   boat   drum   ball   skates   car   blocks
first

1. Write the name of the **third** toy.

__boat__

2. Write the name of the **seventh** toy.

__car__

3. Circle the number that is **greater**.

(56)   42

4. Circle the number that is **greater**.

34   (43)

5. Circle the number that is **less**.

25   (19)

6. Circle the number that is **less**.

(52)   55

7. Write the number that comes just **before** 68.

__67__ , 68

8. Write the number that comes just **after** 68.

68, __69__

9. Write the number that comes **between** 81 and 83.

81, __82__ , 83

10. Ann picked a number **between** 36 and 38. Write the number that she picked.

36, __37__ , 38

11. Write these numbers in order from **least** to **greatest**.

79, 73, 77

__73__ , __77__ , __79__

12. Write these numbers in order from **least** to **greatest**.

98, 51, 62, 29

__29__ , __51__ , __62__ , __98__

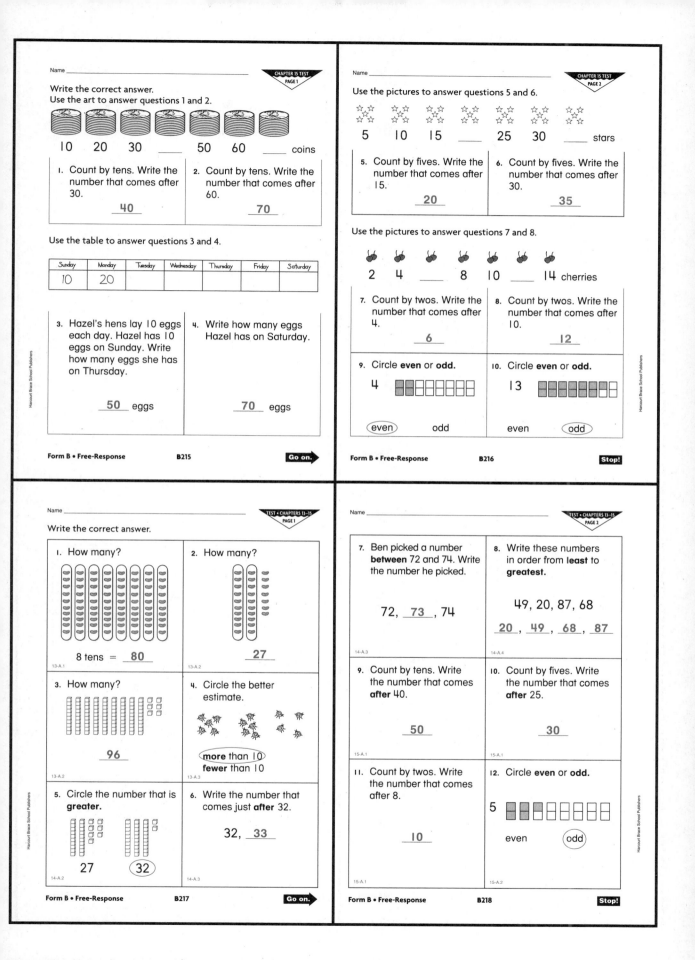

Name _____

Write the correct answer.

1.

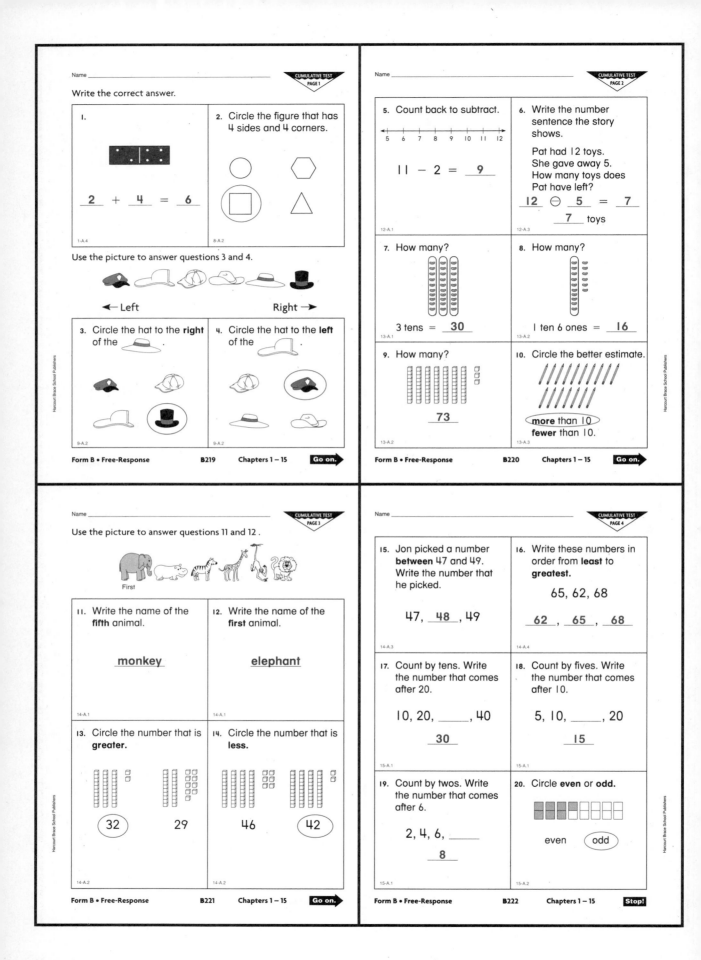

__2__ + __4__ = __6__

1-A.4

2. Circle the figure that has 4 sides and 4 corners.

8-A.2

Use the picture to answer questions 3 and 4.

← Left   Right →

3. Circle the hat to the **right** of the 🎩 .

9-A.2

4. Circle the hat to the **left** of the 🎩 .

9-A.2

Form B • Free-Response   B219   Chapters 1 – 15   **Go on.**

Name _____

5. Count back to subtract.

5 6 7 8 9 10 11 12

11 − 2 = __9__

12-A.1

6. Write the number sentence the story shows.

Pat had 12 toys. She gave away 5. How many toys does Pat have left?

__12__ ⊖ __5__ = __7__

__7__ toys

12-A.3

7. How many?

3 tens = __30__

13-A.1

8. How many?

1 ten 6 ones = __16__

13-A.2

9. How many?

__73__

13-A.2

10. Circle the better estimate.

more than 10
fewer than 10.

13-A.3

Form B • Free-Response   B220   Chapters 1 – 15   **Go on.**

Name _____

Use the picture to answer questions 11 and 12 .

First

11. Write the name of the **fifth** animal.

__monkey__

14-A.1

12. Write the name of the **first** animal.

__elephant__

14-A.1

13. Circle the number that is **greater.**

(32)   29

14-A.2

14. Circle the number that is **less.**

46   (42)

14-A.2

Form B • Free-Response   B221   Chapters 1 – 15   **Go on.**

Name _____

15. Jon picked a number **between** 47 and 49. Write the number that he picked.

47, __48__ , 49

14-A.3

16. Write these numbers in order from **least** to **greatest.**

65, 62, 68

__62__ , __65__ , __68__

14-A.4

17. Count by tens. Write the number that comes after 20.

10, 20, _____, 40

__30__

15-A.1

18. Count by fives. Write the number that comes after 10.

5, 10, _____, 20

__15__

15-A.1

19. Count by twos. Write the number that comes after 6.

2, 4, 6, _____

__8__

15-A.1

20. Circle **even** or **odd.**

even   (odd)

15-A.2

Form B • Free-Response   B222   Chapters 1 – 15   **Stop!**

Free-Response Format • Test Answers

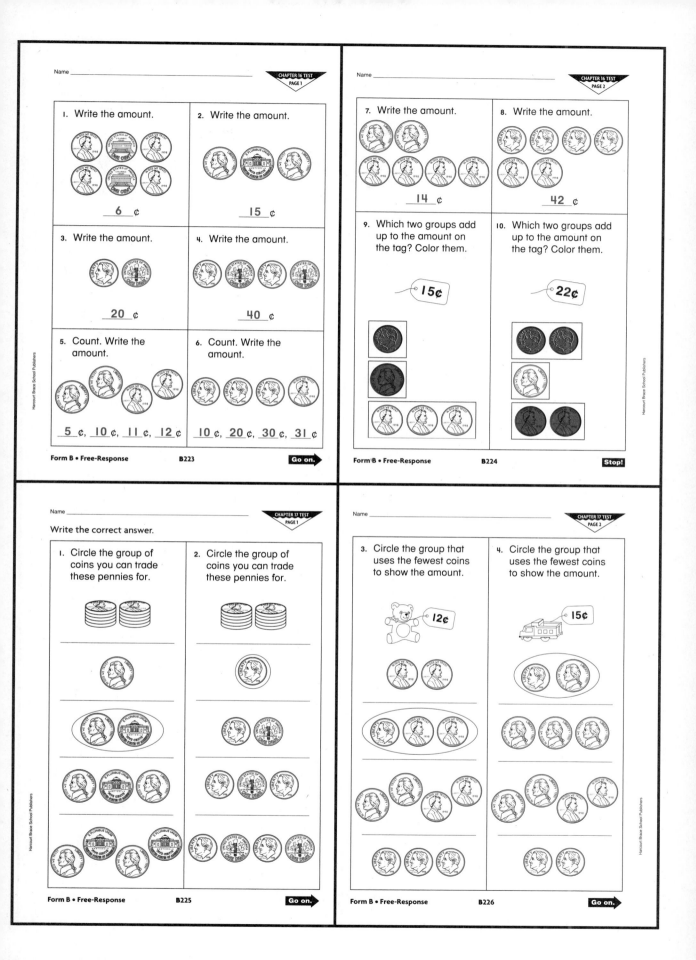

Name _____

Circle the group of coins you need.

5. 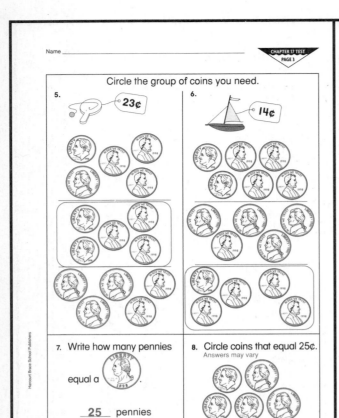 23¢

6. 14¢

7. Write how many pennies

equal a 🪙.

___25___ pennies

8. Circle coins that equal 25¢.
Answers may vary

Form B • Free-Response   B227   Go on.

Name _____

9. Circle what you could buy with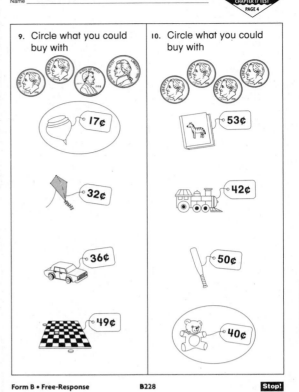

- 17¢
- 32¢
- 36¢
- 49¢

10. Circle what you could buy with

- 53¢
- 42¢
- 50¢
- 40¢

Form B • Free-Response   B228   Stop!

Name _____

Write the correct answer.
Use the calendar to answer questions 1 to 6.

January

Sunday	Monday	Tuesday	Wednesday	Thursday	Friday	Saturday
			1	2	3	4
5	6	7	8	9	10	11
12	13	14	15	16	17	18
19	20	21	22	23	24	25
26	27	28	29	30	31	

1. How many months are in one year?

___12___ months

2. Which day comes just after Sunday?

___Monday___

3. On which day does this month begin?

___Wednesday___

4. On which day is January 28?

___Tuesday___

5. What is the date of the first Saturday in this month?

January ___4___

6. How many days are in this month?

___31___ days

Form B • Free-Response   B229   Go on.

Name _____

7. Does this happen in the morning, in the afternoon, or in the evening?

in the __morning__

8. Does this happen in the morning, in the afternoon, or in the evening?

in the __evening__

9. Circle the one that takes longer to do.

write your name

write a story

10. Circle the one that takes longer to do.

carry the ball

throw the ball

Form B • Free-Response   B230   Stop!

Free-Response Format • Test Answers

Write the correct answer.

1. What time is it? Write the time that is on the clock.

___6___ o'clock

2. What time is it? Write the time that is on the clock.

___11___ o'clock

3. Read the clock. Write the time.

_4:00_

4. Read the clock. Write the time.

_10:00_

5. Draw the hour hand and the minute hand to show the time.

3:00

6. Draw the hour hand and the minute hand to show the time.

8:00

7. Write the time.

1:30

8. Write the time.

5:30

9. Does it take **more** than a minute or **less** than a minute to turn on a light?

__less__ than a minute

10. Does it take **more** than a minute or **less** than a minute to ride to school?

__more__ than a minute

Write the correct answer.

1. Write the amount.

___20___ ¢

16-A.1

2. Write the amount.

___12___ ¢

16-A.3

3. Circle the coins that show the amount on the tag. 13¢

16-A.5

4. Circle the answer that shows the amount using the fewest coins. 21¢

17-A.2

5. Circle the coins that equal a .

17-A.4

6. Circle what you could buy with

53¢ 50¢ 49¢ 45¢

17-A.3

Use the calendar to answer questions 7 and 8.

February

S	M	T	W	T	F	S
						1
2	3	4	5	6	7	8
9	10	11	12	13	14	15
16	17	18	19	20	21	22
23	24	25	26	27	28	

7. On what day is February 14?

Friday

18-A.1

8. What is the date of the first Tuesday in this month?

February ___4___

18-A.1

9. Which takes longer?

18-A.3

10. Write the time.

2:00

19-A.1

11. What time is it?

4:30

19-A.1

12. Which takes less than a minute to do?

19-A.2

Free-Response Format • Test Answers

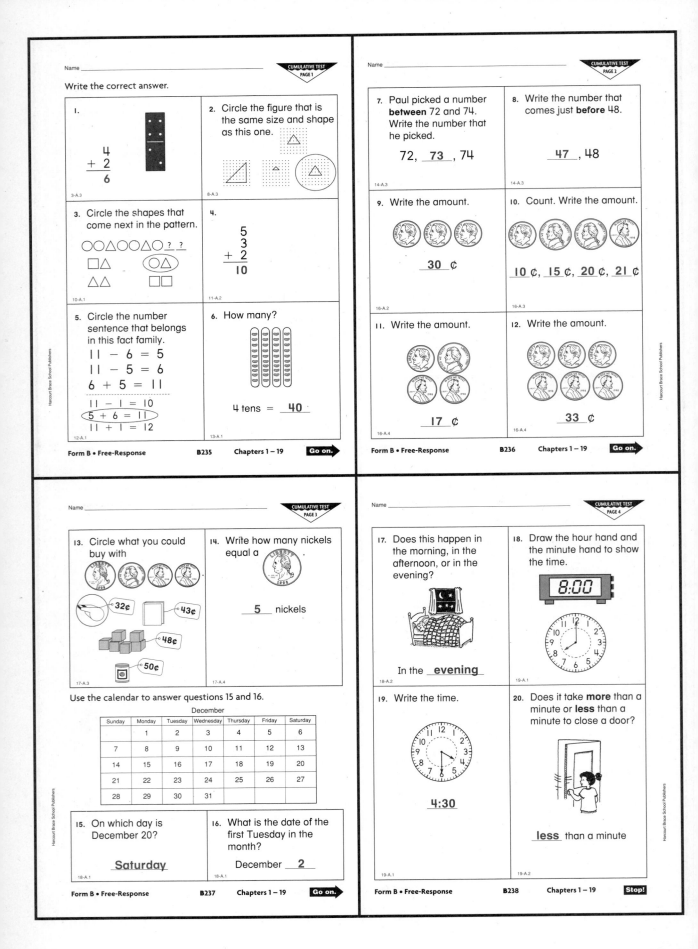

     Free-Response Format • Test Answers

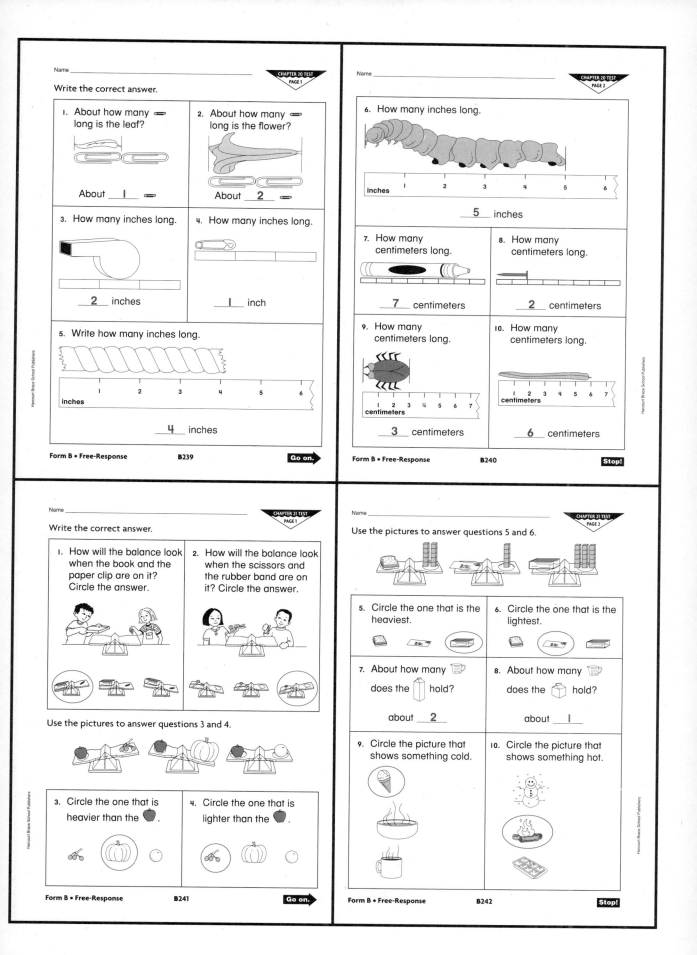

Name

Write the correct answer.

1. About how many ⊂ long is the leaf?

About ___1___ ⊂

2. About how many ⊂ long is the flower?

About ___2___ ⊂

3. How many inches long.

___2___ inches

4. How many inches long.

___1___ inch

5. Write how many inches long.

inches | 1 | 2 | 3 | 4 | 5 | 6

___4___ inches

Form B • Free-Response   B239   Go on.

Name

6. How many inches long.

inches | 1 | 2 | 3 | 4 | 5 | 6

___5___ inches

7. How many centimeters long.

___7___ centimeters

8. How many centimeters long.

___2___ centimeters

9. How many centimeters long.

centimeters | 1 2 3 4 5 6 7

___3___ centimeters

10. How many centimeters long.

centimeters | 1 2 3 4 5 6 7

___6___ centimeters

Form B • Free-Response   B240   Stop!

Name

Write the correct answer.

1. How will the balance look when the book and the paper clip are on it? Circle the answer.

2. How will the balance look when the scissors and the rubber band are on it? Circle the answer.

Use the pictures to answer questions 3 and 4.

3. Circle the one that is heavier than the 🍎.

4. Circle the one that is lighter than the 🍎.

Form B • Free-Response   B241   Go on.

Name

Use the pictures to answer questions 5 and 6.

5. Circle the one that is the heaviest.

6. Circle the one that is the lightest.

7. About how many 🥤 does the 🧃 hold?

about ___2___

8. About how many 🥤 does the □ hold?

about ___1___

9. Circle the picture that shows something cold.

10. Circle the picture that shows something hot.

Form B • Free-Response   B242   Stop!

Free-Response Format • Test Answers   303

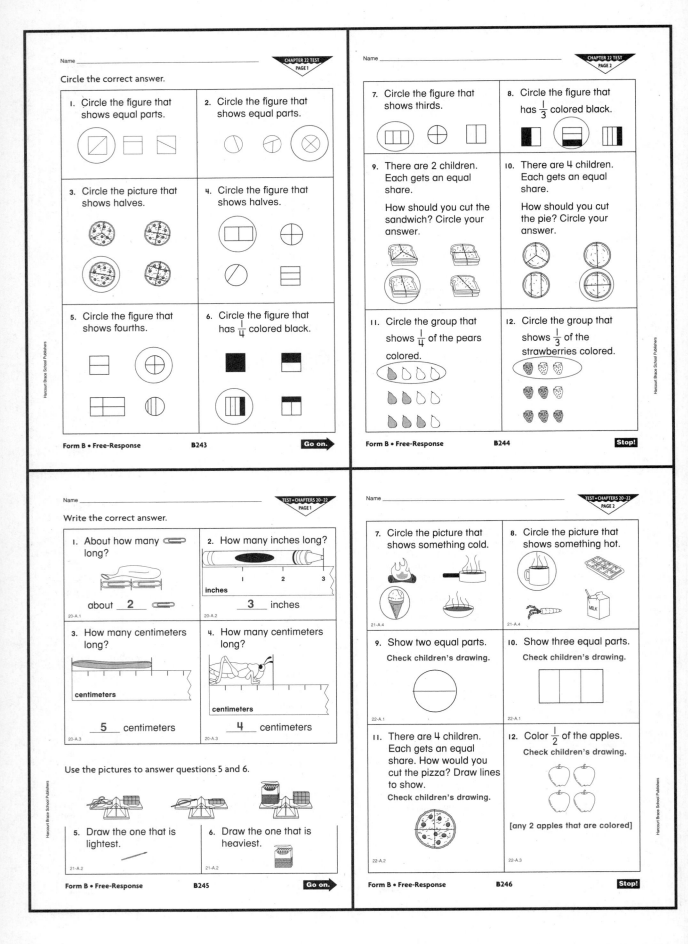

Free-Response Format • Test Answers

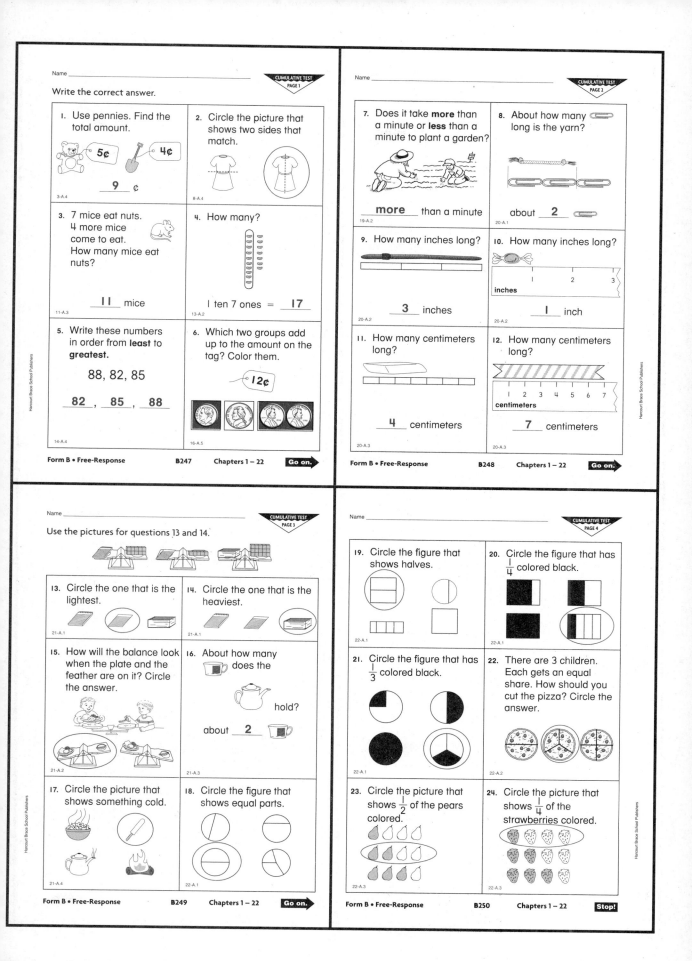

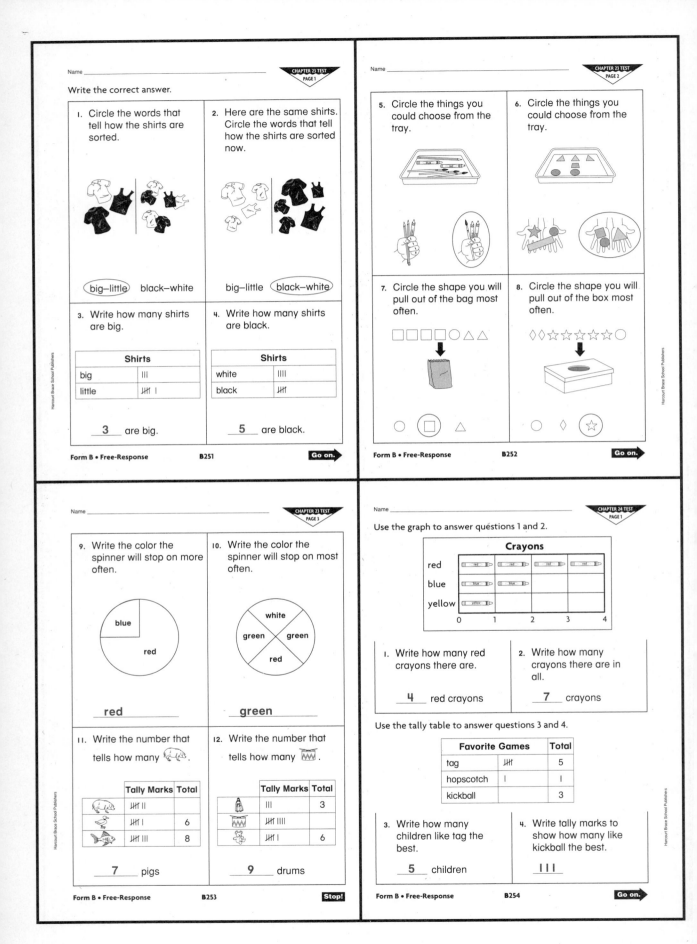

Free-Response Format • Test Answers

Use the graph to answer questions 5 and 6.

Favorite Animals

	0	1	2	3	4	5	6
tigers							
apes							
bears							

5. Write how many children like bears the best.

____3____ children

6. What animal got the most votes?

____apes____

Use the graph to answer questions 7 and 8.

How We Go To School

7. Write how many children ride the bus to school.

____7____ children

8. Write how many more children walk than ride the bus.

____2____ more children

Use the tally table and the graph to answer questions 9 to 12.

	Pictures We Drew	Total
Al	I	1
Kim	III	3
Sam		2
Jane	IIII	4

Pictures We Drew

9. Make tally marks to show how many pictures Sam drew.

____II____

10. Write how many pictures Kim drew.

____3____ pictures

11. Write who drew the most pictures.

____Jane____

12. Write how many more pictures Kim drew than Al drew.

____2____ more pictures

Write the correct answer.

1. Circle the words that tell how the items are sorted.

black–white
(circle–square)

23-A.1

2. How many shapes are square?

Shapes	
triangle	JHT
square	III

____3____ are square.

23-A.1

3. Circle the shapes you could choose from the tray.

23-A.2

4. Draw the shape you will pull from the bag most often.

Check children's drawing.

23-A.2

5. Which color will the spinner stop on most often?

red
green   blue

____red____

23-A.3

6. Which number tells how many 🐁?

	Tally Marks	Total
🐭	JHT	5
🐱	III	3
🐹	IIII	

____4____ 🐁

23-A.3

Use the graph to answer questions 7 and 8.

	Animals	Total
ducks		3
pigs		4
chickens		5

7. How many chickens are there?

____5____ chickens

24-A.1

8. How many animals are there in all?

____12____ animals

24-A.1

Use the tally table and the graph to answer questions 9 to 12.

Favorite Fruits		Total
apple	I	1
banana	IIII	4
grapes		3
pear	II	2

Favorite Fruits

9. Make tally marks for how many like grapes best.

____III____

24-A.2

10. How many like pears best?

____2____

24-A.2

11. Which fruit do the most people like best?

____banana____

24-A.2

12. How many more people like grapes best than like apples best?

____2____

24-A.2

Free-Response Format • Test Answers

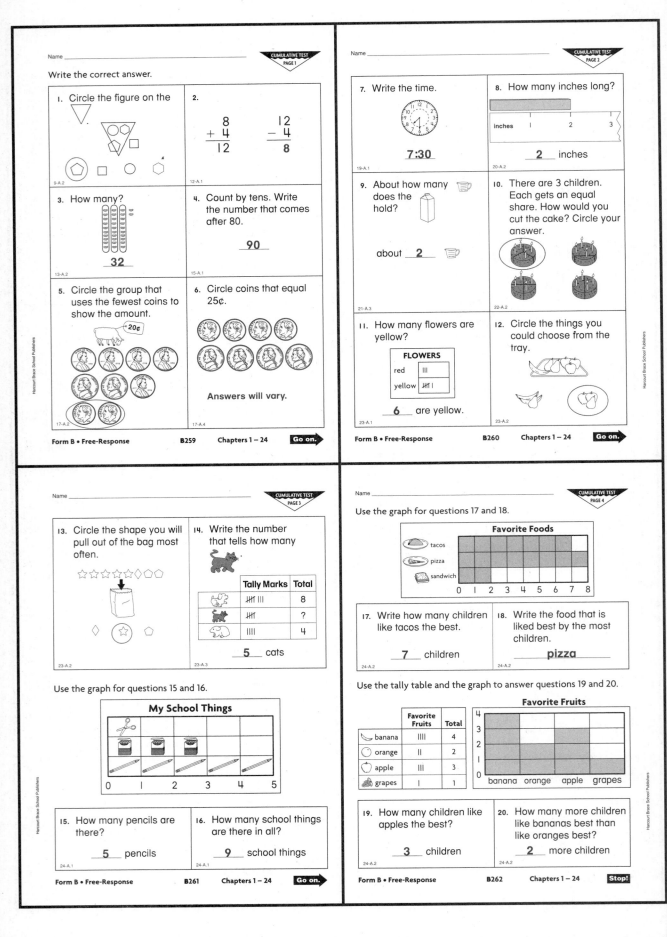

Name _____

Write the correct answer.

1. Circle the figure on the

9-A.2

2.

$$\begin{array}{r} 8 \\ + 4 \\ \hline 12 \end{array} \qquad \begin{array}{r} 12 \\ - 4 \\ \hline 8 \end{array}$$

12-A.1

3. How many?

32

13-A.2

4. Count by tens. Write the number that comes after 80.

90

15-A.1

5. Circle the group that uses the fewest coins to show the amount.

20¢

17-A.2

6. Circle coins that equal 25¢.

Answers will vary.

17-A.4

Form B • Free-Response   B259   Chapters 1 – 24   **Go on.**

Name _____

7. Write the time.

7:30

19-A.1

8. How many inches long?

inches   1   2   3

2 inches

20-A.2

9. About how many does the hold?

about **2**

21-A.3

10. There are 3 children. Each gets an equal share. How would you cut the cake? Circle your answer.

22-A.2

11. How many flowers are yellow?

FLOWERS

| red | III |
| yellow | JHH I |

6 are yellow.

23-A.1

12. Circle the things you could choose from the tray.

23-A.2

Form B • Free-Response   B260   Chapters 1 – 24   **Go on.**

Name _____

13. Circle the shape you will pull out of the bag most often.

23-A.2

14. Write the number that tells how many

	Tally Marks	Total
	JHH III	8
	JHH	?
	IIII	4

5 cats

23-A.3

Use the graph for questions 15 and 16.

My School Things

0   1   2   3   4   5

15. How many pencils are there?

5 pencils

24-A.1

16. How many school things are there in all?

9 school things

24-A.1

Form B • Free-Response   B261   Chapters 1 – 24   **Go on.**

Name _____

Use the graph for questions 17 and 18.

Favorite Foods

tacos
pizza
sandwich

0   1   2   3   4   5   6   7   8

17. Write how many children like tacos the best.

7 children

24-A.2

18. Write the food that is liked best by the most children.

pizza

24-A.2

Use the tally table and the graph to answer questions 19 and 20.

	Favorite Fruits	Total
banana	IIII	4
orange	II	2
apple	III	3
grapes	I	1

Favorite Fruits

4
3
2
1
0

banana   orange   apple   grapes

19. How many children like apples the best?

3 children

24-A.2

20. How many more children like bananas best than like oranges best?

2 more children

24-A.2

Form B • Free-Response   B262   Chapters 1 – 24   **Stop!**

308   **Free-Response Format • Test Answers**

Write the correct answer.

1.
$$\begin{array}{r} 4 \\ +4 \\ \hline 8 \end{array} \qquad \begin{array}{r} 4 \\ +5 \\ \hline 9 \end{array}$$

2.
$$\begin{array}{r} 8 \\ +8 \\ \hline 16 \end{array} \qquad \begin{array}{r} 8 \\ +9 \\ \hline 17 \end{array}$$

3.
$$\begin{array}{r} 5 \\ +5 \\ \hline 10 \end{array} \qquad \begin{array}{r} 5 \\ +4 \\ \hline 9 \end{array}$$

4.
$$\begin{array}{r} 7 \\ +7 \\ \hline 14 \end{array} \qquad \begin{array}{r} 7 \\ +6 \\ \hline 13 \end{array}$$

5.
$$\begin{array}{r} 7 \\ +8 \\ \hline 15 \end{array}$$

6.
$$\begin{array}{r} 4 \\ +3 \\ \hline 7 \end{array}$$

7.
$$\begin{array}{r} 5 \\ +6 \\ \hline 11 \end{array}$$

8.
$$\begin{array}{r} 9 \\ +8 \\ \hline 17 \end{array}$$

Form B • Free-Response   B263   Go on. ➤

9.
$7 + 7 = 14$

$14 - 7 = \underline{\ 7\ }$

10.
$8 + 8 = 16$

$16 - 8 = \underline{\ 8\ }$

11.
$12 - 6 = 6$

$6 + 6 = \underline{\ 12\ }$

12.
$18 - 9 = 9$

$9 + 9 = \underline{\ 18\ }$

13. Lani read 7 books. Bo read 1 more than Lani. Write how many books they read in all.

$\underline{\ 15\ }$ books

14. Ruth picked some flowers. Pat gave her 3 more. Now she has 6. Write how many flowers Ruth picked herself.

$\underline{\ 3\ }$ flowers

Form B • Free-Response   B264   Stop!

Write the correct answer.

1.
$$\begin{array}{r} 8 \\ +5 \\ \hline 13 \end{array}$$

2.
$$\begin{array}{r} 9 \\ +3 \\ \hline 12 \end{array}$$

3.
$$\begin{array}{r} 9 \\ +8 \\ \hline 17 \end{array}$$

4.
$$\begin{array}{r} 7 \\ +5 \\ \hline 12 \end{array}$$

5.
$$\begin{array}{r} 7 \\ 3 \\ +6 \\ \hline 16 \end{array}$$

6.
$$\begin{array}{r} 6 \\ 2 \\ +6 \\ \hline 14 \end{array}$$

7.
$$\begin{array}{r} 1 \\ 5 \\ +9 \\ \hline 15 \end{array}$$

8.
$$\begin{array}{r} 4 \\ 4 \\ +5 \\ \hline 13 \end{array}$$

Form B • Free-Response   B265   Go on. ➤

9.
$$\begin{array}{r} 7 \\ +5 \\ \hline 12 \end{array} \qquad \begin{array}{r} 12 \\ -5 \\ \hline 7 \end{array}$$

10.
$$\begin{array}{r} 8 \\ +3 \\ \hline 11 \end{array} \qquad \begin{array}{r} 11 \\ -3 \\ \hline 8 \end{array}$$

11.
$$\begin{array}{r} 6 \\ +8 \\ \hline 14 \end{array} \qquad \begin{array}{r} 14 \\ -8 \\ \hline 6 \end{array}$$

12.
$$\begin{array}{r} 5 \\ +9 \\ \hline 14 \end{array} \qquad \begin{array}{r} 14 \\ -9 \\ \hline 5 \end{array}$$

13.
$$\begin{array}{r} 9 \\ +9 \\ \hline 18 \end{array} \qquad \begin{array}{r} 18 \\ -9 \\ \hline 9 \end{array}$$

14.
$$\begin{array}{r} 7 \\ +6 \\ \hline 13 \end{array} \qquad \begin{array}{r} 13 \\ -6 \\ \hline 7 \end{array}$$

15.
$$\begin{array}{r} 6 \\ +9 \\ \hline 15 \end{array} \qquad \begin{array}{r} 15 \\ -9 \\ \hline 6 \end{array}$$

16.
$$\begin{array}{r} 8 \\ +9 \\ \hline 17 \end{array} \qquad \begin{array}{r} 17 \\ -9 \\ \hline 8 \end{array}$$

Form B • Free-Response   B266   Stop!

Free-Response Format • Test Answers

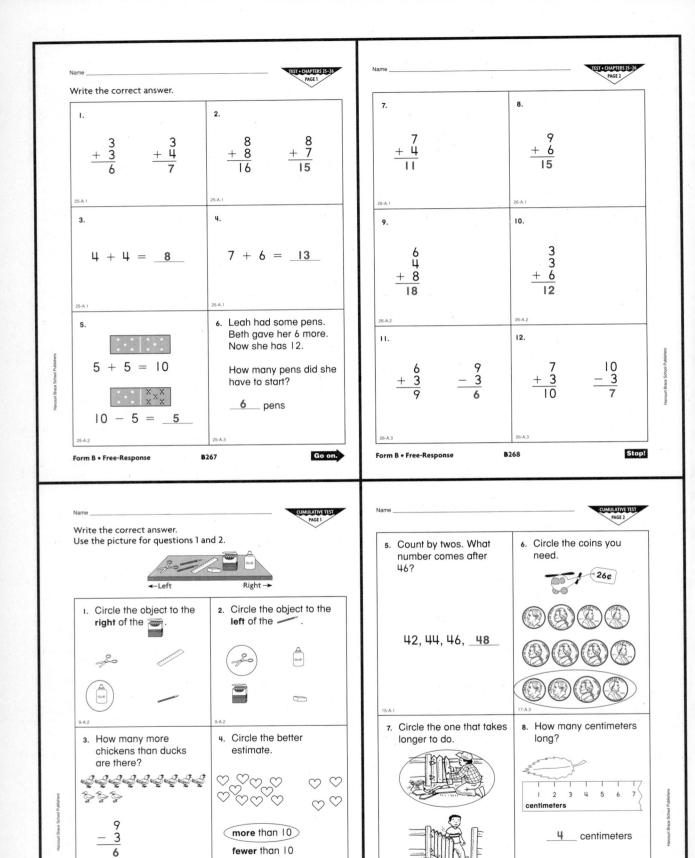

Free-Response Format • Test Answers

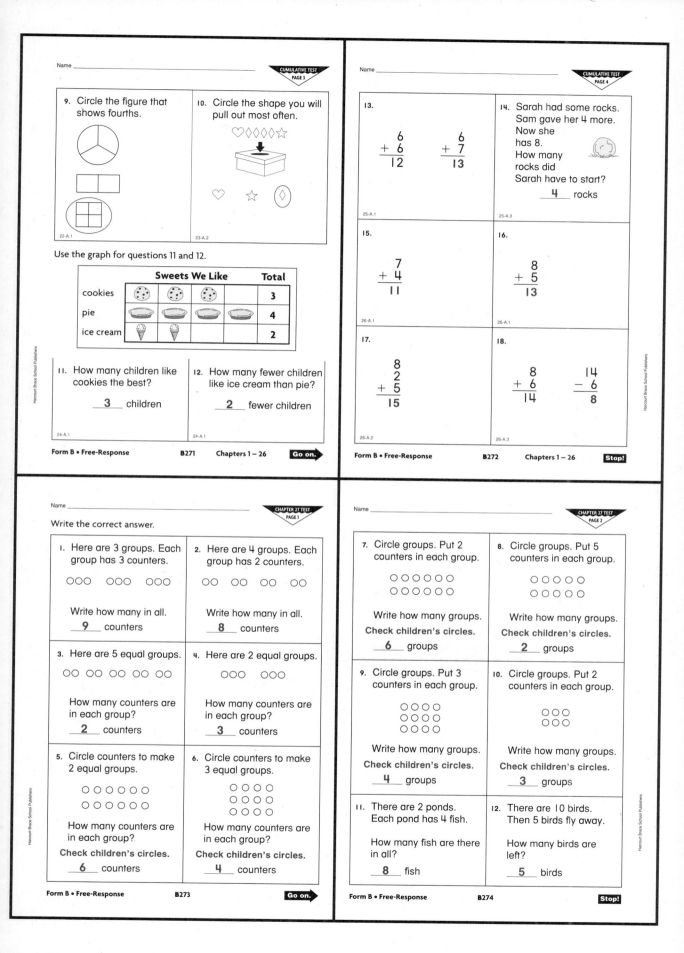

Name ______________________

CUMULATIVE TEST PAGE 3

9. Circle the figure that shows fourths.

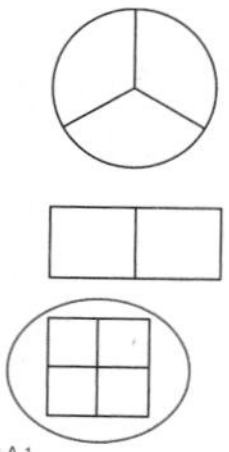

22-A.1

10. Circle the shape you will pull out most often.

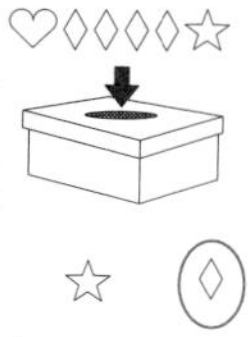

23-A.2

Use the graph for questions 11 and 12.

Sweets We Like
Total
cookies
3
pie
4
ice cream
2

11. How many children like cookies the best?

3 children

24-A.1

12. How many fewer children like ice cream than pie?

2 fewer children

24-A.1

Name ______________________

CUMULATIVE TEST PAGE 4

13.

$$\begin{array}{r} 6 \\ +\ 6 \\ \hline 12 \end{array} \qquad \begin{array}{r} 6 \\ +\ 7 \\ \hline 13 \end{array}$$

25-A.1

14. Sarah had some rocks. Sam gave her 4 more. Now she has 8. How many rocks did Sarah have to start?

4 rocks

25-A.3

15.

$$\begin{array}{r} 7 \\ +\ 4 \\ \hline 11 \end{array}$$

26-A.1

16.

$$\begin{array}{r} 8 \\ +\ 5 \\ \hline 13 \end{array}$$

26-A.1

17.

$$\begin{array}{r} 8 \\ 2 \\ +\ 5 \\ \hline 15 \end{array}$$

26-A.2

18.

$$\begin{array}{r} 8 \\ +\ 6 \\ \hline 14 \end{array} \qquad \begin{array}{r} 14 \\ -\ 6 \\ \hline 8 \end{array}$$

26-A.3

Name ______________________

CHAPTER 27 TEST PAGE 1

Write the correct answer.

1. Here are 3 groups. Each group has 3 counters.

○○○ ○○○ ○○○

Write how many in all.

9 counters

2. Here are 4 groups. Each group has 2 counters.

○○ ○○ ○○ ○○

Write how many in all.

8 counters

3. Here are 5 equal groups.

○○ ○○ ○○ ○○ ○○

How many counters are in each group?

2 counters

4. Here are 2 equal groups.

○○○ ○○○

How many counters are in each group?

3 counters

5. Circle counters to make 2 equal groups.

○○○○○○
○○○○○○

How many counters are in each group?

Check children's circles.

6 counters

6. Circle counters to make 3 equal groups.

○○○○
○○○○
○○○○

How many counters are in each group?

Check children's circles.

4 counters

Name ______________________

CHAPTER 27 TEST PAGE 2

7. Circle groups. Put 2 counters in each group.

○○○○○○
○○○○○○

Write how many groups.

Check children's circles.

6 groups

8. Circle groups. Put 5 counters in each group.

○○○○○
○○○○○

Write how many groups.

Check children's circles.

2 groups

9. Circle groups. Put 3 counters in each group.

○○○○
○○○○
○○○○

Write how many groups.

Check children's circles.

4 groups

10. Circle groups. Put 2 counters in each group.

○○○
○○○

Write how many groups.

Check children's circles.

3 groups

11. There are 2 ponds. Each pond has 4 fish.

How many fish are there in all?

8 fish

12. There are 10 birds. Then 5 birds fly away.

How many birds are left?

5 birds

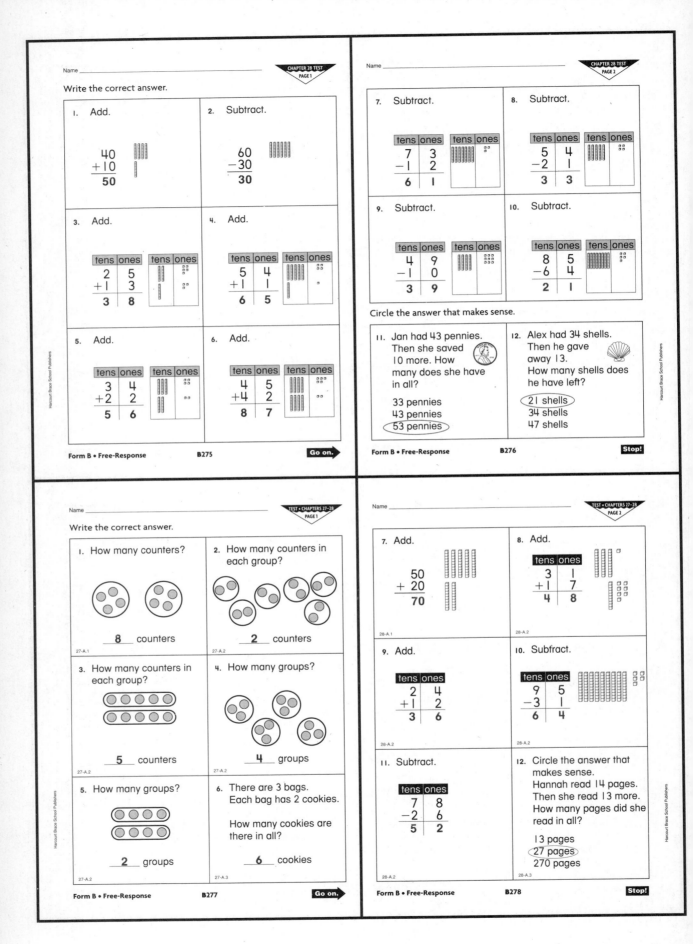

Write the correct answer.

1. Add.	2. Subtract.
40 +10 50	60 −30 30

3. Add.

tens	ones
2	5
+1	3
3	8

4. Add.

tens	ones
5	4
+1	1
6	5

5. Add.

tens	ones
3	4
+2	2
5	6

6. Add.

tens	ones
4	5
+4	2
8	7

Form B • Free-Response   B275   Go on.

7. Subtract.

tens	ones
7	3
−1	2
6	1

8. Subtract.

tens	ones
5	4
−2	1
3	3

9. Subtract.

tens	ones
4	9
−1	0
3	9

10. Subtract.

tens	ones
8	5
−6	4
2	1

Circle the answer that makes sense.

11. Jan had 43 pennies. Then she saved 10 more. How many does she have in all?

33 pennies
43 pennies
(53 pennies)

12. Alex had 34 shells. Then he gave away 13. How many shells does he have left?

(21 shells)
34 shells
47 shells

Form B • Free-Response   B276   Stop!

Write the correct answer.

1. How many counters?

__8__ counters
27-A.1

2. How many counters in each group?

__2__ counters
27-A.2

3. How many counters in each group?

__5__ counters
27-A.2

4. How many groups?

__4__ groups
27-A.2

5. How many groups?

__2__ groups
27-A.2

6. There are 3 bags. Each bag has 2 cookies.

How many cookies are there in all?

__6__ cookies
27-A.3

Form B • Free-Response   B277   Go on.

7. Add.

50
+ 20
70
28-A.1

8. Add.

tens	ones
3	1
+1	7
4	8
28-A.2

9. Add.

tens	ones
2	4
+1	2
3	6
28-A.2

10. Subtract.

tens	ones
9	5
−3	1
6	4
28-A.2

11. Subtract.

tens	ones
7	8
−2	6
5	2
28-A.2

12. Circle the answer that makes sense.
Hannah read 14 pages. Then she read 13 more. How many pages did she read in all?

13 pages
(27 pages)
270 pages
28-A.3

Form B • Free-Response   B278   Stop!

Free-Response Format • Test Answers

Write the correct answer.

1. Circle the number sentence that belongs in this fact family.

$9 + 2 = 11$

$2 + 9 = 11$

$11 - 2 = 9$

$\boxed{(11 - 9 = 2)}$

$9 - 2 = 7$

$7 + 2 = 9$

12-A.1

2. How many?

___57___

13-A.2

3. Count by fives. Write the number that comes after 35.

☆☆☆	☆☆☆	☆☆☆	☆☆☆
25	30	35	

25, 30, 35, ___40___

15-A.1

4. Write the amount.

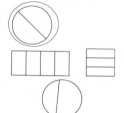

___32___ ¢

16-A.4

Use the calendar for questions 5 and 6.

May

Sunday	Monday	Tuesday	Wednesday	Thursday	Friday	Saturday
				1	2	3
4	5	6	7	8	9	10
11	12	13	14	15	16	17
18	19	20	21	22	23	24
25	26	27	28	29	30	31

5. On which day does this month begin?

___Thursday___

18-A.1

6. What is the date of the last Friday in this month?

May ___30___

18-A.1

7. Read the clock. Write the time.

 11:00

19-A.1

8. Circle the picture that shows halves.

22-A.1

9.

$\begin{array}{r} 8 \\ + 8 \\ \hline 16 \end{array}$ $\begin{array}{r} 8 \\ + 7 \\ \hline 15 \end{array}$

25-A.1

10.

$\begin{array}{r} 4 \\ 3 \\ + 4 \\ \hline 11 \end{array}$

26-A.2

11. How many counters?

___9___ counters

27-A.1

12. How many in each group?

___2___ counters

27-A.2

13. How many groups?

___5___ groups

27-A.2

14. There are 6 pens. Each pen has 2 pigs. How many pigs are there in all?

___12___ pigs

27-A.3

---

15. Bo sees 9 deer. Then 2 deer run away. How many deer are left?

___7___ deer

27-A.3

16. Subtract.

$\begin{array}{r} 50 \\ - 40 \\ \hline 10 \end{array}$

28-A.1

17. Add.

tens	ones
2	5
+ 1	4
3	9

28-A.2

18. Subtract.

tens	ones
9	4
- 5	1
4	3

28-A.2

19. Meg had 31 pennies. Then she saved 25 more. How many does she have in all?

6 pennies

(56 pennies)

130 pennies

28-A.3

20. Lee had 26 cards. Then he gave away 14. How many cards does he have left?

2 cards

(12 cards)

40 cards

28-A.3

Free-Response Format • Test Answers

Management Forms

Test Answer Sheet

This copying master is an individual recording sheet for up to 50 items on the multiple-choice (standardized) format tests.

Grading Made Easy

This percent converter can be used for all quizzes and tests. The percents given are based on all problems having equal value. Percents are rounded to the nearest whole percent giving the benefit of 0.5 percent.

Individual Record Form

One copying master for each content cluster of chapters is provided. Criterion scores for each learning goal are given for the chapter test. The student's total scores are recorded at the top of the page for chapter tests, the multi-chapter test and the cumulative test. The scores for each learning goal can also be recorded. You can use the Review Options that are listed on the form to assign additional review for the student unable to pass the test.

Formal Assessment Class Record Form

The scores for all the tests can be recorded for your class on these record forms. The Criterion Score for each test is given.

Learning Goals

The learning goals for the entire grade level are provided. These goals are referenced throughout the program. Each test item is referenced to a learning goal. You may wish to use these pages to cross-reference the Math Advantage Learning Goals with local, district, or statewide benchmarks.

Name_____ Date_____

Test Answer Sheet

Test Title_____

1. Ⓐ Ⓑ Ⓒ Ⓓ
2. Ⓐ Ⓑ Ⓒ Ⓓ
3. Ⓐ Ⓑ Ⓒ Ⓓ
4. Ⓐ Ⓑ Ⓒ Ⓓ
5. Ⓐ Ⓑ Ⓒ Ⓓ

6. Ⓐ Ⓑ Ⓒ Ⓓ
7. Ⓐ Ⓑ Ⓒ Ⓓ
8. Ⓐ Ⓑ Ⓒ Ⓓ
9. Ⓐ Ⓑ Ⓒ Ⓓ
10. Ⓐ Ⓑ Ⓒ Ⓓ

11. Ⓐ Ⓑ Ⓒ Ⓓ
12. Ⓐ Ⓑ Ⓒ Ⓓ
13. Ⓐ Ⓑ Ⓒ Ⓓ
14. Ⓐ Ⓑ Ⓒ Ⓓ
15. Ⓐ Ⓑ Ⓒ Ⓓ

16. Ⓐ Ⓑ Ⓒ Ⓓ
17. Ⓐ Ⓑ Ⓒ Ⓓ
18. Ⓐ Ⓑ Ⓒ Ⓓ
19. Ⓐ Ⓑ Ⓒ Ⓓ
20. Ⓐ Ⓑ Ⓒ Ⓓ

21. Ⓐ Ⓑ Ⓒ Ⓓ
22. Ⓐ Ⓑ Ⓒ Ⓓ
23. Ⓐ Ⓑ Ⓒ Ⓓ
24. Ⓐ Ⓑ Ⓒ Ⓓ
25. Ⓐ Ⓑ Ⓒ Ⓓ

26. Ⓐ Ⓑ Ⓒ Ⓓ
27. Ⓐ Ⓑ Ⓒ Ⓓ
28. Ⓐ Ⓑ Ⓒ Ⓓ
29. Ⓐ Ⓑ Ⓒ Ⓓ
30. Ⓐ Ⓑ Ⓒ Ⓓ

31. Ⓐ Ⓑ Ⓒ Ⓓ
32. Ⓐ Ⓑ Ⓒ Ⓓ
33. Ⓐ Ⓑ Ⓒ Ⓓ
34. Ⓐ Ⓑ Ⓒ Ⓓ
35. Ⓐ Ⓑ Ⓒ Ⓓ

36. Ⓐ Ⓑ Ⓒ Ⓓ
37. Ⓐ Ⓑ Ⓒ Ⓓ
38. Ⓐ Ⓑ Ⓒ Ⓓ
39. Ⓐ Ⓑ Ⓒ Ⓓ
40. Ⓐ Ⓑ Ⓒ Ⓓ

41. Ⓐ Ⓑ Ⓒ Ⓓ
42. Ⓐ Ⓑ Ⓒ Ⓓ
43. Ⓐ Ⓑ Ⓒ Ⓓ
44. Ⓐ Ⓑ Ⓒ Ⓓ
45. Ⓐ Ⓑ Ⓒ Ⓓ

46. Ⓐ Ⓑ Ⓒ Ⓓ
47. Ⓐ Ⓑ Ⓒ Ⓓ
48. Ⓐ Ⓑ Ⓒ Ⓓ
49. Ⓐ Ⓑ Ⓒ Ⓓ
50. Ⓐ Ⓑ Ⓒ Ⓓ

Total Number of Test Items

Number of Test Items Wrong	4	5	6	7	8	9	10	11	12	13	14	15	16	17	18	19	20	21	22	23	24	25	26	27	28	29	30
1	75	80	83	86	88	89	90	91	92	92	93	93	94	94	94	95	95	95	95	96	96	96	96	96	96	97	97
2	50	60	67	71	75	78	80	82	83	85	86	87	88	88	89	89	89	90	90	91	91	92	92	93	93	93	93
3	25	40	50	57	63	67	70	73	75	77	79	80	81	82	83	84	85	86	86	87	88	88	88	89	89	90	90
4	0	20	33	43	50	56	60	64	67	69	71	73	75	76	78	79	80	81	82	83	83	84	85	85	86	86	87
5		0	17	29	38	44	50	55	58	62	64	67	69	71	72	74	75	76	77	78	79	80	81	81	82	83	83
6			0	14	25	33	40	45	50	54	57	60	63	65	66	68	70	71	73	74	75	76	77	78	79	79	80
7				0	13	22	30	36	42	46	50	53	56	59	61	63	65	67	68	70	71	72	73	74	75	76	77
8					0	11	20	27	33	38	43	47	50	53	56	58	60	62	64	65	67	68	69	70	71	72	73
9						0	10	18	25	31	36	40	44	47	50	53	55	57	59	61	63	64	65	67	68	69	70
10							0	9	17	23	29	33	38	41	44	47	50	52	55	57	58	60	62	63	64	66	67
11								0	8	15	21	27	31	35	39	42	45	48	50	52	54	56	58	59	61	62	63
12									0	8	14	20	25	29	33	37	40	43	45	48	50	52	54	56	57	59	60
13										0	7	13	19	24	28	32	35	38	41	43	46	48	50	52	54	55	57
14											0	7	13	18	22	26	30	33	36	39	42	44	46	48	50	52	53
15												0	6	12	17	21	25	29	32	35	38	40	42	44	46	48	50
16													0	6	11	16	20	24	27	30	33	36	38	41	43	45	47
17														0	6	11	15	19	23	26	29	32	35	37	39	41	43
18															0	5	10	14	18	22	25	28	31	33	36	38	40
19																0	5	10	14	17	21	24	27	30	32	34	37
20																	0	5	9	13	17	20	23	26	29	31	33
21																		0	5	9	13	16	19	22	25	28	0
22																			0	4	8	12	15	19	21	24	27
23																				0	4	8	12	15	18	21	23
24																					0	4	8	11	14	17	20
25																						0	4	7	11	14	17
26																							0	4	7	10	13
27																								0	4	7	10
28																									0	3	8
29																										0	3
30																											0
31																											
32																											

Individual Record Form

GRADE 1 • Chapters 1-2

Child's Name _____

Test	Chapter 1	Chapter 2	Chapters 1-2	Cum Chs 1-2
Date				
Score				

LEARNING GOALS

		Form A CHAPTER TEST				REVIEW OPTIONS					
		Test Items			Criterion	Lesson	Teacher's	Workbooks			
Goal #	Learning Goal	Concept	Skills	PSolv	Scores	page #	Edition	P	R	E	PS
1-A.1	To use concrete materials to model addition story problems	1-2			1/2	25-26	TR-p26A p. 25A: AOC 1 RAL-p26A	1.1	1.1	1.1	1.1
1-A.2	To add on 1 or 2 to find sums to 6	3-4 5-6			3/4	27-28 29-30	TR-p28A p. 29A: AOC 1	1.2 1.3	1.2 1.3	1.2 1.3	1.2 1.3
1-A.3	To use pictures to find sums	7-8			1/2	31-32	INC-p32A	1.4	1.4	1.4	1.4
1-A.4	To write and solve addition sentences to represent addition story problems			9-12	3/4	33-34	p. 23C: LCC 1 p. 33A: AOC 1	1.5	1.5	1.5	1.5
2-A.1	To use concrete materials to model subtraction story problems	1-2			1/2	39-40	p. 39A: AOC 1 INC-p40A	2.1	2.1	2.1	2.1
2-A.2	To subtract 1 or 2 to find differences from 6	3-4 5-6			3/4	41-42 43-44	TR-p44A p. 45A: AOC 1	2.2 2.3	2.2 2.3	2.2 2.3	2.2 2.3
2-A.3	To write and solve subtraction sentences to represent pictures			7-10	3/4	45-46	p. 37C: LCC 2 p. 45A: AOC 1	2.4	2.4	2.4	2.4
2-A.4	To use the strategy *make a model* to solve addition and subtraction story problems			11-12	1/2	47-48	p. 47A: AOC 1, AOC 2	2.5	2.5	2.5	2.5

Key: AOC–Activity Options Column **BB**–Bulletin Board **PG**–Practice Game **LCC**–Learning Center Card **RAL**–Reaching All Learners
TR–Troubleshooting **INC**–Inclusion

Individual Record Form

GRADE 1 • Chapters 3-6

Child's Name _____

MATH ADVANTAGE

Test	Chapter 3	Chapter 4	Chapter 5	Chapter 6	Chapters 3-6	Cum Chs 1-6
Date						
Score						

LEARNING GOALS

Goal #	Learning Goal	Form A CHAPTER TEST Test Items Concept	Skills	PSolv	Criterion Scores	REVIEW OPTIONS Lesson page #	Teacher's Edition	Workbooks P	R	E	PS
3-A.1	To use counters to understand the Commutative Property of Addition	1-2			1/2	59-60	p. 59A: AOC 1	3.1	3.1	3.1	3.1
3-A.2	To identify combinations of addends with sums to 10	3-4 5-6			3/4	61-62 63-64	p. 61A: AOC 1	3.2 3.3	3.2 3.3	3.2 3.3	3.2 3.3
3-A.3	To add basic facts to 10 in vertical and horizontal formats	7-10			3/4	65-66	TR-p66A	3.4	3.4	3.4	3.4
3-A.4	To use the strategy *make a model* to solve addition problems with money			11-12	1/2	67-68	p. 67A: AOC 1	3.5	3.5	3.5	3.5
4-A.1	To use the *counting on* strategy to add	1-2 3-4			3/4	73-74 75-76	p. 71C: LCC 4 p. 73A: AOC 1	4.1 4.2	4.1 4.2	4.1 4.2	4.1 4.2
4-A.2	To use counters to show doubles and write the facts	5-6			1/2	77-78	TR-p78A	4.3	4.3	4.3	4.3
4-A.3	To find sums for addition facts to 10		7-10		3/4	79-80	p. 79A: AOC 1	4.4	4.4	4.4	4.4
4-A.4	To use the strategy *drawing a picture* to solve problems			11-12	1/2	81-82	TR-p82A	4.5	4.5	4.5	4.5

Key: AOC–Activity Options Column   **BB**–Bulletin Board   **PG**–Practice Game   **LCC**–Learning Center Card   **TR**–Troubleshooting

Individual Record Form

Individual Record Form

GRADE 1 • Chapters 3-6 (continued)

Child's Name _____

LEARNING GOALS

Goal #	Learning Goal	Form A CHAPTER TEST — Concept	Skills	PSolv	Criterion Scores	Lesson page #	Teacher's Edition	Workbooks P	R	E	PS
5-A.1	To identify combinations of ways to subtract from numbers 10 or less	1-2 3-4			3/4	87-88 89-90	TR-p88A	5.1 5.2	5.1 5.2	5.1 5.2	5.1 5.2
5-A.2	To subtract in horizontal and vertical formats	5-8			3/4	91-92	p. 91A: AOC 1	5.3	5.3	5.3	5.3
5-A.3	To identify fact families with sums to 10	9-10			1/2	93-94	INC-p94A	5.4	5.4	5.4	5.4
5-A.4	To use subtraction to compare two groups of 10 or less			11-12	1/2	95-96	p. 95A: AOC 2	5.5	5.5	5.5	5.5
6-A.1	To use the *counting back* strategy to subtract	1-2 3-4	5 6		4/6	101-102 103-104	p. 99C: LCC 6	6.1 6.2	6.1 6.2	6.1 6.2	6.1 6.2
6-A.2	To subtract zero and subtract to find a difference of zero	7-8			1/2	105-106	INC-p106A	6.3	6.3	6.3	6.3
6-A.3	To find sums and differences for addition and subtraction facts to 10		9-10		1/2	107-108	INC-p108A	6.4	6.4	6.4	6.4
6-A.4	To use the strategy *drawing a picture* to solve problems			11-12	1/2	109-110	INC-p110A TR-p110A	6.5	6.5	6.5	6.5

Key: AOC–Activity Options Column   **BB**–Bulletin Board   **PG**–Practice Game   **LCC**–Learning Center Card   **TR**–Troubleshooting
INC–Inclusion

Individual Record Form

GRADE 1 • Chapters 7-10

MATH ADVANTAGE

Child's Name _____

Test	Chapter 7	Chapter 8	Chapter 9	Chapter 10	Chapters 7-10	Cum Chs 1-10
Date						
Score						

LEARNING GOALS

Goal #	Learning Goal	Form A CHAPTER TEST Concept	Test Items Skills	PSolv	Criterion Scores	Lesson page #	Teacher's Edition	Workbooks P	R	E	PS
7-A.1	To identify solid figures		1-3 4-6		4/6	121-122 123-124	p. 119C: LCC 7 p. 121A: AOC 1	7.1 7.2	7.1 7.2	7.1 7.2	7.1 7.2
7-A.2	To sort solid figures by attributes	7 8			1/2	125-126 127-128	TR-p122A	7.3 7.4	7.3 7.4	7.3 7.4	7.3 7.4
7-A.3	To use the strategy *make a model* to identify how many cubes are used to build a figure			9-10	1/2	129-130	p. 129A: AOC 1	7.5	7.5	7.5	7.5
8-A.1	To identify plane figures	1-2	3-4		3/4	135-136	p. 133D: PG p. 135A: AOC 2	8.1	8.1	8.1	8.1
8-A.2	To sort plane figures by the number of sides and corners	5-6	7-8		3/4	137-138	p. 129C: BB	8.2	8.2	8.2	8.2
8-A.3	To identify figures that have the same size and shape		9-10		1/2	139-140	p. 139A: AOC 1 TR-p140A	8.3	8.3	8.3	8.3
8-A.4	To identify a line of symmetry in plane figures	11-12			1/2	141-142	p. 141A: AOC 1	8.4	8.4	8.4	8.4

Key: AOC–Activity Options Column **BB**–Bulletin Board **PG**–Practice Game **LCC**–Learning Center Card **TR**–Troubleshooting

Individual Record Form

GRADE 1 • Chapters 7-10 (continued)

Child's Name _____

| LEARNING GOALS | | Form A CHAPTER TEST | | | | | REVIEW OPTIONS | | | | | |
| | | Test Items | | | Criterion | Lesson | Teacher's | Workbooks | | | |
Goal #	Learning Goal	Concept	Skills	PSolv	Scores	page #	Edition	P	R	E	PS
9-A.1	To identify plane figures as open or closed	1-2			1/2	147-148		9.1	9.1	9.1	9.1
9-A.2	To classify objects by position	3-4		7-10	4/6	149-150 151-152	TR-p150A	9.2 9.3	9.2 9.3	9.2 9.3	9.2 9.3
9-A.3	To locate positions on a grid		5-6		1/2	153-154	INC-p150A	9.4	9.4	9.4	9.4
10-A.1	To identify, reproduce, and extend patterns	1-2	5-6	3-4	4/6	159-160 161-162	p. 157D: BB p. 159A: AOC 2	10.1 10.2	10.1 10.2	10.1 10.2	10.1 10.2
10-A.2	To create patterns	7-8			1/2	163-164	TR-p164A	10.3	10.3	10.3	10.3
10-A.3	To analyze and correct patterns	9-10			1/2	165-166	TR-p166A	10.4	10.4	10.4	10.4

Key: AOC–Activity Options Column **BB**–Bulletin Board **PG**–Practice Game **LCC**–Learning Center Card **TR**–Troubleshooting
INC–Inclusion

Harcourt Brace School Publishers

Individual Record Form

GRADE 1 • Chapters 11-12

Child's Name _____

Test	Chapter 11	Chapter 12	Chapters 11-12	Cum Chs 1-12
Date				
Score				

LEARNING GOALS

		Form A CHAPTER TEST				REVIEW OPTIONS		Workbooks			
		Test Items			**Criterion**	**Lesson**	**Teacher's**				
Goal #	**Learning Goal**	**Concept**	**Skills**	**PSolv**	**Scores**	**page #**	**Edition**	**P**	**R**	**E**	**PS**
11-A.1	To use strategies such as *counting on* and *doubles* to find sums to 12		1-4 5-6 11-14	7 8	8/12	177-178 179-180 183-184	p. 175D: BB p. 177A: AOC 1 TR-p180A	11.1 11.2 11.4	11.1 11.2 11.4	11.1 11.2 11.4	11.1 11.2 11.4
11-A.2	To add three addends with sums through 12		9-10		1/2	181-182	TR-p182A	11.3	11.3	11.3	11.3
11-A.3	To solve addition story problems by acting them out and writing addition sentences to represent the problems			15-16	1/2	185-186		11.5	11.5	11.5	11.5
12-A.1	To use mental math strategies such as *counting back, relating addition and subtraction,* and *fact families* to find differences to 12	1-2 5-6	3-4 9-10		5/8	191-192 193-194 197-198	p. 189C: LCC 12 TR-p192A	12.1 12.2 12.4	12.1 12.2 12.4	12.1 12.2 12.4	12.1 12.2 12.4
12-A.2	To compare groups of objects to find the differences between them	7-8			1/2	195-196	p. 195A: AOC 1	12.3	12.3	12.3	12.3
12-A.3	To solve addition and subtraction story problems by writing a number sentence			11-12	1/2	199-200	p. 199A: AOC 1	12.5	12.5	12.5	12.5

Key: AOC–Activity Options Column **BB**–Bulletin Board **PG**–Practice Game **LCC**–Learning Center Card **TR**–Troubleshooting

Individual Record Form

Individual Record Form

GRADE 1 • Chapters 13–15

Child's Name _____

MATH ADVANTAGE

Test	Chapter 13	Chapter 14	Chapter 15	Chapters 13-15	Cum Chs 1-15
Date					
Score					

LEARNING GOALS

Goal #	Learning Goal	Form A CHAPTER TEST — Test Items — Concept	Skills	PSolv	Criterion Scores	REVIEW OPTIONS — Lesson page #	Teacher's Edition	Workbooks P	R	E	PS
13-A.1	To count groups of tens, identify and write the number	1-2			1/2	211-212	p. 211A: AOC 1	13.1	13.1	13.1	13.1
13-A.2	To count groups of tens and ones to 100, identify and write the number	3-4	5-6 7-8 9-10		5/8	213-214 215-216 217-218 219-220	INC-p220A TR-p220A	13.2 13.3 13.4 13.5	13.2 13.3 13.4 13.5	13.2 13.3 13.4 13.5	13.2 13.3 13.4 13.5
13-A.3	To use 10 as a benchmark to estimate a quantity as more than or fewer than 10	11-12			1/2	221-222	p. 221A: AOC 1	13.6	13.6	13.6	13.6
14-A.1	To identify ordinal numbers from *first* through *twelfth*		1-2		1/2	227-228	INC-p228A	14.1	14.1	14.1	14.1
14-A.2	To compare two numbers and identify which number is greater or less	3-4 5-6			3/4	229-230 231-232	p. 225D: PG p. 229A: AOC 1	14.2 14.3	14.2 14.3	14.2 14.3	14.2 14.3
14-A.3	To identify numbers that come before, after, or between other numbers	7-9		10	3/4	233-234	TR-p234A	14.4	14.4	14.4	14.4
14-A.4	To order numbers (less than 100) from least to greatest or from greatest to least		11-12		1/2	235-236	p. 235A: AOC 1	14.5	14.5	14.5	14.5
15-A.1	To count by twos, fives, and tens to 100	1-2 5-6 7-8		3-4	5/8	241-242 243-244 245-246	p. 239D: PG TR-p246A	15.1 15.2 15.3	15.1 15.2 15.3	15.1 15.2 15.3	15.1 15.2 15.3
15-A.2	To identify a number as even or odd	9-10			1/2	247-248	p. 247A: AOC 1	15.4	15.4	15.4	15.4

Key: AOC–Activity Options Column **BB**–Bulletin Board **PG**–Practice Game **LCC**–Learning Center Card **INC**–Inclusion
TR–Troubleshooting

Individual Record Form

GRADE 1 • Chapters 11–12

Child's Name _____

MATH ADVANTAGE

Test	Chapter 16	Chapter 17	Chapter 18	Chapter 19	Chapters 16-19	Cum Chs 1-19
Date						
Score						

LEARNING GOALS

		Form A CHAPTER TEST				**REVIEW OPTIONS**			
		Test Items			**Criterion**	**Lesson**	**Teacher's**	**Workbooks**	
Goal #	**Learning Goal**	**Concept**	**Skills**	**PSolv**	**Scores**	**page #**	**Edition**	P R E PS	

Goal #	**Learning Goal**	**Concept**	**Skills**	**PSolv**	**Scores**	**page #**	**Edition**	**P**	**R**	**E**	**PS**
16-A.1	To count groups of pennies and groups of nickels and give the value	1-2			1/2	259-260	TR-p260A	16.1	16.1	16.1	16.1
16-A.2	To count groups of dimes and give the value	3-4			1/2	261-262	INC-p262A	16.2	16.2	16.2	16.2
16-A.3	To count combinations of nickels and pennies and give the value	5	7		1/2	263-264	INC-p264A	16.3	16.3	16.3	16.3
16-A.4	To count combinations of dimes and pennies and give the value	6	8		1/2	265-266	p. 257C: LCC 16 p. 265A: AOC 1	16.4	16.4	16.4	16.4
16-A.5	To use the strategy *make a model* to identify coins to use to buy an object			9-10	1/2	267-268	p. 267A: AOC 2	16.5	16.5	16.5	16.5

Key: AOC–Activity Options Column   **BB**–Bulletin Board   **PG**–Practice Game   **LCC**–Learning Center Card   **INC**–Inclusion
TR–Troubleshooting

Individual Record Form

GRADE 1 • Chapters 16-19 (continued)

Child's Name _____

LEARNING GOALS		Form A CHAPTER TEST				REVIEW OPTIONS		Workbooks			
Goal #	Learning Goal	Test Items			Criterion Scores	Lesson page #	Teacher's Edition	P	R	E	PS
		Concept	Skills	PSolv							
17-A.1	To trade pennies for nickels and dimes	1-2			1/2	273-274	p. 271D: PG	17.1	17.1	17.1	17.1
17-A.2	To use combinations of coins to show a given amount using the fewest coins	3-4			1/2	275-276	p. 275A: AOC 1 TR-p278A	17.2	17.2	17.2	17.2
17-A.3	To identify the coins needed to purchase an item		5-6	9-10	4/6	277-278 281-282	p. 277A: AOC 1	17.3 17.5	17.3 17.5	17.3 17.5	17.3 17.5
17-A.4	To make combinations of pennies, nickels, and dimes that represent the value of a quarter	7-8			1/2	279-280	p. 279A: AOC 1	17.4	17.4	17.4	17.4
18-A.1	To read a calendar		1-2 3-6		4/6	287-288 289-290	p. 285C: LCC 18	18.1 18.2	18.1 18.2	18.1 18.2	18.1 18.2
18-A.2	To sequence events	7-8			1/2	291-292	INC-p292A TR-p292A	18.3	18.3	18.3	18.3
18-A.3	To estimate which of two tasks will take more time			9-10	1/2	293-294	INC-p294A TR-p294A	18.4	18.4	18.4	18.4
19-A.1	To tell time to the hour and half hour		1-2 3-4 5-6 7-8		5/8	299-300 301-302 303-304 305-306	p. 297D: BB TR-p306A	19.1 19.2 19.3 19.4	19.1 19.2 19.3 19.4	19.1 19.2 19.3 19.4	19.1 19.2 19.3 19.4
19-A.2	To estimate the time needed to do a task as more or less than one minute			9-10	1/2	307-308	EXT-p308A	19.5	19.5	19.5	19.5

Key: AOC–Activity Options Column **BB**–Bulletin Board **PG**–Practice Game **LCC**–Learning Center Card **INC**–Inclusion
TR–Troubleshooting **EXT**–Extension

Individual Record Form

GRADE 1 • Chapters 20–22

Child's Name _____

MATH ADVANTAGE

Test	Chapter 20	Chapter 21	Chapter 22	Chapters 20-22	Cum Chs 1-22
Date					
Score					

LEARNING GOALS / Form A CHAPTER TEST / REVIEW OPTIONS

Goal #	Learning Goal	Concept	Skills	PSolv	Criterion Scores	Lesson page #	Teacher's Edition	P	R	E	PS
20-A.1	To use nonstandard units to measure length	1-2			1/2	319-320	TR-p320A	20.1	20.1	20.1	20.1
20-A.2	To measure the length of objects in inches	3-4	5-6		3/4	321-322 323-324	p. 317D: BB p. 321A: AOC 1	20.2 20.3	20.2 20.3	20.2 20.3	20.2 20.3
20-A.3	To measure the length of objects in centimeters	7-8	9-10		3/4	325-326 327-328	p. 325A: AOC 1	20.4 20.5	20.4 20.5	20.4 20.5	20.4 20.5
21-A.1	To estimate, then weigh, using a balance to determine which of two objects is heavier	1-2		3-4	3/4	333-334	p. 33IC: LCC 21	21.1	21.1	21.1	21.1
21-A.2	To estimate, then weigh, using nonstandard objects	5-6			1/2	335-336	TR-p336A	21.2	21.2	21.2	21.2
21-A.3	To estimate, then measure, about how many cups a container will hold	7-8			1/2	337-338	TR-p338A	21.3	21.3	21.3	21.3
21-A.4	To classify the temperature of objects as hot or cold	9-10			1/2	339-340	TR-p340A	21.4	21.4	21.4	21.4
22-A.1	To identify equal parts, halves, fourths, and thirds of a whole	1-2 3-4 5-6 7-8			5/8	345-346 347-348 349-350 351-352	p. 343C: LCC 22 TR-p352A	22.1 22.2 22.3 22.4	22.1 22.2 22.3 22.4	22.1 22.2 22.3 22.4	22.1 22.2 22.3 22.4
22-A.2	To visualize results of sharing equal parts to solve problems			9-10	1/2	353-354	p. 343D: PG	22.5	22.5	22.5	22.5
22-A.3	To identify equal parts of a group	11-12			1/2	355-356	INC-p356A	22.6	22.6	22.6	22.6

Key: AOC–Activity Options Column **BB**–Bulletin Board **PG**–Practice Game **LCC**–Learning Center Card **TR**–Troubleshooting **INC**–Inclusion

Individual Record Form

GRADE 1 • Chapters 23–24

Child's Name _____

Test	Chapter 23	Chapter 24	Chapters 23-24	Cum Chs 1-24
Date				
Score				

LEARNING GOALS

		Form A CHAPTER TEST				REVIEW OPTIONS					
		Test Items			Criterion	Lesson	Teacher's	Workbooks			
Goal #	Learning Goal	Concept	Skills	PSolv	Scores	page #	Edition	P	R	E	PS
23-A.1	To sort objects and record data in a tally table	1-2	3-4		3/4	367-368	TR-p368A p. 365C: LCC 23	23.1	23.1	23.1	23.1
23-A.2	To use data to determine if an outcome is certain or impossible, or which event is most likely	7-8	5-6		3/4	369-370 371-372	p. 369A: AOC 1	23.2 23.3	23.2 23.3	23.2 23.3	23.2 23.3
23-A.3	To make predictions and record data in tally tables	9-10	11-12		3/4	373-374	INC-p374A	23.4	23.4	23.4	23.4
24-A.1	To record and interpret data in picture graphs	1-2			1/2	379-380	INC-p380A	24.1	24.1	24.1	24.1
24-A.2	To count, record, and interpret data in tally tables and bar graphs	3-4	5-6 7-8 9-10	11-12	7/10	381-382 383-384 385-386	p. 385A: AOC 1 TR-p384A	24.2 24.3 24.4	24.2 24.3 24.4	24.2 24.3 24.4	24.2 24.3 24.4

Key: AOC–Activity Options Column   **BB**–Bulletin Board   **PG**–Practice Game   **LCC**–Learning Center Card   **INC**–Inclusion
TR–Troubleshooting

Individual Record Form

GRADE 1 • Chapters 25-26

Child's Name _____

MATH ADVANTAGE

Test	Chapter 25	Chapter 26	Chapters 25-26	Cum Chs 1-26
Date				
Score				

LEARNING GOALS

Goal #	Learning Goal	Form A CHAPTER TEST — Test Items			Criterion Scores	REVIEW OPTIONS — Lesson page #	Teacher's Edition	Workbooks P	R	E	PS
		Concept	Skills	PSolv							
25-A.1	To find sums to 18, using mental math strategies such as *doubles, doubles plus one,* and *doubles minus one*	1-2, 3-4	5-8		5/8	397-398, 399-400, 401-402	TR-p402A	25.1, 25.2, 25.3	25.1, 25.2, 25.3	25.1, 25.2, 25.3	25.1, 25.2, 25.3
25-A.2	To write the related addition and subtraction number sentences for doubles fact families	9-12			3/4	403-404	p. 395C: LCC 25, p. 403A: AOC 1	25.4	25.4	25.4	25.4
25-A.3	To solve story problems by *making a model*			13-14	1/2	405-406	INC-p406A	25.5	25.5	25.5	25.5
26-A.1	To add basic facts with sums 11-18 by using *making a ten and more*	1-2	3-4		3/4	411-412	p. 411A: AOC 1, TR-p412A	26.1	26.1	26.1	26.1
26-A.2	To add three numbers with sums 11-18 by using *doubles* or *making a ten strategy*		5-8		3/4	413-414	p. 413A: AOC 1	26.2	26.2	26.2	26.2
26-A.3	To use inverse operations to finds sums and differences to 18	9-12, 13-16			5/8	415-416, 417-418	p. 409D: PG, p 415A: AOC 1, TR-p416A	26.3, 26.4	26.3, 26.4	26.3, 26.4	26.3, 26.4

Key: AOC–Activity Options Column **BB**–Bulletin Board **PG**–Practice Game **LCC**–Learning Center Card **TR**–Troubleshooting **INC**–Inclusion

Individual Record Form

MATH ADVANTAGE

GRADE 1 • Chapters 27-28

Child's Name _____

Test	Chapter 27	Chapter 28	Chapters 27-28	Cum Chs 1-28
Date				
Score				

LEARNING GOALS

Form A CHAPTER TEST / REVIEW OPTIONS

Goal #	Learning Goal	Concept	Skills	PSolv	Criterion Scores	Lesson page #	Teacher's Edition	P	R	E	PS
		Test Items						Workbooks			
27-A.1	To make equal groups and count to show how many in all	1-2			2/2	429-430	p. 427D: BB TR-p430A	27.1	27.1	27.1	27.1
27-A.2	To put objects into equal groups to determine how many in each group and how many groups	3-4 7-8	5-6 9-10		6/8	431-432 433-434	INC-p432A	27.2 27.3	27.2 27.3	27.2 27.3	27.2 27.3
27-A.3	To solve problems by drawing a picture			11-12	2/2	435-436	p. 435A: AOC 1	27.4	27.4	27.4	27.4
28-A.1	To add and subtract tens	1-2			2/2	441-442		28.1	28.1	28.1	28.1
28-A.2	To add and subtract tens and ones	3-4 7-8	5-6 9-10		6/8	443-444 445-446	p. 439C: LCC 28 TR-p444A	28.2 28.3	28.2 28.3	28.2 28.3	28.2 28.3
28-A.3	To choose a reasonable estimate to solve problems			11-12	2/2	447-448	p. 447A: AOC 1	28.4	28.4	28.4	28.4

Key: AOC–Activity Options Column   **BB**–Bulletin Board   **PG**–Practice Game   **LCC**–Learning Center Card   **INC**–Inclusion
TR–Troubleshooting

Formal Assessment

Class Record Form

School / Teacher	Inventory	Chapter 1	Chapter 2	Chapters 1-2	Cumulatives 1-2	Chapter 3	Chapter 4	Chapter 5	Chapter 6	Chapters 3-6	Cumulatives 1-6	Chapter 7
Criterion Score	15/22	8/12	8/12	8/12	16/24	8/12	8/12	8/12	8/12	8/12	16/24	7/
NAMES **Date**												

ool	Chapter 8	Chapter 9	Chapter 10	Chapters 7-10	Cumulatives 1-10	Chapter 11	Chapter 12	Chapters 11-12	Cumulatives 1-12	Chapter 13	Chapter 14	Chapter 15
cher												
Criterion Score	8/12	7/10	7/10	8/12	14/20	11/16	8/12	8/12	15/22	8/12	8/12	7/10
MES　　　　　**Date**												

Formal Assessment

Class Record Form (continued)

MATH ADVANTAGE

School / Teacher	Chapters 13-15	Cumulatives 1-15	Chapter 16	Chapter 17	Chapter 18	Chapter 19	Chapters 16-19	Cumulatives 1-19	Chapter 20	Chapter 21	Chapter 22	Chapters 20-22
Criterion Score	8/12	14/20	7/10	7/10	7/10	7/10	8/12	14/20	7/10	7/10	8/12	8/
NAMES — Date												

	Cumulatives 1-22	Chapter 23	Chapter 24	Chapters 23-24	Cumulatives 1-24	Chapter 25	Chapter 26	Chapters 25-26	Cumulatives 1-26	Chapter 27	Chapter 28	Chapters 27-28	Cumulatives 1-28
Criterion Score	16/24	8/12	8/12	8/12	14/20	9/14	11/16	8/12	12/18	8/12	8/12	8/12	14/20

ool

cher

MES   **Date**